Which Way Now?
The 3 lives of Barbara Toy

Lesley Wildman rca

Copyright © 2025 by Lesley Wildman
All rights reserved. No part of this book may be reproduced in any form or by an electronic or mechanical means, including information storage and retrieval systems, without permission in writing from the publisher, except by a reviewer who may quote brief passages in a review.

First Edition: 2025.

ISBN 978-1-7395944-9-7 (paperback)

Published by WILD ideas publications – www.wildideas.tv

Every effort has been made to trace or contact all copyright holders. The publishers will be pleased to make good any omissions or rectify any mistakes brought to their attention at the earliest opportunity.

In loving memory of
Terri and Ian Wells

Introduction

Such a cliche, who would believe me? What was I to do, stand and watch the evidence of an extraordinary life be destroyed?

Barbara Alex Toy came unexpectedly into my life, her story rising from the unwanted dishevelled piles of papers and mountains of photographs, films and slides, all hidden away in what turned out to be an artist's attic/garret. Having learned it was all destined for destruction, I harboured it all, the evidence of her inner thoughts and concerns in hundreds of letters she'd written home to her beloved mother. Surrounding myself with the remains of her life, collating and researching Barbara Toy, her courage, sheer grit and tenacious need for freedom, a certain solitude emerged. On the edge of obsession, it felt like she had moved in with me, her questions mine, her hardships mine, her tragedies mine.

In 1950, when Barbara's first solo expedition took place, advances in the motor industry meant it was only a matter of time before the places she longed to visit would be overtaken by tourists. Barbara's need to explore the world was a journey of a very different kind. She chose to reinvent herself from actress, theatre and film producer, playwright to adventurer, and to add a frisson of danger, she would do so alone. Excited by a childhood story of the desert, told to her by her father, she crossed remote deserts, jungles and plains, cities and countryside, making a life time decision to search the world for the freedoms she yearned for. She left the successful career she had forged for herself during the hard times of the Blitz in London. Surviving on little was a challenge she had to rise to, which lasted for the rest of her life. She had sought the limelight and the glittering life of the stage, the parties, the glamour and the fame. None of it gave her the longed-for knowledge of knowing her true self, the way the open plains of the wild offered to the lone traveller. The patriarchal world she was born into fell away once she took to the open road, going her own way, in her own way.

Relying many times on her humour, her wits, and charm, written on the cover of her first book, *A Fool on Wheels*, was a description of her tenacity. Saying she would often ride on her luck and with a dogged determination to do it her way. Agreeing it didn't always happen that way and stating she had the time of her life and would have faced any peril for the thrill. With the help of strangers and the obstruction of officials, she battled through the bureaucracy of borders, financial and physical difficulties with an unwavering belief in humanity in all it guises. An Australian newspaper described her ability to put people on their best behaviour and anxious to help.

She was a petite, 5ft 2" in heels, 8 stone Australian woman who made London and latterly the Cotswolds in England her base. She journeyed through the conventions of her time to learn of all religions, new places and new relationships, capturing the romance in all aspects with a wit and sense of daring. From battling the casting couch of theatre and film, the unequal wages for women, to her choice of partners, Barbara was a true pioneer of life.

Through this collection of loving letters to her mother in Australia, lies the story of each journey's toll, success and the soul-searching discoveries she makes along the way.

I introduce to you, Miss Barbara Alex Toy…

Chapter 1
'This can't be I'

I was in an attic room with a flimsy fading airmail letter in my hand, suddenly aware that I had been lost in a poignantly personal letter for some time, to the mother of a lady called Barbara Toy. But I was there to help Terri, not add to her problems.

When my dear friend, Ian Seymour Wells, passed away, and at the request of his widow Terri, I was more than happy to take on the burden of sorting through the remains of his studio. As a fellow artist, I recognized it as a privilege and recalled happier times, chatting to Ian outside a Chipping Norton café. He would take a route round the small square known as Middle Row, visiting 3 cafés during the space of a morning. His favourite, encouraged people to sit outside at grey marble tables with ornate iron chairs, under coloured umbrellas or heated lamps. This part of the town would bustle with tourists and locals strolling along the pedestrianized street, where Ian would draw their likeness as they passed by. The black biro drawings on delicate pink sheets of the Financial Times would be folded away out of sight if anyone approached. Ian was only too happy to discuss the art of others, it was his passion, but he was desperately secretive, almost embarrassed about his own. Only upon entering his studio, did I see the vast collection of folded papers covered from edge to edge with most beautiful and intricate drawings. (Fig 1)

The attic studio was piled with old pots, jars, paints, old artists materials, papers, a lifetime of collecting. Aside from a meter square of carpet, there was no room to move. Canvases were propped in every corner and stacked carelessly on top of each other, all covered in a fine layer of grey dust. Letters, on blue airmail paper were lodged under old suitcases and partly used art boards. The paintings and drawings were obviously Ian's, as for the rest? Terri informed me that the attic had been his domain and she would only venture far enough to vacuum the square foot of uncovered carpet and no more.

On seeing the letter in my hand Terri, reluctantly and with a blasé tone, shared a little more about the mysterious writer. It belonged to Ian's Aunt, an Australian travel writer, who'd circumnavigated the world, alone. I was stunned at the casual, throwaway comment that seemed to mean nothing to Terri but landed square on my curiosity. The house we were in, she informed me, was the last place this intrepid explorer had settled before her death in 2001. It was a house that took Terri away from her beloved London, the people she knew and the patients she had helped during her time as a health visitor. The anonymity of the London streets was not how it worked in this small working town. Ian and Terri kept themselves to themselves, in a daily routine. As Ian's health deteriorated, she became even more protective of him, keeping all but a few intimate friends away. The house itself, a mill workers cottage, nestled at the end of a sought-after row of Victorian cottages was once tied to the tweed making Bliss Mill. Barbara, it seemed, had chosen the property for its proximity to the small local theatre at the other end of the street.

The day I was summoned to the cottage the roadside entrance was flanked by a toppled chimney pot with a child's plastic blue rabbit nestling among the weeds protruding from its ornate top. The cottage had a small concrete sign 'Snails' that perched above a large wooden garage door. There wasn't a front door as such, just a wooden panelled garage entrance, with a doorbell that sounded like a string of cowbells; the door answering would take just long enough to end the need to ring the bells again. Inside, the garage was crowded with books, old kitchen cabinets, and plastic boxes with, 'to go', written on them. Curious Middle Eastern objects with unusual carvings and lettering sat alongside spanners, ornate shoe horns, dishevelled coats, a large picture of an Arab on a camel, and discarded half open boxes of screws and nails of all sizes. Terri's laundry area sat clean and proud at the end of the room, surrounded by half-finished paintings and pots of hardened paint brushes, stuck in crusted rings of evaporated turpentine. Another door to the tiny lean-to conservatory housed a dark wooden dresser with rose painted plates and overgrown spider plants spilling from its shelves; all pressed up against the moulding Cotswold stone wall of the adjacent abandoned maternity hospital. The vast wall towered over the little cottage and bowed precariously, stretching against the earth filled mound on the other side. Thick impenetrable ivy sucked the mortar from the Cotswold stone wall which loomed over the tiny outside garden. The now derelict Hospital building towered on its hill over the cottage, left to rot as one developer after another ran out of money. Once inside, the treacherous consecutive staircases, with treads barely wide enough to put half a foot on, were Ian's fantasy and abstract paintings, winding past two rooms filled with furniture, clothing, ornate decanters and glasses, sculptures, more paintings and more books. Terri waved a hand to each room telling me most of them belonged to Barbara Toy, Ian's aunt, at least eight of the books she had written, Terri wasn't sure which ones. As the stairs narrowed again, even more art, from another age, hung precariously on the walls and the heavy dark wooden furniture had been squeezed into each corner. It was clear by Terri's reaction none of it was to her taste, it had belonged to the mysterious Aunt. It became apparent that Terri was trapped among the aunt's things barely able to put her own mark on the place, which went some way to explain her indifference to this mysterious explorer.

The glazed panels of the attic room door hazed the view inside with a coating of dust as it dragged against the worn carpet. As I walked in, the scale of the task was over whelming. Photographs were left curled in dusty corners, slide boxes propped at awkward angles and broken, spilling the contents into toppling heaps. A large abstract painting of contorted bodies lay propped slightly away from the wall, I could just see behind it, a big black wooden chest, at least 6ft long. My shoulders sank, was this to be sorted through too? There were two old suit cases, their travel stickers torn off, trollies filled with dried up paints and inks. Files of all sizes left in no particular order were strewn on the floor, placed on old shelving and broken chairs. I reached down towards an upturned cardboard box, drawn to the pale blue airmail letter sticking out. As I read the solemn words on the page I looked back to Terri, she was holding out a large black bin bag; I took it slowly, incredulous at its intention. She wanted rid of it all, it meant mess and clutter, all of which she was anxious to throw away. Terri had longed to have her shy beloved husband's work be the prominent feature of the house; the aunt, Barbara Toy, had been in the way. I looked from the shiny black refuse sack to the letter. The near transparent blue paper barely had the strength to stay flat in my hand but its content had already slipped me to the edges of a past life. I was touched by a mystery and moved by this single letter. I couldn't let this lady go, I had to know more. It seemed Barbara Toy had written to her mother over many years and they had all landed up here, evidence of the old custom to return letters once the recipient had died. Ian had kept it all and they now lay scattered among his equally forgotten works of art.

Naples
22nd October 1930

Dear Mum,

The reason I didn't get the cable earlier, we'd stopped over and I didn't know where we would be, but we got it when we arrived in Naples. I can't write much you will understand and I hope you are alright and will be able to move to new surroundings.

It is so futile to say if only one had done things differently, but it hurts like hell to think I wasn't there. I can't understand it all, just when he could have settled down to enjoy things. How many times I have thought, how he would have loved this and that. Please write and tell me lots of things, I feel so lonely.

We will probably go back to London despite the winter, I must get some work done or something to occupy my mind. We hope to save quite a lot if we stay in London. I know you will let me help you if you need anything.

We were very lucky to be staying at a small place with only an American and a Polish woman. Her son is very nice, and we talk a lot to keep our minds occupied.

I have been very miserable for the last few weeks after having a bad dream about Pop, but I didn't think it was that bad.

I hope you are well and not too sad.
    My love,
        Barbara

Barbara Alex Toy was born on the 11th of August 1908, in North Sydney Australia. The second daughter to an editor and writer in newspapers and magazines, Bert F. Toy. Barbara's mother, Nellie, a nurse, was in correspondence with Barbara until her death at the age of 103 years.
In a later, abandoned attempt at her own auto biography Barbara writes:

'This can't be I'

The first thing I can remember is holding my mother's hand as we walked down the jetty of the yacht club in Sydney harbour. I was three years old. We passed under a huge white arch which was the jaw bone of a whale and on to the jetty where the waters below thundered against the pillars. The vigorous waters of our shores and beaches played a big part in our lives. (The jaw bone is still there).

    We lived across the harbour in Shell Grove Road at the head of a cove of the same name. Our house had been built by an eccentric lady named Mrs Brown, who then bought an entire headland in the harbour and erected a small weatherboard cottage on the sight. From then on, she was known as 'Mrs Weatherboard Brown'. Her design of our house was unusual. There was one huge living room and all the other rooms led off of it; two bedrooms, one for my parents and one for my elder sister, a study, a kitchen and a long veranda. A kookaburra, the laughing jackass, invariably perched on the rail and would wake me in the morning - laughing.

    We had a small billiard table in the lounge and most nights pals of my father would come and play. As a small child I learnt to play snooker, using a butter box to stand on. We had a pianola and our taste was very catholic. With classical music and the latest jazz. Next door was a large stone house with a spreading magnolia tree in the grounds. Each day a pale young woman, who was dying of T.B was brought out to rest under it. If she slept, we would be very quiet. A large Loquat tree and a group of Bamboos ran along a dividing fence. Otherwise, the house was surrounded by thick undergrowth of Lantana bushes known locally as the 'Cat's bush'. This was of great interest to me and my cat, Persepolis. He was wild and very thin for he lived entirely on mice and locusts.

There was no refrigeration as we know it now, but an ice box with a zinc lined compartment which was filled each week with a block of ice.

Sometimes my father, armed with torches and nets, took me and my sister prawning down in the cove. Shinning the torches on the water the prawns swam towards the light and were scooped up in our nets.

My mother had been trained as a nurse, despite her well-off background, and worked during the bubonic plague (after the first world war) during this time no one could leave their house without wearing a white mesh mask over their face. Rather like the Japanese do today when they have a cold. Pity we don't do the same.

Mother was a quiet, self-contained person, given to quoting Dickens, she had a great affection for queen Victoria who she referred to as the little Queen. She spoke of her as if she knew her. Mother had been educated at a convent school even though her mother was bigoted against Catholics, but all those who could afford to send their girls there had the best education. Two of my aunts lost their fiancés in the first world war as did my school mistress.

We had a series of animals for as well as Persepolis, there was his sister Wuzzy, a much more sedate cat who would spend her time sat on top of the piano. We were given two white mice and within two weeks we had sixty, they eventually escaped and neighbourhood was invaded by a breed of piebald mice. An opossum used to hang by his tail from the gutter in front of the kitchen window and my mother fed him slices of bread with tea leaves. Pink and grey Galas (Cockatoos) nested in the large oak tree near my veranda. Later there was a mongrel black and white dog called Tim – the love of my young life.

There was little traffic on the suburban roads, once a week a horse and cart would rumble by. It had a slanting roof with slats, where pairs of rabbits made a furry thatch. They were sold for eighteen pence a pair and the old boy, Shamus, skinned them on the spot. Across the hill on the adjoining cove was the wharf for the ferry boat to the city. My school, Neutral Bay School, was half a mile away and my dog Tim came along, leaving me at the school gate to find his own way home. It was a girl's school and we sang hymns in the playground before we went into class. There was surprisingly little sport, above all, swimming.

My father Bert F. Toy (he signed everything this way) was the literary editor on the Sydney Bulletin and he reviewed the books on its Pink Page. He was, at one time, the editor of the Sunday Times and of the Afternoon Sun and the Sydney Morning Herald. He started the first Australian Woman's Magazine, becoming the editor. My sister was 'Sister Sadie', four and half years my senior, was the Agony Aunt on the same magazine, she was the brains and the looks of the family.

Earlier my father had been a cub war correspondent during the Boer War in Africa and when he described the desert to me, my tummy turned over with excitement, although it was many years before I was able to see the desert for myself.

I was about twelve when Pavlova came to Sydney and a friend of my father invited me to one of the performances. I was completely bowled over by her and left the theatre in a dream. On the way home I boarded the ferry, still in a daze. I remember standing alone in the darkness at the bow of the ferry as it crossed the harbour and seeing its loveliness for the first time. Such was my state of elevation that I forgot to leave the ferry at our wharf and repeated the whole journey a second time to be finally greeted by a very irate and panic-stricken parent.

Christmas day was invariably spent on the beach and we had traditional Christmas dinner at night. None of us had ever seen snow.

Our cinema was a large one storey barn like structure, with a slightly raised platform at the rear where the more expensive leather seats were. Below were just wooden benches. The programs were changed twice a week, a varied collection of films, some epics such as Ben Hur, Death of the Gods and The Seven Commandments. These were announced well ahead and had a live show on stage before the film. The main attraction was a nubile young woman called Dorothy Woolley.

As well as stars, such as Harold Lloyd, Laurel and Hardy, Tom Mix, Charlie Chaplin, Theda Bra and Mary Pickford. There was a hilarious film starring Marie Tempest about a couple who bought a plot of land, built a house and found they had struck oil under it. There was a sketch by the clown 'Pimple', just a backdrop with a bench and a simpering young woman with the catchphrase: 'Oh it's s-lovely to be in s-love with s-ones nother'. The max Sennet comedies had us worried as the heroine was either drowning in a room full of water, or had Clara Bow tied to a track before the advancing train. When tension had become almost unbearable and the pianist had played herself into a frenzy, came the announcement on the screen 'To be continued in our next…'

Later the cinema was built with two circles and a Wurlitzer organ. The lights faded majestically and there was an awesome hush, but by then I was growing up, and with a boyfriend and probably didn't see the point of it all.

When I left school, I worked in a rather arty bookshop and gallery, The Roycroft. It was owned and run by an intellectual giant, Mrs Frances Zabel. The library was the meeting place for the literary and musical folk of Sydney, and most visitors from abroad had either been told about the place before they arrived, or were bought in by friends. On Saturday afternoons we had a musical soiree attended by most of the literary and artistic folk of the city. There was a hunger for all types of literature, although when books were ordered they took some time to arrive from Europe. Then, as now, Sydney had several good bookshops.

When we spoke of England we talked of 'going home'. It was the time of the Oxford bags, Brylcream, the Charleston, the Tickle Toe... and jazz. The music was wonderful. I caused a stir by being the first girl in the country to have an Eaton crop hairstyle. Life as a teenager had been carefree, we spent a lot of time on the beaches around Sydney or along the coast, we danced till the early hours in night clubs, dance halls, or in each other's houses and if possible. Or wangled and invitation on board the numerous ships that sailed into the harbour. Sometimes four masted sailing ships on the corn run to Europe, would appear. We took wonderful weather for granted.

When I left the country and sailed in the Esperance Bay (later to be sunk during the second World War), I held the streamers thrown to me from the wharf by my friends and family. They broke as the ship moved away from the quay; I had no idea it would be twenty years before my return.

I would spend the next few days looking everywhere in the attic studio, turning over any bills and letters I could find, there was no more to this memoir. Barbara's idealised past showed the carefree bohemian life she'd lived in a prosperous and growing country, not giving a clue as to why she left. At the time there was no way she would have known what was on the horizon. What was life post the Great War in Australia? My research discovered that at the end of the 1920s, Australia was a male dominated society at the dawn of the 20th century. Males comprised 52% of the general population in 1901 and would likely have represented a large majority of voters, given that prior to 1902, women were entitled to vote in South Australia and Western Australia only. In the second half of the 1920s the Australian economy suffered from falling wheat and wool prices, and competition from other commodity-producing countries. Australia was also borrowing vast sums of money, which came to a halt as the economy slowed. Although for many Australians, the 1920s did indeed herald an exciting new world, the tragic legacies of the Great War and the Spanish flu pandemic, were still felt and innovation in art, aviation and industry proved welcome distractions. This was not to last, by the end of the decade in October 1929, the stock market crashed, and America's invested wealth suddenly lost $26 billion in value. Prosperity had ended. The economic boom and the Jazz Age was over, Australia recorded one of the highest rates of unemployment in the world during the Great Depression. Good reason then for Barbara to turn her back on Australia.

Barbara's effects moved in with me, in my own studio, away from Terri's unwavering attempt to destroy it all. I searched through each of the three hundred letters, piecing together the connections to the objects and salvaged belongings. Her last attempt to put a voice to her early life, seemed sadly short, written on scraps of paper and left untouched for years. When I found the scattered pages of Barbara's memoir, she had written them, decades later, on the back of letters and bills she received in 1991. A letter agreeing to alterations to the house that never happened. A request to have a story about her in the Chiropractic Advancement Associations 'Back Chat' newsletter, she never replied to. And a letter from her solicitor handing her over to another practice due to his diagnosis of cancer. There was also an offer from the American Express company about money off computer equipment she didn't know how to use. The irony wasn't lost as I sat next to Barbara's typewriter and imagined the clatter of the keys as the endless edits piled up beside her. The holdalls of papers stacked under my desk groaned with rewrites, a testament to the endurance of days spent bashing out thoughts and memories of her travels on the small blue typewriter. It was here she returned to her beloved desert through words and photographs for her readers to enjoy. Remembering the first letter, how proud her father would have been.

Among the many tattered and torn letters, was a section of writing by Barbara's mother Nellie to one of Barbara's friends, in 1941. It alludes to the special father - daughter relationship, she had with the man that once called her 'the boy I never had.'

...She is so much like her father and always they were so much to one another. I think it broke his heart when she went away, she feels that also. I assure her that was not so. That he was glad she was living her own life and knew she would always come back to him.

Sadly, this reunion was never to take place. Unhappy at her early marriage, Barbara and her father never reconciled their differences; he was taken ill and died before she could return. The October 1930 letter from Naples, was written by Barbara while she was away on her yearlong honeymoon with her new husband Ewing Sundblom Rixson, a man eleven years her senior. A marriage that took place without the blessing of her father.

A newspaper cutting, found in her archives from the Australian newspaper **'The Sun.'** November 23rd 1930 and goes on to describe her as:

> '...an engaging lass with a head you would love to "sculpt" and a personality you would love to bottle and serve out to humans less fortunate.'

Barbara sporting her trailblazing, Chanel inspired, Eton Crop hair do. 1930

Bertie Toy, Barbara and Sadie's father.

Fun in the back yard, Bertie Toy.

Bertie Toy,
newspaper journalist and editor.

Barbara and her older sister Sadie at the house on Shell Grove Road.

House on Shell Grove Road.

Sadie as a child was part of the newspapers advertising for her father's newspaper.

Sadie, agony aunt of the first Australian Women's magazine, late 1920s.

Fig 1.

Ian Seymour Wells, biro drawings, one of over 600 found in his studio.

Chapter 2
'Introduction to the world.'

Before leaving Australia, Barbara had secured a job in an upmarket book shop in the centre of Sydney. The Roycroft Library and Art Shop on Rowe Street, working for Mrs Zabel. The shop, was well known for its soirées and gatherings of intellectuals and poets. (Fig 2)

In the basement of the bookshop were maps and travel books and it was here that Ewing Sundblom Rixson F.R.G.S. came into the 19-year old's life. 11 years her senior he was already a world traveller, of Finnish descent and acting Consul to Panama, from a then well-known New York Quaker family. Within 3 months they married at a registry office in Woollahra, against her father's wishes. But when Barbara's employer broke her ankle, Barbara had to keep her marriage a secret for the next few months. It was expected that women would not work once married as a later newspaper article from **The Sun,** Sunday, November 23rd 1930, explained.

> 'Don't ever tell me that a woman can't keep a secret.'

In the same article Barbara is quoted as saying:

> 'I'm afraid the gilt is rather off the gingerbread as far as our lark is concerned.'
>
> For thus she terms the on-the-spur-of-the-moment marriage decision and the unconventionality of the proceedings.
>
> The next day she was finally seen wearing her wedding ring.'

Writing regularly to her 'mum' during her yearlong honeymoon trip, some of the 19yr old's comments are caught in the parlance and prejudices of pre-war attitudes, laced with a large pinch of Barbara's naive and crumbling loneliness.

On leaving Australia, her mother saw her off at the dock in Sydney:

Orient line SS Orsova
April 1930

Dear Mum,

Your lovely flowers, for any cabin they're really lovely and make a marvellous show. Also, I smell beautiful and have, for the first time in weeks, a pair of stockings on that haven't a couple of ladders in them. Thank you so much, darling for everything. It's a horrible thing seeing anyone off and you had to hang around for so long, you must have been nearly dead.

We seem to take a long time to get going and as we departed, the heaven's, it was blowing something terrible. However, once out at sea it seemed to settle down and the weather since has been very calm. It's sunny but a bit nippy and I've done nothing but sleep. Gosh I was tired. My other cabin is also full of flowers and some plaintive notes from people who had come to see me off, deciding that I must have changed my mind. I can't think how it happened, but everyone was warned where I was. Also, two papers and the photographer came on and were looking for me. Everything in Sydney from the very start always seem to go wrong with the Press.

The food on board, you'll be glad to hear, is very good and the ships half empty. It's all quite nice but I never like these big liners, and of course it's a dress parade with me bringing up the rear in the latest two seasons removed models. However, once my legs are browned, I'll be able to rely on my figure and a certain caustic wit!

The aunt's flowers are so beautiful and so fresh they should last - all of them - until at least Honolulu. The loud speaker booms out instructions all day long, and little notes about the trips are slipped under the door day and night. Never a dull moment.

I'm slowly drinking my way through a dozen bottles of beer nobody drank. You should have taken them with you. I hope you are not too tired and got home alright. I'll be seeing you soon make no mistake about that. I'll try to write again before we leave Auckland.

My love darling,

Barbara

PS. *You say you would never throw the enclosed away but I am sure they are no good.*

Central Hotellet
Vasagatan 38
Stockholm
Wednesday 1930

Dear Mum,

Yesterday we arrived here and had a perfectly lovely trip through the canal, sunny and almost warm the whole way, and of course it looks it's best as the trees are all coming out. It is a dear little boat and sometimes the canal is so narrow you can touch the trees on both sides. There are about 65 locks, you rise about 165ft, all in all, very curious. The food on board is marvellous, very like the Norwegian food, so now I have got to go on a diet for a week or so. I find it very hard to diet when one does so little exercise and really one doesn't need that much food, but eating passes the time so well.

Stockholm is really built on many islands, so therefore has canals all through the city. Canals are such common things here in Europe and sometimes I think Sydney will look funny to me when I go home, with no water through the city. Ewing has gone to have a sort of Turkish bath; he always does when we stop anywhere. So, I am taking it easy, I should be buying myself a hat as I haven't got any, but I can't be bothered, it is such a bore translating the signs.

Just had a letter from Uncle Jack, I sent him a few of those Chinese rice paper slips, he seemed to like them. He says his wife is a great golfer and his son is too, also saying he has had a letter from you. Also, I had a letter from George. He's a darling boy, always so sweet to me, it will be lovely to see him when we are in England. He is as funny as a fit and such a decent kid. Also had a letter from Dr Bridie, she is the woman I gave my dog 'John' to, she says he is a darling and everybody loves him and that a girl came in a bit like me and he nearly went mad for a minute, but when he found out it wasn't me went and whined in his basket.

Fancy Sadie having an earache poor kid how depressing they are, tell her to cheer up that I had one on the way here and couldn't sit down!

I am a little disappointed in the Swedish people. I expected them to be finer looking, not so far. I think Norwegians like the Germans collectively are the finest looking people. You would be surprised how terribly ordinary the men and women in England look.

In a couple of days, we go to Mariehamn to see Ewing's relations, an old aunt of about 80 and a niece about 40, it ought to be rather fun.

One gets very tired walking here, the pavements are all uneven stones and it's tiring.

Tons of love,

Barbara

SS. Puccini
July 1930

Dear Mum,

    I'm such a clutter brain, I can't remember when I wrote to you. I think I wrote to you about this trip, we are in Catania, Sicily, and we are already treacherously late in starting, but the boat is really very nice and beautifully laid out with new cabins. Tomorrow, we go back to Malta, that's if we do leave. I wish you could hear the noise; the Italians never stop yelling, you would think they were murdering each other, but it is quite alright! I will be glad to see Malta again tomorrow, it is a lovely place.

    This trip is very nice and we travel at night and are in port every day. There is another honeymoon couple on board, a Chinese girl and a young German, they seem very happy. She laughs all the time; she laughs too much, I think it seems wrong, they are evidently very well off and she has wonderful clothes, it's very pathetic, I think.

    On the ferries bay there was a young English lad with a Senegalese wife, it seemed very terrible. The people are so dirty it's awful, one has to close one's mind when having a meal, I hate to think that Cyprus will be like that.

    Yesterday we were at Bari, Italy, a big town visiting the grave and church of St. Nicolas. A thirteenth century church, a huge stone place with a gruesome statue of the saint.

    Here in Catania, in the middle of the city they have unearthed an old Roman theatre, or part of it. It is weird, I am very anxious to get to Naples so we can go to Pompei and Messina the day after tomorrow, where we will be able to see Mount Etna.

    They are shipping a big box of canaries; they are just outside my window and are getting quite tame. I feed them with grapes much to George's (Barbara's dog) annoyance.

    If only we had come on a decent boat, I could have bought Mina and landed her in France. There is no quarantine and everyone carries their dogs on their holidays; how is she, have you seen her? George is a devil, I made him a coat for the cold weather in Norway, he has taken such a liking to it he still wears it and nearly dies of the heat, he *is cute enough to sleep in it, but I can't take it away. I will enclose a photo of me feeding the pigeons in Venice, such an original snapshot!* (Fig 3)

Ewing is getting wild business ideas so we might yet be millionaires, things are getting harder, still it seems we might yet have to live at home with mamma! (Ewing's mother) *I am getting prepared anyway and reading the modern version of the New Testament. I wish you could hear the row; we are three and a half hours late and another boat wants to come in and everyone is talking at once.*

Tons of love,

Barbara

Would it be asking a lot to send me a pot of Thorburn's. My skin is terribly freckled and I can't get anything here to help remove them somehow.

Barbara writing to her sister Sadie in Australia:

Helsingfors, Finland
9th August 1930

Dear Sadie,

I just got your letter, which has taken some time to reach me and laughed and laughed until tears ran down my face. They all thought I was cuckoo.
In mum's first letter she said there was no news from you this week, and the case from Ewing hadn't arrived just a key! The next letter said still no case, just another key from Ewing!
I was surprised to hear you were moving. It was the first I'd heard of it. It seems to me it would always be better for mum to go to a biggish boarding house where she would get some company. Like some of those nice places in Macleary, but of course I don't know.

The garden ought to be nice, funnily enough we have been talking a lot lately about having a farm, Ewing is very keen and he certainly needs something to do, in fact we both do. One is very apt to get crotchety with too little to do. As it is, he reads the paper and gets into a positive fury at every political move by Australia, America and England, to say nothing of the continent! We have been spending a lot of time in Finland, it's nice, more especially because it's cheap. We would need twice the amount in England and also, we can move around here. We have just come here and it is a lovely city with many beautiful buildings and the railway station (Fig 4) is a perfect dream. There are lovely restaurants here and in Sweden. The architecture is nice, and they always play rather good music. We hope, if we can, to stay here for maybe two months and 'save' as Ewing says, which really means we will have a bit of money to get one's shoes repaired.

We hope to get a flat or a cottage, which will be good as Ewing is terribly thin and doesn't eat well, even though we have better food. Heavens I wish I had some money of my own, I always feel so mean travelling around like this and then not having anything at all, if only I had an allowance of my own. But as it is, although we spend a lot, of course on moving around, I spend very little on myself by the way. When I was in France and all by myself, without Ewing (possibly the Cote de Azure), I renovated my black and white dress, do you remember it? It looks not bad at all, luckily, I have got thin again and that always helps. Also renovated the hat to match and wearing it at the new formal tilt making me look like a prostitute but still fashionable. The old dame said to me this morning, 'I think you are a quaint little thing the way you always wear that brown costume'. So, I feel duty bound to go look for another one.

These people are very uninteresting looking, the women, not at all good looking and the men, not much better.

I have been having some lovely Finnish baths, the sweating process is really good, my poor old tummy even seems better. They have some rather nice glass here but I wonder if you should have the bother of cleaning it, if I did send some. Everywhere now sells that 'new pewter' but you probably have that at home.

You don't know how lonely I get sometimes as I have few friends, although Helen, she was always a brick, a dear thing, writes nearly every week and I know that I must mean a lot to her.

It's raining like hell and nearly midnight, Ewing has had a bath and seems to have done the family washing! I have a good view of Helsingfors although through the leg of a pair of underpants, and each door is artistically draft proofed by a nightshirt.

Tomorrow I'll don my old walking shoes (no mean sight) and brave the cobblestone paths (God how I hate them) I'll walk this town from East to West. Good night honey, my love to you all.

Barbara.

Baltic sea on route to Latvia
19th August 1930

Dear Mum,

We are now on our way to Latvia on the dirtiest, lousiest boat imaginable. We got the car on Wednesday and left the same day. We had a lot of repairs done on her and she works like new, for how long oh lord, how long! She has her own eccentricities, that of running out of petrol. Like she did last night when we stopped in Parnu at a quaint old town in Estonia, where we left the boat.

We slept the night at the hotel, quite a modern place and the darlingest room. We went to the local casino where Miss Estonia was on view, a frilly fair doll like girl. Tomorrow, we arrive at Riga, the capital of Latvia where I heard there is a marvellous beach. We got tired of the one in Helsingfors as it had a house on it. Parnu was a dear little place and everywhere one can see the remains of Russian influence, as it was once owned by Russia, and possibly will again.

I'm awfully sorry the old suitcase was so long in coming, you will have expected something nicer by the time it came, there really isn't much as I said, just Sadie's coat. But still if it isn't much trouble, I thought you would like to see them. I don't want anything kept for myself, we don't know what we will do after Riga, but will probably go South through Poland if the bandits aren't too bad. I am writing with a new fountain pen Ewing gave me for my birthday complete with pencil, in black and silver but as you can see, I am having a little trouble with the nib.

We are still undecided as to what we will do for the winter, either go definitely South into the Southern hemisphere or settle down and even if we do freeze enjoy the comforts of our own rooms... rest of letter missing.

Riga, Latvia.
(Date unknown)

Dear Mum,

We got here on Saturday and after meandering around the town, which by the way is quite large, we decided to go down to the beach. It is about 12 miles long. It has many small towns and restaurants along the way and is all very lively.

The only respectable looking hotel was dirty, so we have come here to the Sanitorium which is perfectly lovely, even though a little crude. We have 3 regular meals a day, the first time for many months, and are right on the beach. I walk about 9 miles every day and swim the rest of the time. I've never felt so well since I left home. They call it a Sanitorium but it is not in the same sense as we think of at home. Although there are sick and weak people here, the majority are just families who come because it is on the beach and the food is wholesome and good. But heaven's it's funny, I've never seen so many Jews in all my life. I imagine there are more Jews in Riga than there are Latvians themselves and they are naturally all very rich. This is a strange country and hard to describe, there isn't any, what I call, local colour, as in Holland or say China. No costume and yet there is a strange foreign atmosphere, even more than other countries. I suppose it is because the place doesn't look much different from our own countries, but one does realise how different the people are.

There is fruit everywhere, masses of it such a refreshing sight, lovely fresh apples just off the trees.

The children learn Latvian, German and Russian in their schools so they have a good start in life. Today it is quite cold and there is a sharp wind blowing, but yours truly has become a health crank. Out at 8.30am, dressed in only a bathing suit and a cake of soap, I plunge into the briny, it is cold but lovely, then a run on the beach. Ewing sits looking out of the window shivering at the sight!

Now that you are preparing for spring, we are preparing for a gloomy winter but I have decided I have just got to get used to the cold, so that's all.
Must go now we want to go into Riga to see the sights.

Tons of love,
Barbara

Carlton Hotel
Danzig.
29th August 1930

Dear Mum,

    Here we are at last after many trials and tribulations and perhaps all the good rest at Marienbad did us, undone. I hated leaving Marienbad, I would have liked to have stayed some weeks. I felt so well and the exercise and food made us both good, it would have done if Ewing ate any amount of food, he is so nervy and naturally cross.

    But still, we move on as we generally do and make tracks South to Lithuania. When we got to the border we had to completely turn back to Riga as the passport for the car didn't include that silly little country. So back we went, stayed the night and fixed the passports and whatnots, retraced our steps once again over the most notorious country you could ever imagine. There was a straight road which had, we counted them, only two turns in 50 miles. We then drove to Lithuania where the scenery suddenly changed and is very lovely, with many small green hills and quaint villages, and many lovely geese and ducks which I love to see on the ponds.

    From here we entered East Prussia, always a nerve-racking business for me when we come into German territory. Ewing hates them so and picks a fight whenever possible and is so irritated all the time, I breathed a sigh of relief when we at last passed into Danzig. (Fig 5) *We are in the quaintest and loveliest city I have ever seen; it has a very Dutch flavour about it with many picturesque winding canals, and the oldest loveliest buildings which seem to lay right over the canals. Also, the most modern of buildings and extremely well-dressed women, altogether a very nice combination.*

    The poor old car, like its owners breaking up, notwithstanding the repairs in Helsingfors. Because we dropped off the batteries on the road in Lithuania, she leaks water everywhere.

    It is always very hard to get a quiet room in a hotel in the city, I have been awake from about 5 o'clock with the traffic. Funnily enough it is the only time Ewing seems to sleep, as he is now fast asleep amid the positive roar of the traffic. I will endeavour to dress before he wakes up and go for a walk. It puts me in a good temper and gives him time to defuse his daily dislike of the Germans at the washbasin!

All yesterday we drove through stork country, saw many old storks in the fields and some perched on their ridiculous precarious nests. Two nests were on top of telegraph posts and very big, I don't know how they get them to stay in stormy weather.

It must seem funny living in Pymble, you don't write much about the place, what is it like, who are you going to sell your flowers to?
...will finish this later.

Later...

We drove out of Zoppot, a seaside town, twelve miles from here, which is supposed to be another Monte Carlo but it isn't very nice. It does have some very nice expensive hotels and quite a nice beach if the weather is fine. We may go out there tomorrow for a few days.

Ewing has gone to have a bath, his favourite occupation, bath attendants must be very attractive judging from the number of baths Ewing has! I have been walking around town, a lively business, and feeling rather dowdy, so went and had a manicure now feeling much better.

I can see Ewing looming in the distance looking very clean and more ready for a fight!

Love,
Barbara.

PS. The glint in my husband's eye was the result of six beers and a ham sandwich!

The following was possibly a letter written as her mother made her way to visit them in Italy.

...beginning of letter missing, *... that I may well learn to love the place.*

I am terribly sorry about such few passengers, I do hope you get to play some bridge, let me know. Who'd have thought it would be so empty –

Heaven knows I have rambled, by now your trials and tribulations are over. Take care of yourself, you are rather precious to me; you are all I have got in the world. I'm afraid I am not a very good daughter and rather cross. I am selfish and should have been a man, then it wouldn't have been so noticeable.

Give my love to them all and love to your dear self.

Barbara

Naples
Nov 20th 1930

Dearest Mum,

Your two letters arrived today; it was nice to hear from you. It is nice that you will all be living together and nice for Sadie. You will all be able to enjoy the tea set I sent to her.

Now, I must get some of the handmade handkerchiefs they have here to send, they are lovely also in linen. Do you like cameos? We might be going to Taormina in Sicily soon, people here know of a cottage that a man and wife let out, it is like a mansion for two. It would be nice if we could save some money.

We are both very nervy especially Ewing. We went to Pompei the other day. It was fascinating, especially the roman baths of hot water, the warm then cold, all lovely.

Much to Ewing's delight there was a brothel very well preserved. Over each door there was a picture of the special attractions of the young lady inside in some very weird positions, and at the end of the hall, the counter where the old dame collected the cash. In the street one can still see the wonderful lead pipes that carried the water, and the ruts in the roads where the chariots ran.

I will go out by myself one day, it is the only way to see things, I think.

We have met some weird people, mainly Americans but all rather nice, who give us numerous addresses. We haven't seen much yet although we have been here over a month. I have got so in the way of saying to myself how father would like to see this and that, that I can't bear to go and see things, especially the views that he always loved.

I have enclosed some films that I took in Holland and Venice. Sorry we haven't taken more but the camera only occasionally obliges us by acting.

Did I tell you that by looking out of my window I can see Capri, which was really where Sirens lived and tried to lure Ulysses. Also, about eight miles round the point is the Phlegraean Fields where Dante wrote his Inferno and the old Sybil lived in a cave. I believe it all looks, even now like hell, the vapours hissing out of the ground. I find it hard even now that Homer and Virgil wrote about practically <u>real</u> things and that they can all be traced. Mr Brandyce here knows everything about the places and it is so awfully nice him telling us anything we want to know. He is very kind to me and so is his mother who seems to have more than her fair share of unhappiness. She lost her husband when she was 23yrs with her son just 3yrs. She is very musical and we have many talks. Unfortunately, they both get on Ewing's nerves a bit, I'm sorry because I like them. Ewing can't understand me making friends with people older than myself but I hate younger people.

Things are getting very bad over here, it is obvious there will be another war and he hopes it will wipe out all of Europe as it would make a good new fertilized forest! Ewing's mother is getting very friendly lately and has now given Ewing the Oxford English Dictionary which cost £100! Jeepers how I would have liked the money. Am trying to buy a coat, my green one has ripped right down the front just from sheer wear, but it is hopeless here everything is too big and the prices!

I seem to be rambling, somewhat, don't I? Ewing's asleep and it is nice to talk to you. I started to do some drawing but have given it up now, it doesn't matter. If we go to Taormina, and they have a piano I might learn to play, have always wanted to even if it is only to know the notes. George my dog, is of great comfort to me and knows when I am not feeling very happy. He likes me I suppose, you might think I am mad but he seems to understand me better than Ewing even.

I wish you could see him admiring me when I get dressed and he smells everything in such a funny way, I must get his photo taken to send you.

Ewing gets a tremor in his leg at night, it is his nerves, I think. I gave him some Ovaltine that is food, isn't it?

I will write you again soon
Barbara

Barbara and Ewing spent Christmas 1930 with Konni Zilliacus and his wife. (Fig 6) Zilliacus was a Finnish American and a British Labour minister. He spoke nine languages fluently and was the Secretariat to the League of Nations who he believed could help stop the war as a collective. But the British Government refused to join and Zilliacus resigned when the Nazis invaded Czechoslovakia.

Canadian Pacific
Steamship Liners
Hong Kong
11th February 1931

Dearest Sadie,

Have just got your letter from Avalon and it has made me very homesick. It seems a funny thing I suppose that I would give anything to be home and staying in that cottage with you.

Only the other day in Manila, we got out of the car and went into the fields to watch some coolies threshing rice. It felt so marvellous to be on the field again instead of the incessant watching things from the motor cars. I wish you were here; how lovely it would be and would do you so much good.

It's funny you saying wasn't I scared about the boat rocking, funnily enough nothing scares me. No, I guess it's because nothing matters much and we only die once.

We seem to be right in the middle of the troubles here, looks like a big world war to me. Anyway, civilization is rotting, it is time it was wiped right out. I wish America or England would declare war while we are here, I would join in a minute.

You wouldn't find any difference in me, I haven't changed a bit, except perhaps I have learned to accept things and not kick. Also, I have put on weight, but although it is not good for my figure, I think slightly improves my fizz. Heavens the world is small, I ran into Mrs McEvoy who used to come into the Roycroft but now lives here. I meet Australians everywhere. One American man on board when he heard I was from Australia asked me if I was speaking my own language!

We are not able to go to Shanghai and may not be able to go to Peking or Japan, but won't know for a day or two. It is cold here, such a quick change. Haven't seen much of the place yet as today we are free for independent action. Had a look at the shops, they are very nice, lots of embroidery we used to get at home, I think I'll buy one, I'll keep them till I come home myself. I think if I send them the duty would be very much.

There are some very nice people on board, especially elderly people. I've come to the conclusion that money, where young people are concerned, makes very little difference as far as happiness goes, but it certainly improves elderly people. I envy the old people they are so contented. Heavens the money they spend... There is one young and rather attractive girl who hasn't worn the same dress or coat twice. I suppose they would laugh if they knew we arrived on board with these suitcases. It is the unwritten law of the boat that one gives each of one's stewards 10 shillings a week tip, so you can imagine what that involves with about ten regular stewards and many miscellaneous ones. One old fool gives her table steward £5 a week.

Every day we have a newspaper printed with all the news up to date. Our room has a fan radiator, hot and cold running water, six different lights, meal beds and a thermos jug. I tell you all the tit bits to give you an idea of the boat, I hope it doesn't bore you but it is all so different and new to me, I'm sure you must like to hear all about it.

Mum asked what our class was this trip but we don't know. All depends on what comes out of our meeting with 'mama' as things stand, we can't wander around because we really haven't enough money and anyway, it is time I made some money to help people at least, if nothing else I ought to be useful.

My feet went numb with the cold so will have to go for a walk. Did I tell you that an old dame said to me,' I think you are a quaint little thing the way you always wear that brown costume'. I feel duty bound to go look for another one.

Tons of love darling,
Barbara

Hotel Astoria A. Hanl.
Wein I. Kärnten Strasse 32
Vienna

Beginning of letter missing... *the dear thing he is. It is rather amusing to think of all the acquaintances we have gathered, especially in England, we wouldn't be lonely if we settled in London, although I hate it. But the English countryside and country life certainly gets one thinking. I could live in one of those adorable cottages, although it would be rather like living in a puddle of mud.*

What a mess Europe seems to be in, cheeky Germany and everything, she'll certainly start a war again soon and old England will get it in the neck again. Talk about ingratitude, the Belgians always talk most rudely about the English saying they came too late to help them!

The other night we went to the opera, such a lovely old opera house with dozens of boxes all around the circle and the Royal box was pathetically closed and empty. The opera was Boccaccio rather lovely and tight with the evidently famous Madam Jeritza[1] *was playing, she certainly has a perfectly lovely voice.*

Everyone went out during the interval and ate ham rolls and drank beer, a most happy combination, with evening dress. I didn't wear evening dress as mine is a crumpled mess.

Well excuse all my warbling. Tons of love,

Barbara

---

[1] **Madam Jeritza** an operatic soprano known as 'The Moravian Thunderbolt.'

The Royal Palace Hotel
Kensington, London W
2th April 1931

Dear Mum,

Your parcel hasn't yet arrived - of course, I forget the letters come overland and arrive sooner so the parcel won't be here for some time. About the things we are sending, the wooden beads are from some wood in China I think cherry trees.

The gold lacquer bowl will stand boiling water and washes well. The sign on the letters on the silk handkerchief means 'long life and happiness' The trick box can open in moves pushing different sides and then the top thought may amuse Tal.

The Japanese obi is what the women wear around themselves making a large pad at the back with the long ends as seen on the dolls. Japanese prints are of no value that I know of but I thought rather nice. The cap made of coloured string comes from Jerusalem, had to have something from there! The Japanese socks and shoes are I think rather quaint, the division goes between the toe and the next toe they walk in them with a springy little trot.
They shouldn't charge duty as I have worn them, the socks are quite dirty.

The money box opens this way:
Push the roof forward over the front of the house, slide the back wall up. To <u>put</u> money in slide the top of the door up and in the front. The unmounted earrings I thought Sadie would like; she admired one like it once before. Had great difficulty getting two and now they don't match but maybe alright when made up. I think they are white jade but you needn't mention it as I didn't pay much for them although these are the one thing I really undervalued and if she doesn't want them you won't have much duty on them. Although white jade isn't anything near as dear as green jade. The blue earrings are just curious <u>supposed</u> to be 100 years old.

The cigarette case was a present to me! But I didn't want it, I have sent it on. It is quite a nice and the genuine thing, thought you might dispense of it somewhere.

The kimonos aren't much I'm ashamed to say, you see Ewing said don't bother to get much for his family as they have so much and travel so much, which was all wrong, they expected things and are very simple and thrilled with everything, so I parted with four Kimonos quickly. But from what I see here I'll be able to pick up nicer things here and better. The fur-lined coat I think rather nice and thankfully was only £3. This was due to the exchange but you needn't mention it, I'd advise Sadie to have it recut if she doesn't like the sleeves, that's the only drawback. The embroidery around the edges is genuine old work. The camphor chests are cheap for £1, aren't they? I thought it was a good way of sending things home even if you haven't room for it. We had to put those old clothes in to fill it up, we didn't even have paper but you can dispense with them, also the circular about the Empress of Britain, I thought it would interest you.

That's about all, hope you don't have much trouble. It's raining and miserable here, an awfully pale London. We might buy a car and go around England, can't get anything cheap enough yet. If it wasn't getting winter, I would come home, I can't bear the thought of it any colder, I seem to have been cold for years. Also have got fat and look forty. Did I tell you I found a pearl in an oyster, not very large but was most exciting?

Tons of love,

Barbara

The Royal Palace Hotel
Kensington, London. W
18th April 1931

Dear Mum,

Called today at Australia House and got your two letters but the parcel is not through yet, will be tomorrow probably. I am dying to see it, thank you very much but you shouldn't have spent your money on us like that. Will write more about it when we get the parcel.

Arrived here on Friday evening, terribly cold and wet, it is too miserable for words. I <u>hate</u> London, I don't think I will ever like it, it is the lousiest most miserable *place, full of inferior and deformed people. We struck this place just by chance and a funny thing happen the next day. We were having, just by chance, our lunch in a small Russian cafe and who should walk in but George Draffin, who by the way I knew was in a job out of London, and blessed if he wasn't staying here. He had signed his name just above where Ewing had signed his! So, we have seen a bit of him thank goodness, it cheered us up no end. We just can't decide what to do. Ewing thinks of settling here to do some work but I know he would be too miserable to do much. Then one thought of getting some old second-hand car and seeing a bit of England, perhaps motor up to see Uncle Jack, but I don't know, maybe if Ewing stays here, I might go on to Paris for a while, it's time I learnt French.*

Am hurrying for the mail

Tons of love,

Barbara

There had been so little evidence of Ewing among Barbara's things, no memento of a loving relationship. Only a possible photo in their honeymoon album, just the one. A few scraps of him remained in torn letters to his future brother-in-law Tal (Talwyn) and later to his mother-in-law Nellie, letting her know that living apart from Barbara would be okay as Barbara chose to remain in London while Ewing continued his work abroad.

Two letters from Ewing to Barbara's mother and Sadie's boyfriend, at the time, Tal:

1931

Dear Mum,

Kiitos paljon or if you have forgotten your Finnish, tack so mycket is Swedish for 'Thanks very much' for the handkerchiefs. They are very welcome and you are a dear to send them to me - many thanks.

I hear you won the eyes - gay bird you when you get among the Italians!!

Mum, I love Barbara and will <u>never</u> let her down - don't worry we will be alright even if apart for a little - everything will be okay soon.

My best to Sadie and her boyfriend and much love to you.

Ewing

…. Hotel Tientsin (China)
circa 1931

Beginning of letter missing...*Mr Wood and I went out for a walk. Two US marines came by in a little Austin 7 they waved to us and passed on. A minute later they drove up and asked us to go for a ride, so we piled in and went at a terrific rate for about 10 minutes.*

B and I got the train OK but Mr Wood missed it - it went out like lightning! Later we saw Ltn. Ellis at Peking and had a party! It was 15 degrees and blowing a gale but it wasn't cold at all.

Getting off now at Kyoto (Japan)

Love Ewing

Canadian Pacific Steamship Line Cruises,
Gulf of Aden
Jan 3rd 1932

Dear Tal,

While Bar is out spending some pennies, I'll say hello! Enclosed bits of Australian news might interest you.

Played tennis the dinkum kind on a real court, had a swim in a gorgeous pool and did some work with my dictionary. So, this is a day for you. Oh! played chess also. This is a marvellous boat, it vibrates like a Finale Ford giving birth to a flock of baby Austins.

Ta Ta Tal
Ewing

Canadian Pacific Steamship Line Cruises
(Unknown date)
Emperor of Britain, at Sea.

Dear Tal,

Many thanks for your jolly letter, good of you to think of Ewing so far off.
The straits of Messina look glorious, white snow is a third of the way down. It was cold though, while we were at the straits of Magellan! But the shuttered deck and warm lounge rooms help a lot.

<u>Good, Food</u>! at last! Not that we have starved, but pensioners cooking, especially in Italy is slight and not large in choice. I will send a sample menu.

To Morocco then the Gulf of Corinth, the Canal and then Athens. It is a good thrill for me and Bar too.

The people on board are awfully nice, mostly Americans but some English, French, Norwegian, Danish, several Czechoslovaks, the former Spanish Ambassador to......rest of letter missing.

American Consulate
Finland – Helsingfors
Helsingfors

Dear Mum,

It is hard to realise that you have gone away. Many thanks for your visit - may I say to <u>us</u>? Not just to Europe. And many thanks for coming to Helsingfors, it was lovely.
We got some cider at last, didn't we? And you managed to get me to 'The Exotic' too.
Do you remember Roger standing in all his majesty in the narrow street and we had to back around!? I'll never forget you in your cabin in Copenhagen saying 'I knew it was Ewing'

And when in Italy don't forget your romantic toga darling.

Bunnie wunnie and I are all right Mum, and will be well.

Happy voyage home, lots of fun and love to all my folks in Sydney.

My love to your always

Ewing xx

In a later letter dated July 1953, Ewing was writing to his aunt:

'I still love the memory of my wife Barbara and do not care to marry again.'

From an interview for the Oxford Mail in 1998, and at the age of 90, Barbara explained that her and husband had been travelling extensively when a cable came for him to return to his mother in New York. She declined to go which was the start of an amicable and slow separation. She went on to proclaim herself a lousy wife.

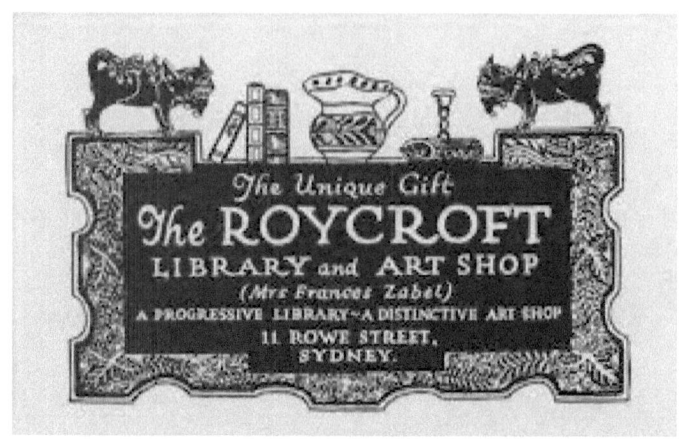

Fig 2

Barbara's work place before leaving Australia

Fig 3

Barbara in Venice, 1930

Photo of Barbara and possibly Ewing in Capri.

Cruise ship at Capri harbour.

Fellow travellers on a beach in Capri, Barbara second from right.

Barbara, Capri.

Barbara second from right, Capri.

Fig 4

Helsingfors (Helsinki) railway station 1930

Fig 5
Dantzig, Poland

Fellow cruise ship travellers.

Mumbai snake charmer.

Shy friends on deck

Panama Canal

Bangkok and Manilla

Rice fields.

Bombay (Mumbai), Ceylon (Sri Lanka) and Java

Bombay (Mumbai), Ceylon (Sri Lanka) and Java

Japan

Japan

China

China

Russia

Fig.6

Finland
May Zilliacus and child.

Belgium

Germany

Menin Gate

River Mozell

Barbara in Sweden

Latvia and Estonia

Barbara on skis, Denmark

Hamlet's Castle.

Austria

Photo taken in France, Barbara on the left.

Barbara at the WWI trenches, Ypres.

A bombed church, Ypres.

Barbara in England. Captioned 'deer me!'

Blenheim, Oxfordshire.

Chapter 3
School for Stars

As winter arrived, Barbara found herself in London alone. With Ewing busy abroad, they didn't meet again until much later. Desperate to start her acting career and bored with doing nothing, Barbara collected the money she needed to produce her acting portfolio photographs. She said in later life, that she came to England with no qualifications and next to no money, but was determined to forge her own career. At the start of her attempt as an actress, and as Australian, she was destined to only play the parts of Cockney maids. While on tour with the play 'A Gay Divorce' she took on a role that required her to sing and dance, neither of which she had done before. She remained with the play despite her inexperience and despite other offers coming along.

London
31st December 1931

Darling,

Just a quick note to wish you a happy New Year, I'll have a drink for you at midnight; going to a rather grand dance in a lovely new frock (can't sit down in it though!) still I can just keep walking.

Just had an offer of a 10-week tour playing Shakespeare, it would be awfully good for me but the money is bad and I don't know want to leave London, I don't think I'll like it.

I'm a hell of a lug...
 Love,
  Barbara

Piccadilly
16th February 1932

Dearest Mum,

Sorry Mrs Draffin hasn't seen you yet she's probably busy settling down with her flock but she will, she wants to see you. Hope you like the material, not much of a present when you have to spend money to get it made up.

You say you are making jam for Sadie; does she sell it in the shop? Oh, and I'm finding it hard to get anything on flowers or florists, there isn't a book published and the florists don't seem to keep catalogues here, but tell Sadie I'm still trying.

After leaving his sisters in Paris, Ewing went on down to Rome, he asked me to come over with the car but we did enough travelling in a car together last year, so I said for him to go down and maybe I would follow him later. So now I am a confirmed grass widow, everybody seems sorry for me but I am really enjoying it very much, doing as I like and having the Minx[2] and going out if I get bored.

I will need to do something soon as it is too expensive here, as I keep saying, I don't mind spending the money but I do like getting something for it.

I'm getting keen on my German now. The little Pekingese I was going to buy has been sold. I'm terribly disappointed, I think I'll buy a Borzoi instead.

This weekend, Dot and I are driving up to Stratford on Avon, it ought to be fun seeing the sights, she doesn't go about much and see things so it ought to be fun.

My dancing is going very well, I'm almost 'top' of the class. It's great fun. George the teacher calls me Barry(?) I suppose he thinks it sounds professional.

---

[2] **The Hillman Minx** was a mid-sized family car that British car maker Hillman produced from 1931 to 1970.

Fancy John Woods doing so well, £25 a week is certainly better than a kick in the pants. By the way Ewing bought me a pair of French panties in Paris, I am dying to see them.

Am enclosing two of my indoor studies, the one in my chemise you made me is very good! The weather here is so good and mostly fine.

Give my love to them all, and a lot for your dear self.

Barbara

London
20th December 1933

Dearest Mum,

I got two letters from you this week, one airmail. I am sorry the last part of your trip home was so monotonous, then I suppose you were tired and keen to get home.

Ewing seems quite settled and has taken an apartment. I haven't heard from him for weeks until today, I suppose he has been occupied. I sent him for Christmas, some pyjamas and a dressing gown and an Australian pudding. A Shetland scarf, a tin of his favourite curry, two tins of Fortnum's toothpaste, a calendar and a long list of what I want. He can't say I am not a thoughtful wife. It is the ghastly holiday time as you know.

God I am nervous about this stupid play on Friday, but I really only have a small part, they made me a sweet young thing and that's rather hard.

More news next week, will write from Marlow.

Lots of love,

Barbara

Barbara writing to her sister:

London
31st January 1935

Dear Sadie,

The dressing gown has arrived and I really don't know what to say, I have never seen anything like it, it was is the loveliest thing I've ever seen and the work the fineness, it is just too lovely. When I think of you making that for me, honestly, I feel like crying or something. I feel so frightened to wear it, I do feel it causes for some auspicious occasion - twins at least! Thank you darling so very much, please know how much I appreciate this. I don't very often get presents, and I mean, to get one like this, is well, I just don't know what to say.

The actress Iris Hoey[3] was here when it arrived, she said she had never seen anything like it. She wants to know if you could let her have the pattern, heaven help me if you can. I can imagine her arriving here at all times of the day and night comparing her handiwork with yours. The slippers are sweet, I really shall look swell in them, I wish you could see them on me. Well perhaps you will soon.

I had a great time in Finland the first real holiday I've had for a long time. I'm glad, for Ewing's, sake that I was a 'success' with his friends, he was very proud. It's wonderful how stage training helps one socially.

If the doctor at the eye hospital said about my eyes is correct, I have nothing to worry about. It is a complaint very common with people living in a hot, glaring climate. A film covers the eyes to protect it from the rays of the sun. In fact, it is much better that it has grown over as it protects the eyes much better. The operation is hardly an operation at all and the simplest one done by that profession. That's all, but it will ease mothers mind, I am off to an eye specialist early next week.

I also had a great time in the country before coming back to London, as I had a little over a week. I took lessons in riding which was great fun, I'm very enthusiastic I would like to take it up. It is a good way to get fresh air and good exercise. Now I am

---

[3] **Iris Hoey** was a British born actress known for her roles in 'Tense moments with Great Authors' 1922. 'Those were the Days' 1934 and 'Just William' 1940

back I am full of hope and trying to get down to some work. There is so much to do and I'm not doing much socially, maybe seeing people for lunches but it's such a waste of time.

I'm going to take singing lessons, if only I had done all these things when I was young. A film agent telephoned today and I have to go to see him this afternoon, he saw my photo somewhere. I hope something comes of it. Unfortunately, I take such a good photo that's it's a bit of a shock when they see me in the flesh!

Iris Hoey is keen to go to Australia with a company, I wish she could arrange it as I would have a pretty good chance of going too, wouldn't it be great!

It worries me that you take tablets to thin you, I think it is bad! Thyroids of course, unless properly ordered by food doctor can make one fat. For me, I find that when I have had so much writing to do, and food around me. But I have got out of the habit of eating bread, potatoes, sweets and cakes and now, I just don't think of eating them. Mind you I can eat an awful lot of meat, vegetables and salads which of course make energy. So, I am pretty trim and work off any flesh I get. It's very different with you I suppose you sit a good deal especially after meals, which is very bad.

London seems very warm after Finland, funny how I have got used to the cold weather. I'm now off to the Caledonian market.

Love,
      Barbara

605 Mount Royal, Marble Arch
W1
9th April 1935

Dear Mum,

I've just got your airmail letter saying you are settling down. I feel so glad for you to have a place of your own. I'm quite sure that if everyone really knew the joy of living on one's own there would never be anybody living together. If you write to me, please use the name Miss Barbara Toy as I like to keep my professional name always in the public eye.

I'm working terribly hard on a scenario for Frank Birch,[4] who is very enthusiastic about it. He says it's a winner, so that encourages me.

I think it's good too, and if I can fit around the technical side of the scenario writing, it seems to me to be the sort of stuff that big films are made of. So far, its child's play the imaginative part is just too easy. In fact, I seem to have too much imagination, I've got too many ideas, I suppose that's why I've always been such a liar!

The last show went well. I played the daughter Susan who elopes. Frank says I am now the principal lead and all I need is heaps and heaps of experience as far as timing goes.

You must remember that for the last year or 18 months, nearly, I've been training steadily so I'm not altogether a new turn. I still study and work with my voice, which is much more improved but still a little hard when I am tired. Also, I'm starting to learn about producing and as soon as the scenarios are finished, I hope to produce a play at the Queen's Theatre (they don't know it yet). Recently bought a wireless, the sweetest thing, about 6 inches by 6 inches in vermillion red. It cost me the large sum four pounds, seven shillings and Sixpence.

I had 3 cables from Ewing on my wedding anniversary. I had forgotten and can't for the life of me remember how many years I have been married.

I am so terribly fortunate to have met Frank Birch, I always hope to meet such a person but was quite resigned to the fact that such things don't happen. He has given me back my confidence and self-respect and made me really ambitious again, believing in me to such an extent that I now believe in myself. He is very like me in lots of ways, very independent. I kind of respect one wanting to be alone, in fact he has the knack of bringing out the best in me, I played the lead in the last one. Now he's having a scenario especially made for him as it seems there is nothing he can't do.

---

[4] **Frank Birch** OBE was a British cryptographer and actor.

He has just been in films, one is called 'School for Stars'[5] *and the other 'Jubilee Window' and his grandmother who lived in a castle at Hampton Court, you remember we went there.*

Well, this is all about me but I know you like to hear about me, except for my work there isn't much else to tell you, I am becoming such an awful bore.

Love,

Barbara.

Among the tatters of the attic horde, I'd found an unusual small, brown, square leather case. The leather was ridged, stiff and flaking at the hinges, the rusted lock was open, thank God. The smell of old leather and the stale perfumes of the make-up made a sickly mixture, the box shaken so many times that the contents stuck together in a tangled encrusted heap. The inside was peppered with grey dust and the 'plastic doll' pink of face powder. Little bottles with torn and fading labels were covered in this mixture, stuck with the grease from tiny squashed tins. There was an odd paper covered crayon that looked like a rouge stick or a thick lipstick. A tiny little Elizabeth Arden pot, no bigger that a ten pence piece, contained a pale green cream, hardened but still showing a small finger print. I removed the little cream pot and wiped away the mess from its black rimmed top. A minute hand-painted figure in a crinoline hooped dress and straw bonnet was just visible. There was no doubting this was Barbara's stage make up case. At the time the box caused some confusion, neither myself or Terri had any idea that Barbara had been an actress.

The box disappeared one day as Terri was venturing into the studio more often as the clearing ramped up, leaving me to wonder if it would have been possible to repair the case. Terri told me she had taken it to the second-hand shop, my feeling was it sadly went to landfill. I had inadvertently placed the

---

[5] **School for stars** made in 1935 was a British romance film directed by Donovan Pedelty and staring the Australian actor Fred Conyngham and British actors Jean Gillie and Torin Thatcher. It was made in Elstree Studios as part of the 'quota quickie'. Produced quickly and cheaply to fulfil the 1927 Cinematograph Film Act, that came into force to ensure the films of a 'British character' were shown, the money returned went to British cinema.

little pot and its tiny fingerprint to one side. I was so pleased it hadn't gone out with the rest. When I explained my liking of the miniature make up pot, Terri thought I was mad. To me it made Barbara's life even more tangible, perceptible by Barbara's touch, she seemed more alive to me than ever.

*London
6th July 1934*

Dear Mum,

I haven't had a call from the theatre yet, hope I soon do. Also, I haven't been to see the film man, hence been getting my clothes in order first and so many people have been taking up my time, I never seem to be able to get away from people somehow.

It is now very hot here in London, and with the sales on it's very objectionable. I saw Margaret yesterday for the first time, we went down to Kew gardens for tea. All the spring flowers have gone and it is all rather sombre. She is a curious girl, between you and me her rapport is going to develop her into a bit of a bore. Anyhow they are sweet and rather appreciative of anything I do, which of course is hardly anything. I don't know about any conquests but Gerry may have some of his work shown with three other artist which is rather exciting.

I met an awfully nice young Australian and we have been going dancing a bit. He's a dear, quite young and dances well. We have been to some funny places together including a nightclub where they were all negros.

There isn't much news, haven't bought anything at the sales because I'm broke.

Tons of love,

Barbara

London
12th December 1934

Dear Mum,

I am awfully sorry I missed the Christmas airmail, but literally I haven't had one minute to myself. Did I tell you I am playing 'Beth' in 'Little Women', so miss cast, should be playing 'Jo' of course.

I won't be going up to visit Ewing for Christmas, can't get away in time as we play until 3 days before Christmas. Anyway, it would be madness to go away just now when I am getting really in touch with people and things, it might mean starting all over again when I come back. Blanche has just come back from somewhere in the country and is going down to Devon, I think quite soon. She likes London but is somewhat lonely I think and likes going home as soon as she is back from Europe.

It has been very mild here this evening. When it is not cold with a vengeance, I might go up to Scotland with some friends for Christmas, I don't know if it is worth the effort for a couple of days. I still have the dog; she is sweet and great company. I must away to bed, this profession gets one into the habit of good plain living.

Tons of Love,
Barbara

London
18th June 1935

Dear Mum,

I really am terribly busy and I'm going to be in a play, touch wood, as 'Miss Neville' in 'She Stoops to Conquer.'[6] it's a very difficult part for me and I have to work at it jolly hard. I'm terribly anxious to be good in it, so I work day and night. The trouble

---

[6] **'She Stoops to Conquer'** is a comedy by Oliver Goldsmith, first performed in London in 1773. It is one of the few plays from the 18th century to have retained its appeal and is regularly performed.

is I am playing opposite a woman of 40, but she doesn't look it, who of course has years of experience and I feel like a Newfoundland puppy all arms and legs.

I have just had a cable from Ewing asking me to go up this July, it is a terrible pity to go just now as all sorts of things seem to be happening here. But I feel I might go even if it's only for a few weeks. There is so much pending, firstly I might go on tour with 'Sweet Aloes'[7]. Also, I have been asked to join a trio to do cabaret work. They are going to Switzerland and Italy during the summer months, it all seems so silly to go away just now...rest of letter missing

London
11th July 1935

Dear Mum,

Just a note as it is mail day, no news, I am flying around getting clothes. On the 24th I am going up to Ewing and I am looking forward to it, will be a rest but want so many clothes. London is full of sales so naturally can't find a decent thing in the shops.

Terribly hot and I haven't a thing to wear. I am feeling much better and when I am away, will be a much better person. News is too hard to tell which is why I don't write my darling but one day I will tell you, don't worry the worst is over. I am lucky to have such a reasonable mind and a philosophy that everything happens for a reason, although I find it fearful. Lots of my ideas are terribly like Christian scientist, which is gratifying when I reason it all out myself. I've seriously found my right level at last.

I have just had my hair permed it is dreadful.

Iris Hoey, the actress who was in the last show with me, is sweet and I see quite a lot of her, she is very like me in some ways, but very lovely.

Why is it that such beautiful women always make such a mess of their lives?

All my love,
Barbara

---

[7] **'Sweet Aloes'** A play in three acts by Jay Mallory

Glasgow
21st September 1935

Dear Mum,

Please forgive the pencil as I'm writing this in bed. Dreadful cold on Sunday and it is Wednesday matinee today. I'm staying in bed until it's time to go to the theatre. It was very bad but one of the boys gave me a draught that practically cured it, it's quite marvellous. It was given to him by a Harley Street Doctor friend and is: 2 grams of caffeine and 8 grams of aspirin (ground up) and put into a chlorodyne[8] draught taken with a glass of hot milk before bed.

Last night my eyes wouldn't stop running and the morning you'd hardly know I had a cold. It's good to know. I'm very thrilled I got quite good notices here, which is surprising as it is the smallest part and especially as Glasgow audiences I supposed to be on the same par as London audiences, only more critical, even more than Edinburgh. Today is the first day it hasn't rained. There is the most marvellous repertory company that play here 1-week and then a week in Edinburgh. I wrote to the producer knowing there was a vacancy and he's coming to see my work if he can manage it. Wouldn't it be marvellous if I got up here for a season?

I'm going to get my eyes seen to next week, I think they are probably very bad.

*My digs this week are lovely, the sitting room with bedroom off, has a big coal fire all day. My landlady is sweet and fusses around with hot water bottles and makes me stay in bed and brings my breakfast in, all for 25 shillings. Theatrical digs are very cheap and I can live easily on my salary. I share with Phyllis, the leading lady. She is sweet but I made a big mistake in sharing really, it's that that has tired me so, not being able to get away by myself. Getting my bank balance straight...*rest of letter missing

There seemed to be large time gaps between some of the letters, this may have been due to her touring with acting troops.

---

[8] **Chlorodyne**. A mixture of laudanum and opium.

Northampton
2nd October 1935

Darling,

Just two letters from you this week, one airmail. I was very worried to hear Sadie wasn't too well, she ought to be careful, I hope she is better now.
This is my last week and I'm just dying to get back to London. Now that I am going, I wonder how I stuck it for so long.

Will write you as soon as I get back in London. No news as just off for the afternoon.
All my love sweet,

Barbara

London
28th October 1935

Dear Mum,

Just an airmail letter for a change. Last week I played a lovely part at the Queen's Theatre, it's the lead in an Ambrose adventure. It is great fun and in the second act which is a dream, I am a cabin boy on a ship. It was right down my street and I think I was pretty good. Everybody is saying I should play Peter pan, but of course I am not a 'name' I couldn't, but if I wasn't going away for Christmas to Ewing, I would try for the understudy of it.

I am having a good clean up and have made an appointment to have my eyes tested again at the doctors tomorrow. My tummy's a bit funny but probably just indigestion! I am really looking quite well and my hair is getting long.

They have been doing a lot of plays and a lot of shows at the Queens Theatre lately, I have discovered that people will come a long way to see a show. I am seriously thinking of trying to do make up with the Shaw Company and go to Australia, and do a season in each of the main towns. The man who produced me in this last play toured in a company out East about six years ago, he would be the man to get. Even if it just paid its way, that would be all we would want, anyhow, I'm keeping it in mind.

Could you possible try once again to send me some Thorburns? I am so sorry to be such a bore about this, it appears that is the only thing that will take the freckles off my back, and they are so bad that I can't wear any dresses at all. Perhaps Thorburn's could send the formula to the chemist here to be made up, as it seems it won't travel. I've never got a bottle as you know.

London is very crowded; I think it is going to be a big season this year. I don't much like the thought of going away…

<u>Next week…</u> so sorry I didn't send this letter last week, also didn't send one by ordinary mail - just lazy.

Anyway, I went to the Doctor and he overhauled me, said I was rudely healthy but a little run-down and gave me a marvellous tonic, which although I have only had about ten doses has made me feel so well and happy with life, that I am going around grinning at everyone. They probably think I have gone mad. Also went to the opticians they say I have a condition common with people living in Australia and hot climates. So, he first gave me some drops but I don't need glasses so evidently, they are quite strong.

I have definitely made my mind up to go to Finland this Christmas no matter what comes along. Iris Hoey who is a great friend of mine and no doubt you have heard of her; she was a very clever and lovely actress in her youth. So, doing some filming and then going to Devon for a week to walk. She is a darling and a bit queer like myself, so we get on well together! Incidentally she is a Christian Scientist and I myself well on the way to becoming one. Went to a dance last Saturday night, the first for many months, I quite enjoyed it.

A young lad of 25 years gave me roses, eminently respectable people are quite panicky about it as he is in love with me. It always amuses me as I am such a harmless person really.

I don't think the air will take another sheet. Much love darling, take care of yourself.

Barbara

When I could get Terri to sit still long enough it would sometimes take a while before she would be willing to talk about Barbara again. I wanted her to tell me more, I couldn't decide if she was hiding something, or knew very little. When I asked about Barbara's repeated 'tummy' troubles Terri mentioned endometriosis; Terri too had been surprised at Barbara's lack of pregnancies and wondered if she was unable to conceive. She wrote of the children in her later letters and always spoke fondly of her sister's boys. Although never having children of her own, among the later collections of Barbara's photographs were many of children. Children in rags begging, some hiding behind their mother's clothes, afraid of the foreigner with a camera. They were tender, sad, charged with an emotion of need, part of a culture and country where such scenes were common place. Barbara's work was her life, whatever she did, it would be all consuming with total dedication, whatever tragedies or circumstances the world threw at her. I could see her hunger for adventure, she would not have settled for the pull of conventions or the ties of a family of her own.

London
Unknown date

Dear Mum,

Just another letter to say that I am sending you by this week's mail a brooch, I hope you like it. This particular kind of work is all the rage here at present and comes from Vienna. I think they are rather lovely. I think I will send it to Sadie and it might not catch the customs. If they ever want to charge you much, I wouldn't accept it if I were you, you can send it back. I will bring them when I come.

I went to the film company today and they said they might take a film test; it would be marvellous if they did, but of course it is all in the lap of the Gods.

Not much news as I am trying to get my Christmas presents fixed this week. It is useless sending things to the aunts, so I am sending them money. I hope they each buy something or something for the whole lot.

Anyhow much love for Christmas darling
* Barbara*

The Broadway Hotel
Worcs.
27th January 1936

Dear Mum,

Just a note from here as I am home tomorrow, I've been here a week and I had the loneliest time. I have been having riding lessons every day, and I have been getting on famously and am very enthusiastic about it, I have decided definitely to take it up I think it will make me get out into the fresh air.

It is curious that I booked my flat for the 28th weeks ago, and of course it is a very important day now with the funeral, everything will be closed. I am very glad to have been in England when the King died, for although it is terribly sad it is always a source of wonder to me at the great love and affection, and the sorrow, the English have for the Royal family.

I feel marvellous from my holiday, it has done me the world of good especially the last two weeks here in England. It has been so restful and healthy; I have done a lot of walking. Did I tell you I spend a few days in Nottingham with friends, but it was so cold!!! I am looking forward to getting home, I have heaps of parcels waiting for me and feel full of pep to get down to work. I suppose I will have some letters from you when I get home also of course.

*I started to canter yesterday, it was marvellous, until then I had only trotted and the groom says I am going to be a good rider...*rest of letter missing

While alone in London, Barbara had many male admirers. The letters made me chuckle, their naive romance and her willingness to dabble in affairs that were inevitably short lived. She seemed detached from her effect on men and played a game of cat and mouse on many occasions. She calculated opinions of men that would raise a few eyebrows even today. She could admire a hero from afar but her natural state was to be free of people.

London
22nd June 1936

Dear Mum,

I think I missed the mail last week I am sorry if I did. I was having one of those hectic times, out every night which is of course a change for me.

My Englishman had come home and we had a few days going around together before we part forever!

It is a funny thing, as much as I like the company of people and going out, it's a glorious sense of peace I get when I find myself alone, and not likely to be going out. If only I could find my true vocation, I would work terribly hard, I think I should get on so terribly well by myself.

Have had a bit of a blow, have found that Wade Moyon is not good for my voice and I have had to go to someone else, starting tomorrow. It has been <u>such</u> a waste of time and money I'm furious.

Coming back to London this time has made me realise that certainly acting is not my profession, although I am going on with it if I get the opportunity, but everything about it is against the grain for me. The people one comes in contact with and the fact of doing long periods of doing nothing. But I do feel something will come out of this for me and the right thing will come along. Anyhow, I will have plenty of time to work because I have got myself into such a mess financially that I can't afford to do anything at all!

I went to the show John Lord is in, he isn't a bit good rather what we call 'Repertory' kind of cut and dried, much too pleasant. I'm afraid he is next door to a 'pansy' it always shows in this world, we have hundreds here, not real pansies but sexless somehow, anything they do is mediocre. I say that but I might be wrong about him, but that's how it strikes me.

Everyone is terribly upset about the flying man, Campbell Black's[9] death. He was such a dear and so loved. So sad for his wife Florence Desmond, she is one of our dearest review artists, I think.

No news in this time, a boring mail of a letter. Forgive me darling.

Barbara

London
1st October 1936

Thanks for the letter,

I can't remember if I sent the photos or not so I will send some off to you, you must think I had forgotten you; I don't keep any but I know you keep them as a record.

I feel marvellous after my holiday and trying to get down to some work. I could kick myself for the waste of time with the Wade Moyon. The woman I'm going to now is marvellous and just what I want, getting my voice ready to put a number over straight away. I'll get used to singing in front of people, she is a real professional herself and I feel inspired and full of hope.

All sorts of things are new, but I'm getting really professional in failing and it's unlucky to talk about them. (Forgot to mention the photos are not good, are really not like me, but will give you an idea at least).

It's funny I feel so much better and happy when I'm working and practicing hard, as I am now, and haven't very many people around me. All my life people have

---

[9] **Tom Campbell Black** was a world-famous British aviator winning the London to Melbourne Centenary Air Race in 1934 with C.W.A. In September 1936 at Speke airport, while waiting to take off in slight fog, another plane collided with his on the runway, the propeller tore through his cockpit, he died later from his injuries.

tried to put themselves on me and persuade me that I should spend more time with people but they tire me, I don't want or need them.

I always feel that if I got a bit of work, I could throw myself into, I would be a very good artist because I would find myself. Does this all sound silly or precocious? I know you're interested and that you're probably wondering what sort of person I've developed into. I try to discipline myself. I have a funny sort of instinct I live by, that generally puts me doing the thing I should, and stops me doing the thing I shouldn't, much to the disgust of my friends who say I miss many opportunities. Which really means I'm not a gold digger. Wish I could get the job, and maybe some money and come home for a while maybe I will next year.

The thought of the Coronation is a nightmare to me. I only hope I get a job out of London for the time, with regards to the flat, I have it only on a weekly basis and they will probably triple my rent for the whole time.

Stephanie Perrotle is having an operation for appendicitis today; she is lucky she had started training at the hospital she gets it all free.[10] *I suppose it is rather selfish of me, but I find her rather a nuisance, when she comes round it's for at least ten hours and wastes my time, she is a nice little girl but of course we have absolutely nothing in common. Anyhow I shall go and visit her, take flowers or fruit and try to feel pious.*

It's terribly cold here, you've no idea, there has been no summer but funnily enough I had to laugh at myself. I found myself thinking how bracing the cold wind was, I am becoming acclimatized at last. I will send the photos by the next mail without fail, you will get them later than the letter though. I will send them to Sadie, there seems to be less fuss with customs.

Love,

Barbara.

---

[10] This was at a point before the creation of the National Health which came into being on 5th July 1948.

Richmond Hill Hotel
Richmond, Surrey

Beginning of letter missing... *hotel is full of rather nice oldish men, they all call me Babs and take great interest in all my doings, they seem likely to liven up working down at the theatre.*

I can't manage to go Thursday morning to serve the free breakfasts while I am down here. (Free food stations set up during the war) *But I send some money instead which is naturally more useful.*

Ewing talks about coming back to England. I wish he wouldn't poor dear, but then I suppose I am too happy for it to last.

Must fly now.
Tons of love, take care of yourself.

Barbara

Barbara and Ewing came together one last time to put on a front as husband and wife, when on a trip to visit her in-laws in New York.

Ian had once described Ewing as a 'remittance man', paid to stay out of the country, mainly New York, to avoid disgracing the family due to his earlier divorce. Ewing had introduced Barbara to the love of travel but their relationship was troubled by his anxieties and the possible philandering of both parties. In an effort to dispel any rumours about their marriage, Barbara wrote in a rare letter to her sister-in-law, Eleanor, after Ewing's death, and one to the family lawyer releasing any clams to a family trust that had been set up for her. Any claims to Ewing's estates were minimal, his New York apartment had been used for storage and sold to pay off creditors after his death, Ewing having settled in California years before.

Barbara and Ewing remained married until his death in 1957, aged 60.

73 St. James Street.
London
April 1958

Dear Eleanor,

Today, at last, after a letter and then a cable, John Orr replied stating facts and I have sent off the letter you asked me to sign. Your letters have shattered me, it is difficult to write.

Dear Eleanor, no one knows the true story of Ewing and me; they'll probably not even go into my autobiography! You suggested I married him for his money, well he had none in Australia, only debts as you must know.

Things were much worse for me; I was disinherited on my marriage and would otherwise have been the owner fine art and bookshop which was to have been my career. Also, would I have refused the money from your mother had I only been after money? Over the years I have had nothing, and some of them, the war years weren't very easy...rest of letter missing.

73 St. James Street.
London
April 1958

Dear Mr Orr,

Thank you for your letter dated 22nd April that I received today. Thank you also for the information about the two trusts now clearly set out.

I hereby enclose a letter that my sister-in-law Mrs Eleanor Cannon wishes for me to sign relinquishing my rights in the 1929 Trust created by Mrs Rixson snr.

Yours sincerely
Barbara Toy

Despite her low income, Barbara had enabled Ian to get out of Australia, to help him become the artist he always wanted to be; to travel and see the world, to capture what he could with his talents. By the late 1970s he had been offered a show at a prestigious Sydney Art Gallery. But within a few weeks his pieces made their way back from Australia, the show cancelled before it opened. He would never show his work again.

Ian, Barbara's nephew, at her encouragement, had spent time as a volunteer in an eye hospital in India where he, unfortunately, contracted TB. Barbara then brought him to England to recover. It was here he met a nurse, Terri, who told me she had seen more of his backside, giving him daily injections, before getting to know the rest of him. They lived together for many years, Ian as stepfather to Terri's three children, only marring a few years before his death.

I'd sat among the many forgotten canvases and over 600 newspaper drawings he had kept a secret, his life work hidden and mingled together among unwanted artifacts and letters of his aunt. Barbara loved art and artists, her bohemian upbringing had encouraged her to take an interest, and now her collection lay dusty and neglected among the debris, alongside the secret paintings and drawings of her nephew.

I wonder what she would have said to Ian to encourage him, what would she say to me now as I look through her 1930s acting portfolio? They are the glamourous and charming photographs of a woman who wanted to be seen. She was not stopped by the unwritten rules of the time, bold, fearless and yes sometime naïve, what an Australian may describe as a 'mettlesome'[11] woman.

---

[11] **Mettlesome.**' Meaning game as Ned Kelly.

Newspaper reviews, 'She Stoops to Conquer 1935

Daily Mirror 1935

Sunday Times 1935.

Barbara's acting portfolio.

Chapter 4
A Gay Divorce

London
(No date given)

Beginning of letter missing...*he has fallen well and truly and they tell me for the first time in his life, he is rather sweet and tall and dark and if I didn't know men so well, I'd say he is a good man. It's the first time, of course, that he has fallen in love with an attached woman.*

The other man I met in January I still see, he's rather sweet, terribly glamourous always wanting to give me things (I never can get used to that although I know I am silly) but he is of a very different type, very wealthy and used to lots of women around him, I should think he's safely married.

I don't know if I am going to Finland yet or not. I don't want to; it is so expensive and <u>so</u> cold. It is no holiday for me at all, in fact it takes it out of me. Anyhow I don't really think Ewing wants me. If I don't go, I'll go up to Scotland to the big hotel at Peebles just for the Christmas and New Year. I would love to do that as a girlfriend is going up with her family and it would be great fun. It is a huge hotel and lots of dancing. But of course, I don't know. If Ewing really wants me to, I'll go.

The photos are not really like me; people say they never seem to be able to fit me in any most natural mood. It is funny when you say you think of me at 18. I can remember when I thought a person of 28 was past everything. I am looking my age these days too, I can never understand why I am not happy, I suppose it is not having the right work.

This letter is one big growl, I am sorry I let off steam, I hope it doesn't depress you too much.

Love,
Barbara

Barbara's marriage had been floundering for some time as the couple spent their time apart, she agonised whether to divorce, changing her mind again and again. Ewing had been reliant on an income provided by his family, earning little himself. Barbara was to have an allowance that Ewing was expected to pass on to her.

Despite her low income, Barbara took acting and dancing classes to improve her craft, she also took a secretarial course as a backup. Desperate to be independent, Barbara struggled with her sporadic allowance and the long periods waiting for an acting part to come her way, subsequently spending the next few years untangling herself from relationships, her work and her growing need for isolation.

Barbara Toy
10th November 1936

Dear Mum,

Just a note, I'm afraid I haven't any news, nothing has happened, in fact less than nothing. I thought we were going off again with the show but that has all fallen through for the present, anyhow it is best not to think of it.

I am contemplating running myself into debt, sorting some marvellous clothes and storming the film studios, it would probably pay in the end, but of course it's a gamble. A friend of mine did that, she went to America, her family have lots of money and gave her some marvellous clothes. She came back all stocked up and walked into a new film company looking a million dollars, got a 7year contract at £75 when working and £15 retaining fee.

It's beginning to get very cold now. I don't know if I am going up to Finland for Christmas or not, frankly I don't want to waste the money, although of course London is dreary during the holidays. By the time you get this Christmas will be over, you will be glad I suppose, won't you?

I always feel awful about my letters they are <u>so</u> dull and all about myself and generally one big whine. I suppose it is writing continuously for so many years they are no longer kind of spontaneous.

I do think it is a pity when something is over, that I didn't choose something that would give me regular continuous work, it would have been much better for my type of mind.

I'll write you this mail if anything happens

Love always,

Barbara

St Regis
Cork Street, Mayfair
London
22nd November 1936

Dear Mum,

I'm afraid I haven't written for some time, and worried that it was too hard to write.

Things are pretty desperate with me as regards Ewing, have cabled for money but none comes. Anyhow it will bring things to a head one way or another. Bertie (Barbara's now boyfriend) *says we are wasting our time we should just go ahead and live together openly, and sometimes I feel like doing so. He's rather marvellous really, and one thinks of what it would mean if he were dragged into it. Ewing would jump at the chance of divorcing me that way. A divorce in any other way would take years and Ewing won't let me out.*

I am finishing at the college this week. Tomorrow is my last chance at getting my 120 words per minute. I'm afraid all the worries will put me back and I don't think there is much chance of me getting it, anyhow I'm having a jolly good try. It is such a disappointment getting so near, but of course I have been too lazy and should have spent more time at the college.

I'll write again later, tell Sadie I'm sorry not to have sent her a letter but I will soon.

Love to all,

Barbara

10th December 1936
(No address given)

Dear Mum,

I feel it is a momentous day to write to you, I have just got news of the abdication. I think it's the ghastliest thing I have ever known and yet I feel so sorry for him. It's unfortunate that he should really fall in love like that and yet I suppose it's only natural that having led the life he has, and travelled and broadened himself, that he would want an experienced woman of the world. At his age he is fussier. It is also dreadful he was going to be so much the right sort of King and now there is this cabbage of a Duke of York with his homely wife, I think it's awful. I heard the news over the wireless at six o'clock while I was having a lesson with my teacher, I could have cried.

London is awful so crowded, one can't move. Heavens how glad I'll be when Christmas is over. I'm not going to Finland it's silly of me to as I am quite ill with a cold and it's so miserable there. I've decided to go in the summer it's better, although Ewing wants me to come and I think he'll be really disappointed.

I've been having trouble with income tax, there is a likelihood of my having to pay back 2 years, I'll be in the soup if I have to.

Last night I had dinner with the people I told you about, I went to a dance with the bachelor (Bertie) *of the party, who has really fallen for me. Rita, the girl who introduced me, says she has never seen anything like it, he's amazing and a flirt but has absolutely changed with me, so kind and gentle and almost goofy! Of course, if it goes on, I shall have to stop it because he's the sort who would want to marry me. The dangerous thing is I feel so at ease and at peace with him - -Bad Sign! He's much more sane and ordinary than most of the young men I know. Rita, who is the most romantic, has quite* made up her mind that it will be the love and the tragedy of his life. She's a scream, anyhow they want us to go away for Christmas, it would be fun and not very expensive. Going to Finland involves me in so much expense, I have to buy all sorts of things I never use here.

At last, I found the right singing teacher for me, I know he'll do wonders with me, although I've only had two lessons. The show, I was going into in the West End came off suddenly because all of this abdication business, it was a great blow to me because it would have been a good chance.

I'm afraid it's going to be rather a sad Christmas here; it will be awful when the King leaves.

Love,
Barbara

Ash Wednesday
10th February 1937

Dear Mum,

Thanks for the airmail letter about the cheque. Although you only sent 2 papers the other one you accidently forgot to put in because the letter wasn't finished! I really don't think there is anything definite or seriously the matter with me. I am pretty sure it is the accumulation of years of living on my nerves and in a more or less unsettled state.

As a matter of fact, I am feeling marvellous now. I have been looking after myself for the first time in my life. I am really quite an ordinary person and if I'd led an ordinary natural life, I'd be quite alright.

About Ewing and myself, don't worry, do as I do, don't think about it. I *know* it will work itself out, the arrangement is suitable and it works for both of us, I feel there is no reason to do anything at the moment.

What I am doing staying here? It is the only possible thing. Anything else that happens to me happens for the good. It has taken me all these years in London to get myself respect and confidence back (it has been a great drawback in my work) I realise, although you always said how hard I am, that I must have been terribly sensitive, the effect certain things have on me, and now boy they have got to go. From now on I have got to look after myself, for if I don't no one will. Don't worry everything will be alright. I am really very happy this last year. I am twice the person I was, to use a trite old saying, I seem to have found myself.

If I can get them off, I will send my new photos this week. Lots of love darling, take care of yourself

Barbara

St Regis
Cork Street, Mayfair, London
April 1937

Dear Mum,

    I was just back from a weekend down by the sea with Bertie, but it was cold and windy after a lovely summer's week up here, it was very disappointing, anyhow it was nice to get away.

    You keep asking what I am doing about Ewing, unfortunately it's impossible to do anything without money. So, all I can do is get on with my life and try and forget about it, and hope his Lordship will want to marry himself. I feel something will happen soon.

    I am starting a job tomorrow down at the Richmond Theatre as assistant Stage Manager, it is nothing much to start with but it means going right through the management side and is the best step to the production side. David got it for me, he is the Managing Director of the theatre and has it in mind to eventually take me into business with him. At least I will learn something and build something up as it seems impossible for me to become a journalist. I would have to start with the secretarial side, and I would never keep a job because of my spelling and general inaccuracy.

Anyhow the theatre is the world I know and if I want to write later on, all this work certainly ought to give me 'copy'. I start tomorrow so will let you know by the end of the week how I am getting along. If I settle down to it, I shall be going to live down in Richmond, which I would love as it is almost country, anything is better than London in the spring and summer.

Lots of love,

Barbara.

816 Mount Royal, London
W1
15th June 1937

Dear Mum,

I think it is better if you write always to me here. If I change my address, I can always airmail you the new address. And sometimes letters of yours go up to Ewing by mistake and it is hard if he opens them, not that anything is said, but you sometimes mention him and things I have told you.

Have just got a note from Stephanie saying her mother arrives this week and she has invited me to tea next Friday. It is going to be such a nuisance but I just can't waste much time with them, I'm very busy and also, don't know them really. Although I have friends, I don't have a 'set' and just seem to go out a lot with men. It's funny how they never introduce you to their men friends!

Anyhow, I suppose I will have to see them. I suppose it is really very selfish of me. But it seems to me I waste so much time and wear myself out with all sorts of people that don't mean a thing to me.

Did I tell you I have been going around a bit with the famous composer of Cochran's[12] New Now? Only trouble is he wants to bed with me so suppose it won't last. As soon as he finds I'm a good girl I think he'll take his inspiration somewhere else!

I often think I sound like one of those awful women to you, who think of nothing else but her conquests. But is seems when you don't know the people I do, that is the only subject that interest them. Also, my bachelor wants to marry me, did I tell you? He's really very sweet and it's a pretty serious thing when a man of nearly 40 falls really in love for the first time. He is the first good man I've met over here. I'm very pleased that I have a good excuse not to marry him, but it is nice to have him around. Sometimes I do think it would be a good idea if I lived with a person like that.

The only trouble with me is I'm too damn lazy. Rita, my friend, who introduced me to him, is all for it as though we are getting married, honeymoon and all! And he has asked me to go to Budapest when he goes on business next month, it all seems to fit in perhaps.

I think an awful lot about Sadie but she seems to me to be having an easy time so far, when does the baby arrive?

Hyde Park is in a mess already with all the seats for the Coronation, good heavens London is going to be dreadful.

No news Mum I'm afraid.

Much love,

Barbara

---

[12] **Charles Blake Cochran,** English theatrical producer and impresario collaborated with composer and song writer Cole Porter on many occasions.

Barbara Toy
Sound City
(Date unknown)

Dear Mum,

I am writing this up at the film studio. I have been up here all afternoon, I have been offered a small part but don't know if it is good enough yet, had great fun up here though, I think I will be doing some stuff soon. In the meantime, I've been drawing people at the studios in the morning, early for them. I get paid 15 shillings a day so it's not bad as it gives me the whole day clear when I am not filming anything, and it at least pays my way.

Have had a horrid thing happen to me a little while ago. I met a famous composer who fell for me very heavily and I think would have done a lot for me. But a girl I know, who was a real gold digger and crazy about getting on at all costs, has gone out of her way to tell him things I said about him and has made a complete mess of things, just my luck as my friends always say. I am too good to my pal friends? I introduce them to all my friends, why shouldn't I? and then they go and do things behind my back. So many are like that yet you expect women should stick together. I don't mind her trying to fascinate him, but why do something so vicious.

I tell you because, of course, I can't mention it to anyone else. Still, I suppose it is all in a day's work. No news but all is very well.

Much Love,

Barbara

24th June 1937

Dear Mum,

Just a note although I haven't much news. Such a lot of things are about to happen that I don't know where I am. It's somehow a very important time in my life I feel. All sorts of people and things are turning out I don't know where I am but I will explain everything when things sort themselves out.

I have met the most extraordinary person, a Doctor of Philosophy, who spent many years out East studying Eastern religions and has lectured all over America. He came to see the play last night with Korda's wife, and asked to be allowed round after to be introduced to me. He has fallen very much in love with me, <u>really</u>. It might be useful with my work. If I fell in love with him myself it would be the real thing, but as yet I don't know.

Please forgive me if I'm vague and thoughtless, I'm full this week with little things.

Love,
Barbara

St Regis
Cork Street, Mayfair. London
(No date given.)

Dear Mum,

I am so very busy now sometimes morning noon and night that I haven't much time for Bertie, he is very sweet about it but he will naturally get fed up. Of course, if we were married, I would come home to him every night. The more I think of it the better it seems that we get married, he likes the thought of me going on with my work. This is so thoughtful, he comes to Richmond for me every night, when the play is on at 11.30 and drives me home. Not many of the modern men would do anything like that. And then, I suppose, if there is any niceness in one at all, you can't help falling in love with someone who is consistently good for you.

Things are a mess financially, but I have ceased to worry anymore, as soon as money arrives, which isn't very often, it immediately goes on rent and bills, the only thing that is really tiring is not having any ready cash. Still, I've been through worse patches and this and money worries are nothing if one is to have any sort of peace of mind.

I am sorry your letter was so down, I'm sorry you have these fits of depression, let's hope that things will be better and when I am theatre manager with a flat in Haymarket, you will come and be with me! As I intend to have lots of children when I get married, if ever, <u>and</u> go on working so I'm going to be pretty busy.

Yes, Rita is sweet to look at, she's a great worry to me. She's got herself mixed up with a married man, it is all so stupid and such a waste, because really, she isn't in love with him. For years now I have had the 'wrong' side of life around me, it's a pity because I have such little faith in anything or anybody. It would do me so much good to be among respectable suburban people again, or married to Bertie and create my own atmosphere.

At the moment anyhow I am very, very happy and working like hell, and at least learning something that ought to lead somewhere eventually. David, you know, who really got me this job, is a director of the theatre and hopes to go into management by himself soon, that's why he is training me, as he has always hoped we could work together.

At the moment I am trying to find him a girlfriend to get his attention that way off me. Unfortunately, as he manages all the stars, he gets all he wants of the glamourous type, and I suppose I am a relief from them.

This has been my trouble all along in my stage career, I never could combine business with pleasure…that's if you call it pleasure.

Must fly now as I have to scour the town for a pair of yellow pyjamas with pink spots for the show.

Lots of love,

Barbara

Yes, Richmond is down past Kew Gardens and the Thames, and Hampton Court is about three quatres of an hour away by London bus.

London
22nd April 1937

Dear Mum,

Just a note to say I have sent the photos this mail for sure, sorry I have been so busy.

All sorts of exciting things are happening but I am superstitious and don't want to tell until things are certain. I am lucky, I have met a man who is a 'talent scout' and a manager of the biggest theatrical and film management over here. At the moment he is taking me around to all the first nights which is terribly useful, for although I don't think he will actually do anything in the way of work for me, he knows everybody and I'm meeting all the right people which is all I want. The other things I will tell you when I'm certain.

My friends always say that I talk myself out of all the films. It seems to be that now I am 28, how much more attractive I really am, and beginning to look my age. The fact is I never knew how to use my scanty charms before.

Am just off to buy some sardines for tonight, it is the first night of the Margaret Rawlings new play.

Goodness, I do wish I could land something; I so badly need clothes at this critical moment.

Bertie is off to Budapest tomorrow his business is upset over there, he's furious he was to go so soon as he had made up his mind up to take me with him later on. Now that he is convinced, I won't marry him he wants to take a flat for me. How do you think I would go in the role of a kept woman!? Afraid I haven't the right mentality for such things.

Must fly.
Love,

Barbara

London
13th July 1937

Dear Mum,

Although it's only Saturday, I'm writing this airmail letter now because goodness knows when I'll be able to write again. I've so much news! Firstly, although I've booked to go on the next boat to Ewing, I'm not going. I've just signed a contract to go away on tour in the 'The Gay Divorce'[13]. I have quite a big part, it suits me perfectly and I have to sing and dance on my own! But nevertheless, I'm terribly determined and working like hell, I'm quite confounded at my own cheek. Today the producer came to me and said I was better than the girl who played the part in London, so that was rather a feather in my cap. But you can imagine my feelings when I'm faced with a chorus of very competent young women who sing and dance most professionally.

Anyhow, I signed a contract and we open on Monday week at Blackpool, I don't see how they can throw me out now. I've never been so happy as I am in this part and realised that I love this sort of stuff, much better than ordinary straight plays. He has promised to put me in pantomime at Christmas if I'm any good, that would be fun.

Oh, at the moment when I'm not hopelessly scared, I'm very happy. Even now when I think of the opening night I go into a cold sweat. It is funny how things just happen; a man saw my photograph in a theatrical magazine we have here, and just asked for me. When I saw him, although I said I couldn't sing much or dance, he said 'oh we can fix it' so I took his word for it.

I feel terrible about Ewing having booked everything, but if I didn't take this time, I might never get another and it would seem such a waste after all this time in London. Also, it will help me reduce my overdraft somewhat. I'm giving up my flat and spending all my time just distributing my belongings about my friends, it's ghastly harsh as I'm rehearsing all day and nearly all night (having come in so late) I have no time to

---

[13] J. Hartley Manners' play **'The Gay Divorce'**. A musical comedy with songs by Cole Porter. The film version starred Fred Astaire and Ginger Rogers 1934.

buy anything. By the way, please address all my mail to Australia house as they are more reliable about forwarding mail. I'll let you know when I'm coming back.

Funny thing happened the day before I got this job, I went with a friend to the fortune teller and she didn't say a word about Ewing, but said I would have an offer of a job. She said it would lead to something quite big so here's hoping.

Darling my good fairy has looked after me again with some good, solid work to help mend my rather bruised old heart.

All my love my sweet, hope you are thinking of me.

Love,
Barbara

Norddeutscher Lloyd
Bremen
16th November 1937

Dear Mum,

As you see I am writing on my way back to London as I decided to go to Finland after all. Ewing has stayed with his people and will, I think, stay till after Christmas, I don't really know. I don't know if it was right of me to come back, but I feel no matter what happens life Ewing would, in the end, drag me down. We have given up the idea of divorce at the moment so please don't mention it.

He was sweet to me before I left and very generous but the way he spends money like water, even on me, and is eternally in debt, is so disappointing to me always. I am sending Ian a lovely bowl and spoon from Tiffany's. I hope they like it, it's so very lovely, I think.

The crossing has been very quiet, not many people on board, rather rough but still it is fine.

The young man in the deck chair next to mine, turns out to be the one-time world champion Jim Braddock. Doesn't mean much to me but it seems to for everyone else. Any how I am grateful to him, he's been very sweet to me all this trip.

It is the loveliest boat I have ever seen, but I will be glad to get back to London. This has been a lovely holiday but a little tempestuous, everything is such a muddle and all so useless really. There is an awful irony in doing things, as I do, that could be so marvellous if one was at peace.

Forgive me, I try not to write dreary letters.

Ewing's so sweet, so good and also, so damn bad. Darling if you sometimes think I ought to stay with him I want you to know that the main thing I am frightened of is his temper. I don't talk much about it, but I don't want you to think I am just being silly and throwing away a lot.

My love to you my sweet, I am going to work like hell when I get home and try and get some sort of pattern in my life

Much Love,

Barbara

88 Litchfield Court
Richmond
London
31st November 1937

Dear Mum,

I am writing this ordinary mail so the news will be a bit short I suppose. It is Tuesday and I feel a bit tired. We had a first night last night, a three-set play and we rehearsed all day then going straight on when we had finished on the show. It is a bit of a strain considering we were working all day Sunday, setting the different sets and lighting them. It is amazing to me sometimes how I stand the continuous work; I must be very strong.

Tonight, is the first night of one of our shows that has dancing in it. I do hope it is a success as we get a percentage on all shows leaving the theatre garden.

Our scenic artist who is also on the board of directors, is producing a play, it is going to be fun. He is much more interested in his sets than anything else and rather resents the artist being on stage at all, they seem to him to just blot out the landscape! He is the most amusing and interesting person, have I ever told you about him? He lived for years in the Sahara and was there when the war broke out. He's a darling and luckily for me has a bit of a 'thing' about me, which makes working at the theatre much easier. He covers my mistakes for me! He wants me to help him with his production which is of course what I have always wanted to do. But unfortunately, now I am director I just haven't the time.

It is funny about my flat. I came down here one Sunday, in a hurry, and went to Litchfield Court to get a small one room flat, but for the moment they hadn't got one, so they put me in a very nice three room one for the time being. As I thought, there are quite a few people here letting and this seems to be the same price as the small one. It is a pity you aren't here; I have a very nice spare bedroom, James (the canary) is such good company!

Did I tell you Bertie has come to live at Richmond, he really is crazy?

Lots of love,

Barbara

Barbara writing again to her sister Sadie:

St. Regis,
Cork Street, Mayfair. London
17th February 1938

Dear Sadie,

I'm writing this early this week as soon as the work actually starts, I don't seem to get a minute.

The snaps, as I have told mum last mail, have arrived. Oh, they are lovely, what a darling he is, you must be proud. I like the ones of you in the street what a pity you didn't look up for the sitting down ones. He seems so alive; you just can't believe he's so young the darling. Of course, Bertie just nearly had an apoplectic fit when I showed them to him, he's the sort that if I ever did say I'd marry him he would give me twins on the way to the church.

So glad you like the bowl, I thought it was fun too, I was beginning to worry about it coming.

Mum asked me to get Lilian a brooch, I forgot to tell her, I'll have a look around for it only they were the rage a year ago when I sent mums and is often the way now, they are now 'out' and hard to find. Evidently, I only have Saturday mornings to shop in!

I have sold my car, I hated parting with her but I use her so seldom and infrequently now, and I just haven't the money to run her now. Also, can borrow Bertie's when I urgently need one.

Mum also says my note paper reeks of prosperity but actually I pay what I did at Mount Royal, but then I arranged that with the management, I'm pretty good with that sort of thing. It is marvellous now one can haggle over money and beat people down if you have a few good clothes on.

I haven't much news these days, I feel too tired to go out much, so am consequently very dull but I console myself with the fact that it is only for six months. I think the journalistic course might be a help to me. I've always thought if I'd had some ground work or preferably had someone like you around me, I would have written. At least now I will be starting at the beginning with someone to correct me as I go along.

At the college I have chummed up with a young girl from Cambridge, she is easily the tallest girl there and I'm the shortest so we look a fine pair, she's a dear like a big ungainly colt.

I think Mother must not get all my letters, she says I've never told her who Rita is, but I have. She's a Scott and is staying at Mount Royal and she doesn't really have to work, but about four years ago she was to be married to a boy in the Sudan and a week before she sailed out to marry him, he was trod on by a...rest of letter missing.

St. Regis Hotel
Cork Street, Mayfair
London
21st February 1938

Dear Mum,

I feel I had better answer your letter while I have the time, we have today off as it is mid-term or something, I don't really know why I get the holiday but I'm grateful to have it anyway. One day away from typewriters, gramophones and big busted young women!

I got an ordinary letter from you today in which you mention my having no substantial financial arrangement. But as you know they have me there, I am dealing with 'religious' people and they are the most hard, unsympathetic and callous people alive.

Mama says '...but Ewing you can't give Barbara an infinite sum or allowance as you only have what I give you' she is a very clever woman. But I will never be bitter about money, I have seen too many people unhappy because of it, bitterness over an artificial thing like money is, I think, a living death. Naturally I shall do what I can as I am attached to a lot from them. But I cannot force anything, and try not to let the unsettled state of things get me down.

Yes, Bertie and Rita have come a lot into my life since I came back, especially Bertie, he belongs to that school of thought that thinks if you want a thing enough you will get it in the end. He does, luckily get what he wants. I only wish I could love him, then of course things would be sensible if Ewing would divorce me. I'll just live with Bertie. But as yet I don't love him, though heaven knows I should, even if it is only through sheer kindness. I didn't know a person could love as much as he does or be so good. Sometimes I think I ought to marry him to at least make someone happy, but then if I wasn't happy myself it seems I would lead him a dog's life - it's all very confusing.

Anyhow he believes in me and realises I have a career no matter what and it was really his influence that started me off on this course. Funnily enough I wouldn't be surprised if I didn't drop into journalism, anyhow I am going to try my hardest at freelancing whilst I am doing this course.

Did I say that Bertie gave a dear little red fox coat for Christmas it is sweet, I must have my photo taken for you to see it?...

I lifted my head from this letter, only the night before, ready to leave 'Snails' for home, Terri had jumped up quickly, stopping me before I could leave. She'd grabbed an old linen bag from behind a large chair in the little conservatory. Opening it she held aloft a screwed-up fur mass and asked me what she should do with it. There was a skin backing which meant the fur was real, I couldn't hazard a guess as which poor animal had met its demise to make what looked like a very small red fur jacket. It had been kept for years in a contorted shape, turning into a crisp and crumbling state, beyond repair. Looking at me and seeing my blank response, too tired to deal with any more, Terri put it back in the bag and back behind the chair. I never saw it again. As I'd walked home, I imagined Barbara at a first night review in that red fur jacket and pearls, young and open to her burgeoning life in theatre and film.

Back the next day, I'd shut myself away, collating more letters and immersing myself in Barbara's world, the time and places she had known, once again. The coincidence caused a further connection, and an understanding of the distance of time, the tragedy of loss and a life contorted into a bag to be thrown away. Not this time Barbara, not this time!

…Things are very unsettled politically here at the moment and with Mr. Eden's resignation Lord knows what will happen. It might mean a general election, if so, labour will probably get in and then Lord help us all. Hitler's mood in Austria is just another example of nations just shuffling in and taking what they want while their neighbours just look on. I think <u>anything</u> will be allowed to happen for the sake of so-called peace. But in Austria's case, I think in the end it's right. Austria hates Germany because she fears her, but now whether she likes her or not, being bound up with her will eventually give her a sense of security. I don't know if it all interests you, but here it is all very important, as war seems so inevitable.

You talk of sending some money and coming over, by then I will have some money after this course is over, I must. I am going to take a wee flat and then you will have to come and see me, maybe Ian and all.

I am just off up to see an exhibition of Bertie's furniture, since he has met me, he has been fuelled with ambition and has now started importing furniture as well as making it. He says I am an expensive proposition and I let him think so! They are importing lovely stuff from Hungary and Belgium and shortly he is saying now that he will start on other things as well. It would be fun to be a buyer and go over and source all the stuff.

I am doing a clay work of Ian from the shot of him in the pram, if it is any good, I'll have it cast and sent over. I wish I had a better one of him for copying, Heaven's he's lovely.

I am very worried about my hair; it is so terribly thin at the temples. I think I really ought to have it shaved, I think it is a Toy characteristic. Do you know of anything good for it? The trouble is it is so fine.

The weather had been dreadful these last two weeks, the wind just goes right through one. I have never really got used to it, but living with central heating makes life much easier. Lots of sleet now and mud, the trouble is one gets no exercise at all.

I have to laugh when I think of us, Sadie and me, how we are getting on, I never can realise I am a woman of 29 it's so silly. I often wonder if I was too young to leave. The other day I was asked, at the college, how old I was and for professional reasons only, I became rather proud of my age and not looking at it, I said I was 26 and then 2 girls just laughed and said they thought I was 22 at the most. It is really only a figure, though my face first thing in the morning… oh God!

    Lots of love,
        Barbara

LATER…

Dear Mum,

I have just found that I haven't posted this letter to you in the last mail, having written it so early too! But once the week actually starts, I seem to go like a wild cat at a nice busy week. I've seen three lovely plays. 'Othello' with Anthony Quail down at the Old Vic, a lovely production of Dodsworth[14] *with Gladys Loofer and her new husband in 'Mourning Becomes Electra'*[15] *that starts at 7pm and goes on till 11.30pm.*

Also went to a dance with all Bertie's family, rather an ordeal. Am just off to bed, as it is Sunday, for an early night. We had a lovely spring day today. I'm looking forward to this spring, it is lovely to have some definite work waiting for one.

    Love,
        Barbara.

---

[14] **Dodsworth:** was a three-act play by Sidney Howard based on the 1929 novel by Sinclair Lewis. Through the title character, it examines the differences between American and European intellect, manners, and morals.

[15] **Mourning Becomes Electra**: is a play cycle written by American playwright Eugene O'Neill.

St. Regis
Cork Street, Mayfair
London. W1
6th May 1938

Dear Mum,

I am writing this in bed, I've got the most terrible hangover, was out last night with Bertie, I had some bad champagne, as I like to blame it!

So, I've woken up early and can't even write quickly, might jerk my head! Had a row with Bertie yesterday and we were celebrating to make it up.

I suppose Bertie adores me as much as any man ever adored a woman, but even he has to be put in his place. Sometimes I feel I'd love to 'give up' and just go and sit in a corner and be myself.

By the way Bertie got the sweetest note from Sadie about the bunny, it's nice of her to write, heavens he was thrilled.

This is Whitsun week and I didn't go away but moved into another flat here, much nicer really, looks out on the street and is a bit brighter, my other one looked into a well and I got a lot of noise in the small hours.

Have I ever told you Bertie also lives in this block of flats? He is quite mad, of course, I had thought of moving to another block and not surprising he said he'd go too, really London must think we are a crazy couple.

I hadn't bought a dress, at least only one dress since I came back from America, so imagine how sick I was of myself. Well, I went out and bought three right off like that! I got them from a warehouse I go to. First one is a kind of suit in black narcissus, wanted it to wear to restaurants at night. When I am not dressing up it's very plain but I think very smart, I wear very plain things. I often wonder if I have got into plain things to hide. Anyhow it's got a plain skirt and the top is the new hip length with long sleeves and buttons all the way down the front, tiny buttons, and a kind of yolk of flowered material applied on, it's just that little touch that makes it.

The other model they have been using, is wool and I wanted something to wear at the weekends going into the country. It has a blue tint, a lovely dark blue, the top is a loose hip length coat with a rather wide stripe of the same blue and a kind of lime green, sounds funny but it is rather nice with a blaze of green in a full circle. It is going to be hell to match things with. Then as I was going the woman who has the warehouse, it's one of the best houses in London, she supplies all the class shops around Knightsbridge and Bond Street, a lot of places take Worth and Chanel, although they wouldn't admit it, she was talking to me about one of their big houses who had ordered tiny dresses for a customer, sending very small measurements. When they got it, they said the dresses were too small. She was saying that because they were a dead loss to her. I tried one on and it fitted me better than anything I've ever had. So, I took one! It is navy blue and terribly plain, has short sleeves and the mink trimmed waist and welts, it looks really awfully nice. I know it is silly, but it is wonderful what a few nice clothes can do.

Went to see 'Operette' [16] *Cowards new play the other night, loved it, very sentimental, I cried copiously but I still loved it, it's curious but Coward is becoming just a little old fashioned and prissy I think it is funny to see it.*

I am still trying for my 80 in shorthand, it seems I always shall; my writing is so against me, I get it wrong so often and because my writing is so untidy, I can't read it back. It annoys me that such a little thing beats me, unfortunately we have a month's holiday in August and when we come back, I will be all out of practice. I am going to try to get a job on a magazine maybe as a secretary first. My journalist mistress who works on a magazine will let me know how to go about it, I find I am pretty good at it all and have lots of ideas for anything she asks us to do. It's just I should be given a purpose, wouldn't be surprised if I was good at advertising, will send you an ad I did when I get it back from her. My drawing will help me there. I am not going to drawing classes anymore I found it was too much for me, but will take it up again as soon as this course stops.... if ever!

I have to laugh, already I have had the offer of jobs as people's secretaries, all kinds, and here am I the worst, untidy, inaccurate, inefficient person at the college, it is the joke of it.

---

[16] **Operette** is a musical in two acts composed, written and produced by Noël Coward. The show is a period piece, set in the year 1906 at the fictional "Jubilee" theatre. The story concerns an ageing Viennese operetta star, who warns the young ingenue not to marry a nobleman. The piece premiered in 1938.

I miss my car terribly now that summer is here but am glad really that I sold it before. Ewing sends me just hardly enough to live on at the moment and I really, except for my rent, don't spend anything. I am trying to sell my piano, but you only get what you get for a second-hand piano.

Do send shots of Ian as soon as you take them, and when is his birthday, I can't remember the date? I'm mad I don't.

I am thinking of getting a dog, a wire haired foxy, Bertie says he will take it to the factory every day, so it would have a good life, the only thing is I think it would be more his dog, he is the sort of person whom dogs like. He is very keen.

Bertie is a bit of a problem, I don't know what would happen if I went away or fell in love with anyone, he has become absolutely dependant on me, and is interested in nothing else. It is a kind of obsession. It must be lovely to finally find the person you have been looking for like that, at least he has that.

When I get a steady job, I will get a flat and then you can come over and see me, it would be very exciting but it will be a warm flat, I can guarantee that.

It's strange but the winters don't worry me so much now, with central heating it just doesn't matter. It will be better now, I'm naturally not so nervy and more settled. Fortune tellers will take me through that, maybe I will come home and be a special correspondent.

My hangover is working off so I think I will go for a long walk. Does your knee still make you walk crook wise? You and Bertie would be a fine pair, he gets water on the knee, would you believe it, I rub it with 'Sodex'.

It is funny, every day on my way to college I call in at a Lyons Tea House near here, and have a cup of coffee and some prunes, the same every morning and now the waitress just brings it and never asks me what I want. Seems funny to get the personal touch like that here in London. Don't forget the snaps.

Lots of love, darling, to you all,

Barbara

The White Hart Hotel
Sonning-on-Thames
24th April 1938

Dear Mum,

I didn't write to you from Devon, I didn't seem to get the time. We had rotten bad weather, fine but very cold and windy and as the hotel was cold, we spent most of the time in the car. But it was a lovely rest, I didn't even have to think, and feel much better for it. Bertie dropped me here on his way to London, to finish off my last few days of holiday. It's a dear little hotel but cold and I'll be rather glad to get back to my nice warm flat again. I realise how impossible it would be for me to spend winters here if I didn't have central heating.

I shall have to put my back into things these next few months to get through this course, it is a bit of an effort but I am determined to do it, though goodness knows what I'll make of it all! After that I am probably going to do something about my private life, I am getting too old to let things ride any longer - though <u>what</u> the Lord only knows.

Had my fortune told; did I tell you? She said I will be married within the year and have 2 lovely children which seems rather good to me.

Finally, old England is at last stirring and we are at last making definite efforts to protect the people from air raids, there are air raid practices regularly and everyone is advised to get in notices, trained staff and first aid materials, and to seal up one room as a gas proof chamber. I suppose it is dreadful, but sometimes I feel that if we are going to have a war, I wish they would start and get on with it.

Do send me more photos of Ian, how old is he? When was his birthday again?

Must fly, the village mail.

Love,
Barbara

The St. Regis Hotel
Cork Street and Old Burlington Street, Mayfair
London
W1.
10th June 1938

Dear Mum.

Thanks for going in again about the policy, it appears I owed the money as I didn't pay the premiums. Yes, I think it will get transferred here. I am enclosing two pictures of me and a nice one of Bertie when down in Devon, also one of an old bridge with Bertie. I think it is pretty good as it's only a 12/6 kodak cameras. It is a queer get up I am in; I was so cold I had to wear my coat. This is my skunk coat that Ewing gave me before he left for New York. They were taken about 9 o'clock in the morning in a high wind so I don't think they are too bad.

Tomorrow, I go for my first test, 70 words a minute in shorthand, I am not very confident of passing but from now on we get tested every week so next week ought to see me through. I find shorthand really difficult. There is so much memorizing to be done and I just can't see how people can think so fast, anyhow I am persevering.

My finances are in a filthy mess, this rather makes me worry and I'm afraid upsets my work. Ewing says that things are so bad that he can only send me a little each month, it is hardly enough to live on. I just <u>don't</u> know what to do. It will be criminal if I can't finish the course now that I've gone so far, but don't really see what I can do.

Everything seems such a mess, I wonder sometimes why I go on...well you never know, I might get a marvellous job and be the prime minister secretary before I'm through! I will write how my test went next mail.

Lots of love,

Barbara

London
7th September 1938

Dear Mum,

As I am getting out my writing paper, I find I didn't send my last letter to you, written the day after I got back, so I will try and send them both together. I have now had almost a week back at college, I will be very glad when it is all over it tries me so. I feel, already as if I haven't had a holiday at all. I wonder how I managed to stick it so long. I find I have lost my speed very much and I only have about two weeks more of my course, if I want to get my 120, and my certificate, I will have to take an extra month at least. I really think I ought to, having gone to such a good college, the certificate will at least show what I can do. There is a chance that if I get a good job and start on a definite writing career, that would be what I want. But then I argue with myself, couldn't I write in America, when I have established myself in the family?

However, I suppose it will work itself out. I just know this I will do something definite quite soon.

Am dying to get Ian's photograph, has it been sent? I am writing this to catch the mail, I'm in a hurry so will write so I will write more next mail.

Yes of course I will send them airmail from now on.

Love,
Barbara

Barbara made the decision to stay London as the world began to prepare for war, unaware of the scale of what was to come. The journey from false beliefs of a short war, to the years of destruction and chaos had begun.

Sunday
3rd September 1939

Dearest Mum,

It is strange but I feel much more worried about you today than anything else, because I know you will be worrying quite unnecessarily about me.

It is just about 5.30pm and we are waiting for the King's speech. Bertie has just gone to take his people down to the country, they left it till today. I only hope he gets back before dark as the blackouts are so thorough and it is almost impossible to drive anywhere, in any case we will probably have an air raid tonight.

You would have laughed, at eleven this morning Bertie came to say that war had just been declared and almost immediately the air raid warning began to blow. So, we upped with our gas masks, closed all the windows and put James in the bathroom with the lights out then shut the door. Then went down to the basement where all the other tenants were, all in different stages of dress and undress. When nothing happened, we all trouped back again and out comes James who had settled down for the night. We just had a cigarette, looked sheepishly at each other and off it goes again, and once more the windows, the canary, the gas masks, and the basement. It was another false alarm. They were evidently testing the alarms. But we really did think Mr. Hitler was a bit quick on the uptake.

It's no-good talking about all this, the stupidity and waste, I have always said it wouldn't happen, and I can't even yet think that it has come. But I suppose I am just an ostrich.

But I do say mum don't worry about me if I stay in London, I am as safe as anything because this building is eight stories high and made of concrete, I just couldn't be blown up. It is only the noise and tension that I will have to worry about. One can't at the moment say what is going to happen, we may get very few raids or we might get a long one trying to break up the morale of the country. But at last, thank God, we will soon know, which puts an end to the awful waiting.

If the theatre reopens, they have asked me to stay on and not join up as they are going to be terribly hard pushed for people. I'll be much more use there than anywhere else.

I suppose, of course, if they decide not to reopen theatres, we will have to join the ambulances who are really in need of drivers. If I stay at the theatre I will have to stay down there as the sirens will be bad at night and with the air raids happening it would mean me staying down there in any case.

If Germany hasn't got any help, it might not be too long a war, but it seems all Europe will be bought in soon.

I hope you can read this; I'm thinking about you today and hope you are not worrying. I'll see if I can send you a cable tomorrow. James (my canary) is flying, and each time he comes out he lands on my hand for a second. But unfortunately, I don't suppose we will let him out from now on. I will write as often as I can, and if I don't it is probably because the letters wouldn't reach you.

All my love darling.

Barbara

Bertie kindly wrote to Barbara's mother Nellie during this time, to reassure their relationship was one of great care and understanding. The letter also gives us another glimpse of Barbara's struggles with Ewing:

Beginning of letter missing...*She will gradually reform her self-confidence - do not worry about that; it will not come suddenly, but the mere fact that she has really made a success of this deal will help to restore it. Only I am afraid she is working too hard - the hours at the theatre are long, but she is sticking it very well and I have that from other sources.*

I do feel, however, that especially in this wartime, it is essential that Barbara should have some work. I am sure she would be very restless and most unhappy if she was doing nothing and I think that hard work is better than no work at all. No one likes to feel that the country is at war, fighting for its existence, that they are doing nothing helpful to help with some form of entertainment for the people, she is certainly doing her share in these difficult days.

*Especially appreciate the very kind things you said of me. I can only say that Barbara has done more for me than I can ever do for her. She is a very sophisticated woman and I have learnt more from her and have a truer perspective on life, its values, from Barbara in the few years I have known her than ever before. I need only say that I value her friendship and affection so very much. And on saying this I could say a lot more but I know that you, as her mother, well understand...*remains of letter missing.

91 William Edward Place
Sydney, Australia

Dear Bertie,

What a kind person you are writing to me to reassure me about Barbi. I really worry about her when I feel anything could happen to anyone in London. Now I feel things are not quite so alarming.

No, I do not know what you British people are going through, we here could never realise if what we imagine is quite bad enough, what a people you are. I am proud to be of the same nationality.

A letter from Barbi written last November arrived last week telling me a piece of news about yourselves. She writes that she was fine and that I should be pleased and I am, it is the best thing that has happened to her since leaving Australia, she deserves it, and I hope that for you it will be just right.

She has had quite a lot of worry and things have always been just a little too much, she is my little girl, can I say that. But she has always had a lot of courage to face those things, which did surprise me. As a child she was the shyest but chirpy sort of person. You can perhaps understand what I felt at her courage at leaving us to go so far away, she was notably very young.

I often wonder if she will come back to Australia to see us, I tell her it is for him, as I went over to see her seven years ago, how long it is and how I still miss her as much as ever.

Barbi mentioned she was going to spend time with your people, and was looking forward to it as it will be the first bit of home since leaving Australia. Underneath her little reserve there is a tremendous love of home and all it means. I am hoping that one day she will have the opportunity to escape herself.

Forgive me for talking such a lot about her but to me she is a very fine person, and I am very proud of her. I don't know why I tell you these things but you have been so wonderful writing to me as you do, that I feel you are interested.

When I read of the dissemination of London's buildings I could weep, they are so unusual with all that finery and history in them. They are so fascinating to one who has always lived with modern things. My first sight of that sort of thing was Naples, through my cabin window and that old castle ruin on a hill, it was like a picture I had once seen, I could not realise it was real. I have never forgotten that first sight all my life and really, it is something to think back on. Strangely enough people are not interested in things you tell them. Myself, I have always wanted to know about them. It is perhaps that the liking of it can't impress them like the reading of it. But there it is, one just finds oneself living it alone.

Wasn't it dreadful your place being bombed? I do hope that you will be able to get somewhere soon. Being British I could guess you would do something about that, what people you are, I can't help admiring you all for your wonderful spirit and we all feel, out here, that we do too little. Also, how lovely to escape all you have gone through, we do try to do our bit with men and women working day and night, helping to raise money.

Tell Barbi there is a letter from Ewing if she gets this one before hers arrives. Will address it % Welwyn as I am not sure which will be your address from now on. By the time I have finished one letter my hand goes to pieces, have hurt my middle finger and at present it feels very tired. I do hope you can read what I have written. I will try and get one to Barbi by the same mail, one doesn't know these days when that will be.

Again, my grateful thanks to you for everything and hoping all is well with you.

Much love to you,

From Barb's mother.

Barbara's freedoms did not curb during her time with Bertie. He may have, given her a sense of stability, but her tenacious searching for experience still bubbled underneath.

St. Regis, Cork Street, Mayfair
London
19th March 1939

Dear Mum,

Just a short note to tell that there is nothing to say! It's Sunday and very cold and windy, a very appropriate day considering the news. This time I don't see how war can be averted, unless all the countries combine to frighten Hitler. It's of course a case of all we people who don't approve of Granny Chamberlain being able to say 'I told you so' because now we have a really formidable enemy who will be very hard to suppress, and will cost many thousands more lives, still, if it is inevitable, well it is now no use worrying.

Bertie is finding it hard to throw off his cold and can't get rid of his cough, I never know with sick people, whether they like to be left alone or not. Anyhow I seem to spend my day making orange juice. Bertie is getting rather worried about his old uncle, sister and niece who are on the Italian liner doing a Mediterranean cruise, they are that sort of family rather, who worry about things all the time.

James, my canary is really very sweet, he is quite tame now and knows me very well, he spends most of the time flying around the room and just loves it when I use the typewriter, he sits on the top of his cage in front of me and watches most intently, he is pretty awful when I have company though, he gets so excited that he won't stop singing and I have to send for the porter to take him downstairs where, he sings away as though he had been there all his life.

The daffodils and crocuses are all out now they are really lovely, the spring always makes me restless though. It is very strange that I feel like I'm going away somewhere, I can't get it out of my mind, although I haven't anywhere, at the moment, that I could possibly go to.

I have a new young man, at least he's not so young (I never seem to get them young) he is divorced from his wife and has a young daughter of six, she is sweet, always said I would like a ready-made family! Funny how men stick true to type, they all tell me that I'm very like his wife, only younger of course. He also lives here, as does Bertie, life is a little hectic and amusing and just what I wanted, I suppose I'm spoilt but I do love variety and being made a fuss of, and after all why not, one is an old woman long enough!

No more news but I'll write again next week.

Love to them all,

Barbara

Spring 1940

Beginning of letter missing or redacted[17]...*safe and we have an excellent air-raid shelter. The only thing that worries me is what to do with James my canary, he hasn't a gas mask. I will have to invite him into my own with me!*

Unfortunately, the theatre is going to shut in two weeks' time which means I shall be out of a job. I shall join the Transport Corps I think and I will send you a photograph of myself in uniform.

The weather here has been too lovely for words, I have never known such a spring I had to laugh in your last letter ....

---

[17] During World War II, censorship of civilian letters to and from places abroad was practiced between allies and enemies alike.

Missing section *...you think. This is common sense. I'm not being morbid and if anything should happen to me, please believe me, I <u>know</u> that I am one of the people who can very well be done without. Nothing will happen to me, I am really too thick-skinned.*

I shall send a photo of me in uniform.

Love to all at home.
Barbara

I suppose it's strange but I wouldn't have missed all this for the world!

In London, all but the Windmill Theatre closed at some point during the Blitz of 1940-41. The Shaftsbury and Queen's theatre were destroyed; Drury Lane was hit but the bomb failed to explode. Working in theatres at that time became increasingly difficult as male actors and technicians were conscripted, earlier openings and the lack of materials for costumes and scenery put strains on creating financial successes.
Barbara's living conditions were sparse, the areas she lived in were not the expensive locations they are now.

Chapter 5
Siamese cat in trousers.

Richmond
4th May 1940

Dear Mum,

If I can find it, I am enclosing a snap of one of the authors took of me, it is after a long day of dress rehearsing so you can make allowances, they all say it is pretty awful, but I think it is good and how it is a snap 'au naturelle'!

Have just been too busy for words doing everything myself since Tansy has been away. It is a marvellous profession of course but unfortunately too much for me. It is really a man's job and I have given in my notice. I have come to the stage where I know it is impractical to go on and do justice to the job. I will have a holiday and look for something else. I have hope for joining 'Ensa'[18] and going to France with a play, it would be grand.

They are very upset about my going, they have offered to get me a secretary and raise my salary, which is very satisfying but even so, the job is just drudgery with never even a Sunday off. It is a good thought to know they were satisfied with me.

No news really, the war doesn't bear thinking about, goodness knows what we are in for now. Haven't seemed to have heard from you all in ages. Will write later when I have more time.

Love,
Barbara

---

[18] In 1939 theatre producer Basil Dean set up the Entertainments National Service Association (**ENSA**) to provide entertainment for British troops. In 1940 ENSA also began arranging concerts for British civilian workers.

Richmond
29th May 1940

Dear Mum,

Excuse the pencil but I have lost my pen. I am very ashamed not to have written before but it is so hard to write when things move so fast, the only thing one seems thankful for is another day, the food and the weather. As you can see by the date things are at their blackest, but they will get better from now on, it's treachery we have fought up to now and we will just have to dig in for the long, long fight. We have at last got our government in order.

We have been putting on some lovely plays lately but it is hard to put one's mind to work that's the only thing. We have a grand play this week by the authors of 'Ladies in Retirement'[19], it has some beautiful acting in it. I am rather proud of the set as I dressed it myself completely, I think it looks rather good. I wish I had photos of all my sets.

I do hope you aren't worrying about me, it would be foolish, firstly because I am well out of London, secondly, I feel this whole thing is much more important than thinking of any one person.

Terribly funny, I have just bought myself a lovely white sheepskin rug, at last, I have just finished paying for it, I had it on HP for months. The other day when I was shaking it out of my window to freshen it up, five floors down cause a great fuss as the thought it was a parachute!

Your last letter had a bit cut out of it by the sensor, it makes one awfully curious of course. Unfortunately, you have written on both sides of the paper so most of the letter was gone.

---

[19] **Ladies in Retirement** by Edward Percy and Reginald Denham: Based on a famous murder which actually took place at the end of the 19th century and set in the 1880's, this play became one of the most successful and the most frequently performed in the modern repertoire.

  Bertie is expecting his factory to be taken over any minute now poor darling all his work for nothing.

  I'm afraid there is not much news.
    Will write you soon
     Love,
      Barbara

In 1940 several high explosive and incendiary bombs hit the St. James area while Barbara was in repertory at Welwyn Studios. Barbara had moved her career to the burgeoning film industry and out of London. At Welwyn Studios,[20] Hertfordshire, she met up again with a friend Norman Lee, a British writer, director and producer of low budget films. They co-wrote the play, 'In the palm of your hand' in 1940, going on to co-write the plays, 'Lifeline' and 'The Moon to Play With', Barbara under the pseudonym Norman Armstrong. Lifeline was a play of the Merchant Navy in three acts produced in 1942. Norman Lee joined Barbara again in 1948, when they co-wrote a screenplay for the B movie 'The Monkey's Paw.'

Welwyn Studios,
Welwyn Garden City, Herts.
26th November 1940

Dear Mum,

  I keep writing letters and then can't remember whether I've posted them or not. I suppose I have. We have all but finished the picture as far as the 'shooting' goes and all that has to be done is to put it together. With effects and music and the like. It has been

---

[20] In 1931, **Welwyn Studios** was taken over by John Maxwell's Elstree-based British International Pictures (BIP), and later became part of Associated British Picture Corporation (ABPC). It was mainly used for supporting features and to accommodate overflow productions from the main complex at Elstree.

great fun and I have learnt a lot and would now like to go to another studio, as this place isn't one of the really first-class studios.

We have been having a quieter time of it lately up here as far as the 'blitz' goes although poor old London[21] seems to be still getting it in the neck. I hope to go down to Bertie's sister's place down in Devon, I think I told you; it will be fun to be in a private house again. Bertie is very keen that I go.

We have decided to get married somehow or other, it does seem a waste of time and I now feel that even if Ewing were to divorce me, it is better than hanging on here like this with nothing to look forward to. I'm sure you'll be pleased too.

Bertie is such a good man, and I am very lucky indeed, I'm sure I don't really deserve it. He was very pleased to get your letter it was nice of you to write to him.

I am sorry I didn't send you anything for Christmas or any money, it is forbidden to send any now, however after the war we will make up for it.

Give my love to Sadie and Ian, and a big hug for yourself.

Barbara

*Welwyn Studios
Welwyn Garden City, Herts.
19th December 1940*

Darling Mums,

I have just received a letter from you dated October 30th with a lot cut out. Some of the things you say in your letters, I think you must get only half of my letters to you, although I suppose that is only to be expected.

---

[21] On April 9, 1940, Germany simultaneously invaded Norway and occupied Denmark, and the war began in earnest. On May 10th, German forces swept through Belgium and the Netherlands in what became known as "blitzkrieg," or lightning war.

You ask me what I look like and such things, it is pretty difficult to give an accurate description of oneself without appearing self-centred and conceited...my hair is quite a lot darker and I wear a platinum streak in front, which is considered very much part of me by my friends.

I still have <u>most</u> of my figure, weighing about 8 stone. Look pretty well preserved, I think, but a bit scraggy about the neck. (Barbara at this stage would have been 32yrs.)

I am considered quite sophisticated without being blazé. I take an intelligent interest in foods and wines, which makes me popular with the opposite sex, who also seem to find me amusing because I never take them all that seriously, in the heavy sense.

I am really very selfish but have a charming manner, which I believe hides most of it. And lastly, and most importantly, I have most of my inferiority complex left me by Ewing, under control. It all sounds awful reading it over but then you are the only person in the world I could say such things to.

I am getting down the technique of farce writing, and find it rather amusing if a little broad. It's fun to find I can write at all.

Must fly now

Love, Barbara

Welwyn, Herts
11th March 1941

Dear Mum,

It's a long time since I have written to you, I'm afraid; it's so hard to write these days. Somehow the situation doesn't bear thinking about let alone writing about.

We are just casting for our new film and it is a difficult job, everyone seems to be away on war work. We had a bit of a set to about salaries the other day and I got up on my high horse, said I would leave and walked out. My little boss was so upset, he rang me up and they said that one thing was certain, no matter what happened I mustn't leave.

I was rather pleased as I didn't know he felt as strongly as that about my staying. So, I went back feeling my frustration had been quite a lot strengthened.

We will probably be having an Australian in the film called John Hardwick, do you know of him? He's quite a dear - my Australian.

I haven't heard a word from Ewing in months, I'm awfully restless and although Bertie is a dear, one can't expect him to sit and wait for me all his life. Poor darling he's having a wicked time now there is talk of shutting all the factories[22] not working on war work, so his will go!

Spring is at last happening here, the country is so lovely now up here. I will try and take some snaps when the weather looks a bit better.

Give my love to Sadie and Ian, and much love darling.
Barbara.

Barbara returned to work in London in 1943 only to be faced with further bombing raids. She played down the seriousness of the situation when writing to her mother:

London
Wednesday, September 1943

Dear Mum,

Didn't seem to answer your questions in my last letter. About my hair - it's fairish and I have it short now - ever since the V1s and V2s [23] one is up and down all night. I wear it sort of sleek and waved across the back. I am beginning to look my age I

---

[22] **Factories,** during the war, were converted to the production of military items such as tanks, rifles, ammunition, airplanes and ships.

[23] **V1** were short range, **V2** were long range rockets dropped over England to demoralise the country as the tide was turning against Germany. Travelling at speed, they dropped on random targets once their fuel was depleted.

think, like everyone else the reaction to the war is awful, and of course everything here is so dreary.

My figure is still good I think and I am considered quite smart. I'm still pretty moody and people tire me more than ever - I've always been better when I am not cluttered up with people and now that I am writing people at last respect it and don't bother me all that amount.

That's all I think, I can't tell you what sort of person I am. One's always surprised at what other people think one's like. But you wanted a description so there it is.

Bertie bought a banana back from Sweden - the first I have tasted for five years! I know you will think I am potty but when is Ian's birthday and is he eight or nine?

Love,
Barbara

Cable, 4th December 1943
Dear Mum, I have just received a letter from you sent on the 3rd which isn't bad going really. Your cake arrived in very good condition. We haven't had a cake like that for years. It was put up on exhibition as we had all forgotten that cakes could be that good, thank you very much. Bertie made a pig of himself about it - he's really very greedy and loves his food - you would really get on with him as he would certainly appreciate your cooking. I am really busy as we have just put another play on and are getting another ready. Business is pretty good in the theatrical business except that we have a few nuisance raids that always scare people off for a while. I am off to Oxford next week to have a look at one of our shows, do you remember it? There isn't much news I'm very busy as usual and not looking forward to winter at all especially as we didn't have a summer to speak of. Haven't seen anything of John since

the first time, I suppose he is still up North, I think he found me a little formidable. How are Sadie and Ian? you never say much about them in your letters, it's funny to think of Sadie with a growing son. As soon as I am making a substantial amount of money, I'm going to adopt a child - I'm too lazy to have one of my own. Love to all. Barbara.

Cable, 1 June 1944.
Dear Mum, it's ages since I wrote to you but I am really busy with work, up till 9 pm. I have just come back from Worthing on the South coast. I was there when the second front[24] started. We had taken a theatre there and I was performing in the play. London is very quiet at present as of course all the soldiers and men in uniform are otherwise occupied. I wonder if you got the photos that Bertie sent you of the cottage? They are pretty awful but I will be able to send more later on. Love Barbara

Cable, 24th June 1944
Dear Mum, Thought I had better write to you again as you will have heard about our new bombings and may be worried. I think - as you do worry - I ought to say that I promise to send you a cable if by any chance I do get hurt, silly really by then you will know. Things seem to be going pretty well with the second front, it is almost encouraging. We are having a lousy summer and no hot weather at all; I am still wearing suits. The one thing I am always

---

[24] **Second front**: The D-Day landings created a second-front and took the pressure off the Russian allies and made steady progress into territory held by Germany.

thankful for is that I have always worn tailored suits, they have certainly stood me in good stead during the war. Love to all. Barbara.

Cable, 11th July 1944
Dear Mum, I got a letter from you this week in which you were worrying about not having heard from me. It's awfully difficult to write much. I'm really so busy and there really isn't much news. You have no doubt heard a bit about those new bombs[25], they put us on the hop a bit but are not so awful so don't worry about me. London is rather empty of people which is a good thing as it means I can at least get a table at a restaurant! My love to you all. Barbara

31st August 1944

Dear Mum,

Your cake arrived in very good order. It really is very good and much appreciated. Actually, we seem to heading towards want for food and everything else this winter. I'm rather dreading the winter here, one feels like one can't stand much more of this, it is going to get really bad.

I have been trying to send something off to the new baby but it is taking an awful time, there is so much red tape and one has to get permits etc. to send things off still.

Love to all,
Barbara

---

[25] **New Bombs**: Operation Steinbock sometimes called the Baby Blitz, was a strategic bombing campaign by the German Air Force during the Second World War. It targeted Southern England and lasted January to May 1944. Steinbock was the last strategic air offensive by the German bomber arm during the conflict.

Cable, 16th September 1944
Dear Mum, Norman and I have written a new play which is being tried out down at Worthing next week. I'm down here producing it; I think it might be quite good. It's a comedy this time so it ought to be better than 'Delphine' It is called 'In the palm of your hand'. I've had quite a few letters from you but no parcels at all, you say you have sent some, they may of course get lost this end.
We have been having fun and games in London - I'm getting proper fed up!
Love to all. Barbara

73 St James Street, SW1
19th December 1944

Dear Mum,

A parcel has arrived from you with figs, crystalised fruit and jellies in it, they are lovely and a welcome present for Christmas. Thank you very much.

I hope you had a good birthday and got my cable. I have first been having lunch with Jack Harrison who met me in a restaurant and knew me straight away, says I haven't changed in twenty years! He looks awfully well and seems rather sweet. I kept off the subject of his family as I couldn't remember but didn't someone in his family die rather intriguingly?

Bertie got a letter from you and is thrilled you are sending him a parcel. I don't think his block of flats is too safe, I think you should send anything to Farndale.

Love,
Barbara

8 Waterloo Place
London. SW1

Dear Mum,

I love getting anything you send but really, we are well looked after these days. It's only things like eggs and butter we miss. Actually, it is things like clothes that I get really upset about - real silk for blouses etc is often more impossible, but I suppose it is with you too.

Christmas is here again and of course it is a complete farce - there isn't anything worthwhile to buy. I think people are mad to do anything about it.

My love to you all,

Barbara

73 St James Street
SW1
(don't send anything more to 8 Waterloo Place as I am leaving)
2nd June 1945

Dear Mum,

A parcel of fruit and two lots of material has turned up at last, thanks most awfully, the muscatels are marvellous and seem to travel better than anything else. The material is lovely but of course, you shouldn't have sent it, I didn't realise you were also rationed.[26]

It is so strange having peace here and to feel like the walls aren't made of paper anymore, one can go to bed without the eternal gas mask packed ready for a quick exit!

---

[26] **Rationing:** Australia was rationed until 1950, using a coupon method restricting clothing, fuel, and some foods.

London was great fun during the peace celebrations - the crowds were marvellous- just happy and content to walk around looking at the lights again.

The cottage (Fig 7) *is looking pretty good again and is the pride of the village, quite a show home, although there is still quite a lot to be done with the gardens.*

Do you know anyone who knows the theatrical position in Australia, who controls the theatres? A couple of stars I know want to go out if things could be properly arranged.

Will write again soon.

   Love, Barbara

73 St James Street
London
SW1
11th July 1945

Dear Mum,

I am sending an ordinary letter as I am sending the enclosed snaps, some are in the final repairs of the cottage. One is of my dogs, a Peke puppy called Wei...at the moment mostly wee wee! And a very bad one of my girlfriends Moie Charles.[27] (Fig 8) *She is really very lovely to look at and a great friend of mine. She wrote the story of 'The Gentle Sex'*[28] *Leslie Howard's last film. Did you see it? She is always trying to get me to take her to Australia.*

I have been very busy finishing a new play. I am thinking mostly of giving up movies and concentrating on writing, it's a big decision and a risk, but it is what I really want to do.

---

[27] **Moie Charles** was a writer, known for The Gentle Sex (1943), The White Unicorn (1947) and When the Bough Breaks (1947). Later collaborating with Barbara on the transcript of Agatha Christie's book 'Murder at the Vicarage' for the stage.

[28] **The Gentle Sex** is a 1943 British, black-and-white romantic comedy-drama war film, directed and narrated by Leslie Howard.

Bertie is very much for it as he knows what a lot the business takes out of me. It would probably mean I would spend more time at the cottage and life would be calmer, more reasonable and enjoyable.

I do hope Sadie is alright and everything is going well. How old is Ian?

Love and take care of yourself,

Barbara.

I wanted to find out more about Bertie, he supported Barbara for many years, financially and emotionally, on the promise of marriage. He had been a successful businessman owning furniture factories in Leicester until factories were requisitioned during the war. I wonder, did he wait too long, did he have trouble recovering financially after the war? Would he have known about her co-writer Norman Lee, who hounded Barbara throughout their film and play collaborations? In a letter he wrote to Barbara's mother: he seemed pleased to help her in her career:

89 Lichfield Court
Richmond, Surrey
Telephone: Richmond 4333
December 8th 1946

Dear Mrs Toy,

I want to thank you so very much for sending me the parcels of food, which arrived yesterday. Although this is greatly appreciated, such delicacies are hard to obtain here, you should not have to go to this trouble but we don't have a crust of bread here now. Just enough to keep body and soul together. Anyhow it is most kind of you and what you sent will be much enjoyed.

In case this letter should reach you before Xmas is over, I would like to send you my heartiest Christmas greetings with the hope that you will, and your family, have a very happy time together. I send also my wishes for a Happy New Year in 1947. I hope you will have good health and enjoy life thoroughly all year, and during 1947/8 a visit to

England is under consideration. I sincerely hope it may materialize. It is high time you came and gave the 'red country' a sight of you.

Barbara has just had one of her plays put on at the Q Theatre (Fig.9) and it is doing very well. Unfortunately, this week has been terribly foggy and this must have affected people coming from any distance - it took us 2 hrs to get home on the first night - this is just sheer bad luck. (How we envy your Australian summer now - although you do seem to have a lot of rain to judge by the test matches.)

I enclose a copy of the program and also a review from the Evening Standard - these will, I am sure, be of interest to you. Barbara produced the play herself and is rather tired after 3 strenuous weeks, but the play is doing very well...I think she hopes to get another play in the spring - so you see she is becoming quite an established playwright. The reception of 'In the palm of your hand' on the first night was enthusiastic and Barbara herself looked very, very attractive. I think there is no doubt that she has a talent for playwriting and someday will produce a 'winner' especially if she writes it on her own.

England is rather dark just now - winter and its dreariness is well established - we have had some of the worst fogs for years and almost incessant rain for weeks. The work of brightening up London seems so very slow; we are gradually becoming nationalized 'socialized'; the irksome destruction one expected went on to the end of the war and is still with us, it all seems to be full of life but there is still little in the shops. But hope 'springs eternal' now we live with more optimism than reality.

With again my thanks, best wishes and kindness always.

Your sincerely,

Bertie Loch

In an interview for 'The People' newspaper, Barbara explained her love of the stage and being urged on by producers, as a young woman she was beguiled by the prospect of success. Remaining in London during World War II, her acting career led to producing and writing. She became stage director for the J. Arthur Rank Organisation, while managing theatres in Worthing and Bromley. Eventually turning to writing, her co-authored stage adaptations of Agatha Christie's "Murder at the Vicarage," 'Random Harvest" and "The Man in Grey', did well. Her all-male-cast play "Lifeline" was produced in London and New York.'

From Barbara's **London Times** obituary 2001:

> ... During the blitz Barbara was a volunteer ambulance driver.
>
> In 1949, with Moie Charles, she approached her friend Agatha Christie with the idea of adapting her book *Murder at the Vicarage*. Despite her vow never to let anyone adapt her plays, Christie agreed and sanctioned a major change to the denouement. Having opened at The Playhouse in December 1949, it ran for 1,776 performances.

From unnamed Australian newspaper cutting found in Barbara's archives:

'Sydney Writer's Film Script Work in England.'

Latest, news from London of Miss Barbara Toy, is that she helped to produce the picture "The Monkey's Paw", for which she wrote the script from W.W. Jacobs's story.

Miss Toy is also associated with the Connaught Theatre, Worthing, where new plays are tried out for the theatre. A play "The Moon to Play With." In association with the late Norman Lee, Miss Toy also wrote and produced 'Life Line" a story of the merchant navy. She also wrote with him 'In the Palm of Your Hand," a play which will be heard over the air in Australia this year.

Miss Toy left Sydney for England in 1931. She is the daughter of the late Mr. Bert F. Toy and of Mrs. Toy, of Castlecrag.'

There seems to be less attention to accuracy in this small newspaper cutting as Barbara mentions meeting up with Lee many times in her later letters. Researching Lee, he was active at the time as a playwright, novelist, and satirical cartoonist. Norman Lee contributed to such low-budget comedies as 'He Snoops to Conquer' in 1945, a play on the words of 'She Stoops to Conquer' a part in which Barbara herself had played on stage a decade earlier. In their banter, at times uncomfortable, Barbara kept the upper hand and her distance despite Lee's pleading, making the most of his connections and status as a writer. She was still in a relationship with Bertie at this time, and still married to Ewing.

Lee seems to have been instrumental in helping her with her writing and the editing of her first travel book *A Fool on Wheels*. They appear to have had a lasting if distant friendship until his death in 1964. Barbara wrote of him to her mother in 1958:

London
28th September 1958

Dear Mum,

I am so sorry that I haven't written earlier but things are hectic. I have been concentrating on this awful book, which thank goodness, I have just about finished. It isn't good and probably nothing will happen with it; however, it is now off my chest.

Norman Lee, who wrote 'Lifeline' with me has been editing it for me. He, by the way, travels to Australia tomorrow. So, going out to get copies of his book I gave him your address - he's a rough and ready sort of old bay - but an old sweetie. He hasn't much money so won't be there long, but he may look you up. He is rather a fan of mine.

I was broadcasting this week in 'women's hour' but I don't think they recorded it, so don't suppose you heard it.

Very many thanks for the papers and magazines which arrived safely, quite nice photos of the Governor I thought, you all seem to be having fun and games with the Russians. [29]

Love,

Barbara.

I had walked, once again, into the garage entrance at 'Snails' on a rainy morning, waiting as usual for the door to be opened. Terri rattled the keys several times in the lock, I could hear her muffled swearing in the struggle. Throwing up her arms, when the door finally opened, she exclaimed 'it's a nightmare'. A small crust of bread was hanging from her mouth and crumbs had fallen over her jumper, she was hastily brushing them away, at the same time waving for me to enter. I was distracted for a moment as I rarely saw her eat. She would take a few bites of her favourite chocolate eclairs I would occasionally tempt her with, but no more, the rest put away 'for later.'

As I looked around, the garage seemed transformed into a library, one that had been picked up and shaken, the lights off and left to rot. Books of all shapes, sizes and decades, were piled up, lodged in old plastic bags and sagging boxes. The smell of old paper and dust permeated to a dry taste in the mouth. I must have looked stunned as the bright sunlight from the outside gave way to the gloom and dark of the garage. Terri told me to help myself to any of the books, they were all destined for second hand shops and bins. She bustled away to make tea, the custom of my frequent visits, as I stood overwhelmed again. I knew I needed to spend time with Terri, herself a remarkable woman, before delving into the life another. My fondness for Terri grew at each visit, if only she had known how similar she was to Barbara after all.

---

[29] In April 1954 Vladimir and Evdokia Petrov, Soviet spies who were masquerading as diplomats in Canberra, defected to Australia. The defection and the information that the Petrov's passed onto Australian authorities had global implications, through the identification of spy networks around the world. It affected the balance of political power in Australia for decades after the event.

Most of the books were from Barbara's personal collection.

The letters of Gertrude Bell, selected and edited by Lady Bell, D.B.E. 1927

The Well of Loneliness, by Radclyffe Hall[30]. 1928

Travellers Prelude, by Freya Stark. 1950

There were map books, religious texts, and beautifully hand-illustrated books of birds and one of plants. History books of different countries, numerous plays Barbara had written, and all eight of her travel books. There were two audio tapes with the words Barbara written on them in dust-encrusted Tipex. I asked to listen to them later and was told to take them, they were not needed anymore.

Among those treasures was a small shabby book, 'Another Woman's man'[31] by Norman Lee. The prologue to the book gave an insight into his humour and character.

> The Way, I see it.
>
> 'Women should hold themselves like a well-bred horse, but there's no need to whinny.'
>
> 'If you saw enough of Marilynn Munroe, you would get used to her.'
>
> 'Skinny women are usually bad-tempered, like the plump ones.'

---

[30] **Marguerite Antonia Radclyffe Hall** was an English poet and author, best known for the novel The Well of Loneliness, a ground-breaking work in lesbian literature. In adulthood, Hall often went by the name John.

[31] 'Another woman's man.' Norman Lee, 1954. He also wrote the series 'The beautiful Gunner' and 'Lover - say it with Mink!'

'Husbands run in three sorts: prizes, surprises, and consolation prizes.'

'If you let a man make love to you, he finally gets satiated, if you don't let him make love to you, he gets bored. The way I play it they never get bored and never get satiated…'

'When a man lets an old chicken pick him up, he's just a worm.'

'American women are the most spoiled in the world. They ought to be, they are God's own children.'

'It's always open season for males and there are no rules.'

'I am warning you, when women go frail and weak on you, look out! They're after something.'

'Most men prefer a girl to have more under her sweater than under her hat. For self-preservation, I prefer to have it both ways.'

'A lot of girls think they are unbeatable, but a lot of good guys have taken a beating to get them like that.'

Norman Lee.1954, Werner Laurie Ltd. Pgs. 5-6

Lee, also known for his cartoon drawings, illustrated, rather suggestively, many letters and notes to Barbara during the time they worked together on films and plays. Although it appears, she froze him out on many occasions, Barbara later wrote a dedication to Lee in her first book *A Fool on Wheels*, where she thanked him for his encouragement and acknowledged it would not have happened without him.

Telegram:
1944. Norman Lee Columbia Pictures.
Like the description of this guy George. Must meet him
sometime. Let's use him in play. Toy.

Darling Babs,

I like your wire BUT WHAT IS THIS BLOODY IMPERSONAL TOY BUSINESS! – And, why have you stopped sending your LOVE –

You are an aggravating, tantalising little bitch, really!!! Where DO I stand with you? You used to write me the duckiest of little notes and now! – that chilly uninspiring SILENCE. I am the only living man who would keep writing to an ice queen and getting not the effort of one…line in reply.

Don't you know I only thrive on ECOURAGEMENT! – Where were you born: on the Russian steps, or an igloo?

Look –

If I hire George, I will <u>warn</u> you – he'll fall for you. He'll think (the poor soft boob) that your redhead is real and your blue eyes are indicative of sincerity and an emotional nature. He would <u>never</u> believe in the ice princess, that chilly little cow who lives in a steel citadel behind those lying blue orbs. He'll buy you presents because he feels warm-hearted towards you – he'll think you have taste and charm and are one of God's children. He'll think too that you are a clever piece of work, with ideas and ambitions and above all, <u>the sap</u>, he'll think you radiate sex, in your quiet secretive way.

He will want to lay in big double beds with you and kiss you all over and try to penetrate your mind by the way of other channels (metaphorically speaking of course) and he'll even contemplate being true to you, which with a little encouragement he'd actually achieve.

That is because he is a silly big sap and doesn't know you were born of a devil's brew for the sole purpose of tantalising men whom you led up the garden path (the streets have a name for it) for your own sheepish purposes. Now, George is a pal of mine and I don't want to see the poor boob done dirt to.

So, if I catch him getting 'that way' about you I am going to beat the hides off you if you don't give him a break…you love – teasing, double-crossing Siamese cat in trousers.

You have been <u>warned</u>!
Yes, we will put him in the play and I am for the idea now.

Yours,
Lee

The letters and drawings from Norman, were among the copious amounts of paperwork in the attic studio, loosely placed into a large old brown envelope, on which Barbara had marked in bold red letters the word 'KEEP.'

I laughed at the teasing and banter, the richness and the honesty of the collaboration that existed on many levels. The cheek of Norman and the strength of Barbara's character, as however different the times were then, she knew how to handle him. She created relationships that worked well for her, although the effort would eventually tire her.

Despite her skill at handling men, Barbara was still yearning to escape from people, to find herself, to be herself, to be alone.

Barbara and Norman corresponded until his death in 1964. They would send and re-sending letters back and forth adding notes each time, until the letters were almost illegible. (Fig 10)

Cottage bought with Bertie in Devon - pre-restoration.

Fig 7

Fully restored.

Fig 8

Moie Charles at the cottage

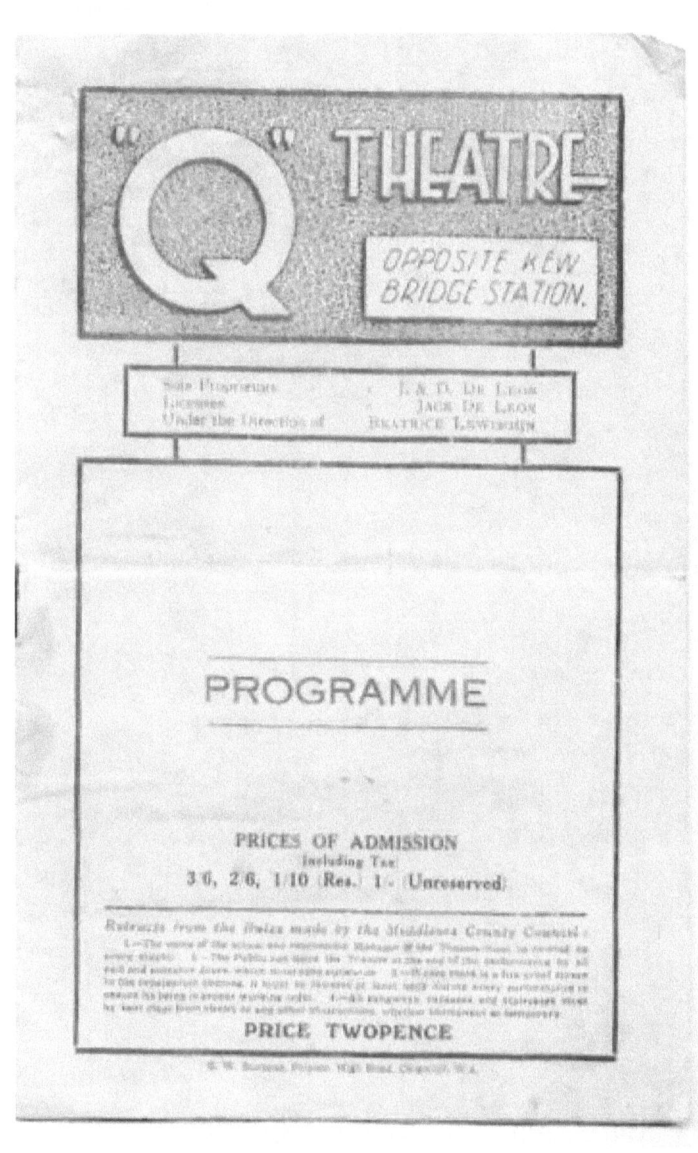

Fig 9

Q Theatre programme

Drawings from Norman Lee

"......and do you really think the
ending is a TEENIE bit immoral...."
"Yeh"
"...well that's my collaborator's bad
influence..... He has the AWFULEST ideas....."

DATE .... 44/5.

THIS WARRANTY GAURANTEES THE BEARER, MISS
B. TOY, A BEDROOM ARMISTICE FOR ..... DAYS
AS FROM .... TO WEEK ENDING ....
AND IS ISSUED SO THAT SHE MAY TRAVEL
UNMOLESTED FOR THE PERIOD STATED, AFTER
WHICH SHE TRAVELS AT HER OWN RISK.¹ (NOTE)
    Signed --- ------------------
              MINISTER OF THE INTERIOR
                 (without portfolio)

> Now why can't men be just friendly without all that shee-shee.... with their damned flowers & kisses & gushy notes they do really make a Girl's life a hell..... and all we want is to just be little palsey-walseys? She taken quite seriously as brother artists..

(I couldnt agree with you MORE.)

← MOLLY.

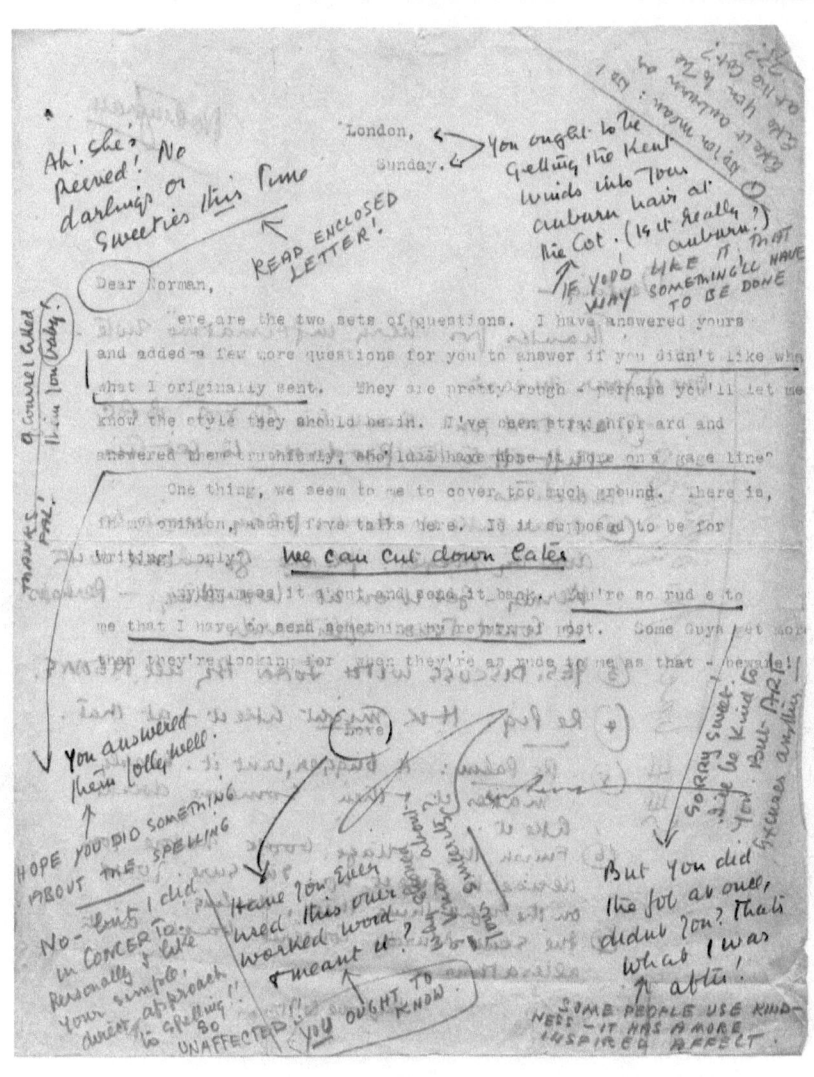

Fig 10

Overwriting of letters sent between Norman Lee and Barbara.

Chapter 6
'The land of milk and honey'.

11th January 1946

Dear Mum,

No sign of your other parcel yet. Don't bother darling to send anymore, I feel awful, you want them for yourself and I am awfully good at scrounging. I'm the black-market belle of St. James's. You seem to have had a good Christmas. It's a pity you aren't being waited on for a change. When do you go home? Did you get the little book I sent you of Normans? He is an absolute pet and has been so kind and helpful to me.

Why don't you know about your father? Has he got skeletons too? Blimey! It is no wonder I am in the theatrical business!

My tooth was painful again yesterday, it is being a real nuisance.

Bertie flew to Finland [32] *on Wednesday for the board of trade about wood. I believe it is really awful over there under the Russians - no food or heating, that's what comes of fighting for your ideals, I suppose if they had sat down like Sweden* [33] *did, they would be in the same happy position as that country.*
    Love,
        Barbara

The leaf tea was a great success, especially with this tooth.

---

[32] **Finland:** In 1944–1945, followed the signing of the Moscow Armistice with the Allied Powers, which stipulated expulsion of Nazi German forces from Finnish territory.

[33] **Sweden** was, subject to British and German Naval blockades, accidental bombings from the Soviets on some cities which led to problems with the supply of food and fuels.

Grand Hotel
Stockholm
20th March 1946

Dear Mum,

We have been here nearly a week and it is all like another world - to see things in the shops and be able to buy them - it takes a lot of getting used to!

Everybody is so polite and relaxed so different from home.

We have luckily had good weather, warm and sunny so far. The exchange is against us which makes everything very expensive but anyway it is nice to see them.

Haven't much time for writing, will write fully when I get home.

Love,
    Barbara

London
30th November 1946

Dear Mum,

I am terribly sorry not to have written for so long, I have been hectically busy. I am in the middle of producing one of our plays and the preparations and castings have been quite a job. I have another eight days before I open and I am still all tied up with it. It is only a 'try-out' but I am hoping something comes of it. I have had some letters from you, let's hope we don't have too bad a winter.

There is no news at present, everyone is going mad about Christmas which is an awful farce as there is nothing at all to buy at reasonable prices.

I hope Sadie is well again. Has she found a house yet? I loved the snaps; Toni had shown me some of them before. How well Sadie looks, she looks about ten years younger than I do.

We have been having lots of rain and floods everywhere, but not much cold yet. I expect it will get bad after Christmas. How are the aunts?

*Love to all,
Barbara*

*London
10th May 1948*

Dear Mum,

Your letter arrived today to say our play had been done. Moie and I were very thrilled and glad you liked it. I would really like to know though how it went; you are naturally bias in our favour. But I would like to know for future plays, if it is the sort of thing they like. Could you let me know what well known plays go down well in Australia? Anyhow, it was nice getting your letter, in fact there are days when everyone's so down here, we almost burst into tears if anyone says anything nice!

Did I tell you my Peke had been ill? Thank goodness he is better now, but still staggering rather drunkenly about. He's awfully sweet though and seems most grateful for all that has been done for him. I am going down to the cottage tomorrow for Whitsun so that ought to put him on his feet. I am taking my 'little woman that does' for me, she regards it as an annual holiday. Although she proceeds to spring clean the entire cottage! Fancy Margo being that way, Moie is very much her type and as good looking. Funny how all my friends are so good looking considering my peculiar visage.

I told you in my last letter that the thread arrived together with the cake and flakes, they were lovely but all I want for some time now. The fruit juice, by the way, that you sent some time ago was awfully good. Some wrappings on the parcels were Sunday papers, could you sometime send me some more. I found them most interesting especially the advertisements.

*Love,
Barbara*

Moie Charles became Barbara's companion for some time, they worked together on several transcriptions, 'Random Harvest' by James Hilton and 'The Man in Grey' by Lady Eleanor Smith.

The pair also worked on Agatha Christie's novel *Murder at the Vicarage* for the stage in 1949. It introduced Miss Marple outside of the books and short stories. (Fig 11) In among the papers of Barbara's archive was a poster of the play that was shown for years in Poland. (Fig.12) This was the only performance of the play that afforded Barbara a royalty payment, despite her efforts to get the play to the stage and its ultimate success, she was to receive a mere £1 a year in royalties, payments which ceased in 2000.

Barbara talked of Agatha Christie in a newspaper interview in 1998 as an amazing woman. During Barbara's Arabian travels, she found Agatha Christie was well known in the area and she visited her on one of her trips, at one of her husband's archaeological digs. She saw Agatha as a friend and knew her as great fun and having a terrific sense of humour.

Barbara also wrote of that meeting with Agatha Christie in her first book, *A Fool on Wheels*. She describes arriving in Nimrud, Northern Iraq, at a long building partitioned in two. Each side was covered with archaeological finds. On entering she was handed several broken pieces and asked to carefully place them on the table. The man handing her the objects was Professor Mallowan, Agatha Christie's husband. As she moved through the room, she saw Agatha at the far end piecing fragments together. Once again, she was greeted without surprise, the concentration and quiet was paramount, it seemed nothing could disturb it.

Barbara had known Christie writing about her husband on a 'dig', in which she saw a great sense of fun, and always imagined what it would be like. It was near the end of the season at the dig, and Christie offered to show Barbara around. As they went through the passage ways and rooms it became clear that there were over two hundred men employed during the two-month excavation.

No letters or correspondence between Agatha Christie and Barbara remain, as anything that did exist between them would have been returned to the Christie estate.

Bertie (also known as Bart and Bert), remained in Barbara's life for many years, tolerating her absences and affairs. Her admiration for the aesthetic of men and women went some way to explain a beautifully preserved photograph, carefully placed in tissue and tucked into a leather embossed folder. All her other photos seemed abandoned and strewn about the attic studio. Who was this magnificent woman? Could it be the women in this tender moment from one of Barbara's books?

Although Barbara writes of a meeting in a temple in her book *A Fool on Wheels*, the place she describes correlates to a visit she made during her honeymoon. We know she found her early married life difficult and this encounter seems to have had a profound effect on her. She describes her meeting with a tall blonde woman, who recognised her loneliness and approached Barbara to help. She had wandered into the Temple of the Jade Goddess in Bangkok, a cool dark place where she was surrounded by the beauty of colourful mosaic tiles. As the beauty of the place overwhelmed her, her contrasting unhappiness became too much. As the woman approached, she offered to sit and talk for a while. As the young Barbara listened to her speak of the independence of mind and body, religions and philosophies, she could feel a return to herself. The woman described her own struggles, resonating with Barbara's own, describing Barbara as a 'fish swimming in the wrong water'.

Later they would meet again, in Bagdad, the end destination of Barbara's first trip. Once again, the unnamed woman, who acknowledged she had feared her new young friend was near suicidal, was grateful to see her as strong and independent as she knew she could be. In the book Barbara explains how she wanted to thank her saviour in person. The chapter in which she talks about this pivotal moment in her life was called "To a lover, even Baghdad is not too far." Could the beautiful photograph be that woman, Billy?

'More books?' I exclaimed, as I stepped over even more old volumes, which by now had spread across the entire garage floor. They were a mixture of beautifully gold embossed volumes and 1970's paperbacks with gaudy jacket designs. I was back with Terri; I not only felt the need to know that as a new widow she was okay, but I genuinely enjoyed her company. Terri's indifference to Barbara had allowed me to discover Barbara for myself, and I loved it. Barbara was rising slowly from the debris; had she been lying in wait for someone to discover? How fortunate was I?

'Everything has to go, what would I want with all these books!' Terri exclaimed with an air of defeat. I didn't know where to turn, a feeling I was getting used to every time I entered the tiny cottage.

'Please Terri, you can't just throw them away, some of them look very old and might be worth selling.' I felt a heart breaking, sinking feeling that yet more of Barbara was destined for the charity shops, or bins. Her library was slowly being decanted to oblivion, scattered to the unknowing edges of the local Oxfam shop. There seemed to be even more books, added each time I arrived, a new pile, travel books and dictionaries this time, a large fantastic two volume collection of hand painted flower plates, two volumes of travel letters written by Gertrude Bell, another Queen of the Desert and, of course, an early copy of Lawrence of Arabia. An autobiography by Freya Stark lay on a swamped dusty desk along with the precious copies of all of Barbara's out of print books, and several religious texts from all denominations. If I'd the money, I would have bought them all from her, but I neither had such funds or the library to house them all.

My sadness jumped to one side when I caught a glimpse of a book, I had coincidentally heard about on Radio 4, only the day before, thank goodness, as I would never have known the significance of it. 'The well of loneliness' by Radcliffe Hall, published in 1928 was subsequently banned for its depiction of lesbian lovers. Suddenly so much began to fall into place. I looked up to see Terri grinning knowingly. 'Oh yes, Barbara loved women too,' she said, catching the look on my face, as she brought in even more books from the sitting room. 'I think she had a lover in Devon, Minna

Dyason[34], she left Barbara all these paintings, the Nolan's, you know, that Australian painter. Lots of the furniture here was Minna Dyason's too, that's why it doesn't fit. This new information seemed to take time for my mind to comprehend as it blended with the question, 'Why didn't you tell me before?'

'When you say Barbara 'loved' Terri do you mean she was gay, bisexual, whatever?' I asked, trying to get to the point, as Terri seemed reluctant to actually say the words.

'She batted for both sides' she replied. ' As far as I know!'

Terri, once again, had a flippant and almost irritated air when talking about Barbara, she swiftly left the room again, something she seems to do whenever the subject moved deeper into the life of Barbara. I felt another door of Barbara's life had opened and I was peering in, not knowing if this secret room was out of bounds or needing the windows finally opening to the air.

Terri, looked at me wryly on her return while coaxing me to go and sit in the tiny living room, on one of Minna's chairs no doubt. She chatted away teasingly before settling in the opposite chair, with a notable twinkle in her eye. The kind you see on a face before the beans are spilt. She handed me an extra strong coffee in a bulbous mosaic patterned cup.

'There were a lot of letters that Ian had put to one side, the ones Barbara had written to different women,' she took a long sip. 'They were love letters,' she explained.

Oh, I thought, we <u>are</u> going there. I looked around. 'Where are they, I haven't seen them among the letters we've already gone through? I can't wait to read them; she was a complicated lady for sure and…' As I get halfway through replying, I can see by the look on Terri's face that something was amiss. She leant in and tentatively said, 'Ian burnt all of Barbara's love letters to women, he wasn't sure how the Aussie lot would

---

[34] **Minna Dyason**, suggested as one of Barbara's lovers.

feel about her if they knew. So he just took a match to them one day.' She was looking in the direction of the little wood burner in the corner of the room. As I followed her gaze, I imagined all the passion and love slowly disappearing into the entangled shapes of the flames and smoke.

'I can only remember what one of them said, it asked why she was so cruel' Terri gave a disparaging shrug.

We sat for a while not saying anything before Terri was, once again, up and scurrying to 'The Donkey' room as she called it. She would fly up the treacherously steep stairs with the agility of a mountain goat. She bought back a yellow decanter she thought I might like. 'I'm running out of room' I said with a sigh, but she wrapped it in newspaper and popped it inside my bag.

Back in my own studio, I tried to find out more on the computer, looking for evidence. Was it true? After bashing away for a good hour there it was.

I got the feeling, from the odd comments in Barbara's letters home, that Ian needn't have worried. The fact that Barbara had kept all the letters up to that point, must have meant they were precious to her, after all, she hadn't kept any love letters from Ewing or Bertie. Norman made it through though!

I knew Terri would spend the rest of the day searching the house, hoping to find a scrap of letter that Ian may have missed. So, I gathered the results of my internet search and took another walk around to Terri's cottage. Taking a seat on the 'Minnie' chair I imparted what I had found. Everything was in reverse and it was me that had the beans to spill....

'I have done some research, Terri, and it seems Barbara would retreat to the French Riviera between travels. It looks like it was her private, dare I say, 'haven.' In a letter home she does her best to put her mother off from visiting her there. Barbara does, however, describe women in some letters and talks to her mother saying, *'you know what I'm like'*. I think there was an unspoken understanding back in Australia about Barbara's sexuality.' I explained, 'at least with her mother.' Terri looked on intently.

'Billy' I continued, 'had come from an upper-class family but she was rejected by them, due to her sexuality. Alfredo Quaglino, a celebrity photographer, and Billy, had set up a bohemian home where the rich and famous would go to play, in Cagnes-sur-Mer on the French Riviera. It was where film stars and artists would go. (A signed Picasso print was found among Barbara's effects). It was a place of free love and partner swapping. It seemed that Barbara had become Billy's long-term lover and she would make many return visits to her.'

Terri replied gently, 'I knew that Ian destroyed the letters, but never really knew who they were to.' She seemed delighted. 'I am so pleased, that Barbara found love, that's a good thing.'

'Yeah,' I said. 'I think so too, we don't need to know all the details, do we?' I was trying to ease any guilt she may have about the burnt letters. 'It must have been difficult for her with the prejudice at the time, although Barbara seemed to ignore such difficulties, she just ploughed on regardless, you've gotta admire that Terri.'

'I guess…good for her, did I tell you I made some biscuits this morning?'

Once again Terri had pushed past Barbara to have herself be the point of my visit, and so it should have been. I'd come to love our chats and she did make a mean biscuit, even if they were for guests only.

Questions continued to battle in my mind. Was it Billy that Barbara sipped tea with in her honeymoon photograph? Fig12 Whatever this relationship held for Barbara, again, it did not tie her down. I have no idea how long it lasted, as Barbara never settled in France for long, despite having her own room in Billy's house and eventually a small flat in the area. Barbara created a life that gave her freedoms of choice, but choices she would continually question.

A scrap of a letter remained from when Barbara was 27yrs old, although the sender's information had been removed only the initials F.V. are left:

My dear & long-absent Barbara Toy:

Your 27th birthday is approaching and I can <u>not</u> let it pass without thinking of you, writing to you and praying for your unredeemed soul...My most cordial congratulations, Bar-ba-ra.

What has become of your long-contemplated career? Did you finish your secretarial studies properly and did you give up on your dramatic ambitions improperly? Are you going to dramatize yourself in real life, or going on distributing stage kisses and attempting suicide on stage?

You are still and remain one of the most fascinating experiments of my life, full of experiments. I am still willing to experiment with your mind, Barbara, and to complicate it further, if you are bored with life-as-such...What has become of your Viennese- Hollywood boyfriend? Is your husband still attached to your image and a prisoner of your beautiful but cold eyes...? What happened to your voice? Certainly, one of the best ringing voices in the universe... I would like to hear your voice again on the phone...

Are you coming to America? To Hollywood? Or would you prefer to come with me to the Hawaiian Islands and swim out in the bay of Waikiki, with all the masculine sharks around you? I hope to spend the winter in Hawaii... and never to return to the so-called civilized world again... I prefer natives to the civilized savages.

Please write me soon and tell me your whole life story...<u>including the story of your heart</u>...since I left you to your destiny.

Hoping to hear from you soon, Bar-ba-ra dear, and wishing you very good luck in everything you undertake in life.

With kindest regards and kissing the top of your nose on your birthday 27-times,

The ex-masseur of your soul,

F.V.

Barbara frequently changed her mind at the thought of another marriage commitment, and at the stigma if divorce, which at the time was considerable. Despite her struggles for freedom and independence. She writes to Bertie to explain her nagging loneliness, as the isolation she yearned for had its own consequences:

No date given

Beginning of letter missing... *I tried to tell you how I valued your last long letter, what it meant to me, can't find the words. Perhaps, like many of us, I am somewhat starved, and at times my expression of feelings becomes a little landlocked as it were. Can you bear with me, do you remember writing to me about a brief interlude, in Cornwall? I think there was a lonely woman? I too had a chance brief interlude, which seems to have unlocked me. With a household and financial worries, plus being let down by those once thought of as friends now that I will not turn on a party at the drop of a hat! I have rather knotted up inside in a ball of defence. I wish I could tell you what is the matter with me.*

    Why does a woman of my age still hope to share moments of magic? You, and only you know what I mean by this. The quality of a day, a night, a certain light, a time of day, Autumn trees, anything that gives a sudden lift of the heart. This brief interlude has helped and unlocked me a little, yet - it has also served to make me know how much I miss you. How much I need someone to share such moments with. How lucky I have been. I shared much with you dear Bertie but know I ballsed it up being afraid to divorce and marry. I have shared so much with you but a thought comes to me. I have had magic alone, shared with children or a man and of course you. Never a woman, I wonder why.

    I may be odd but I am no fool, and know a young man can be sincere, but this was just one evening. What this has done to me is to serve and show me how deeply lonely I am (in the sense of true sharing), and to make me wonder why I never find this with a man 'of suitable age'. I find them hideous and such old bores. Does the spark of dreams wear out quicker in men? I know I was given the chance to marry for a lot of money, but I would be very conscious of what I was doing. I don't expect a lot of life now. I would love my tiny perfect home, security, and someone with whom I can share that once in a while, an uplift to the heart and soul. I am sure you will understand me when I repeat that this brief encounter has unlocked me and to thank you, with a heart full of love and friendship. I remember walking in the Orange Park at dusk, you held out your hand to me. That was magic.

From so long ago I tried not to be soppy with men, I remember a young boy on a yacht in Mosman Bay and how sheltered I kept my feelings. Now I wish all those men to Hades, so I could sail the seas with you. I remember everything.

This is the third time I have written this letter to you. I destroyed the other two. This one I will send. I ask you to forgive me for writing such a long letter all about myself. When I say I am lonely, I know you will understand this too, not just having someone to natter too, plenty of that! Just a little home, and someone 'on the side' to share a little with.

Second day…

Did I mention, at some stage, make a comment that I felt a sense of having been unlocked? British understatement. I could write and write to you forever. The reason is, to me anyhow, quite obvious. I am not, stress NOT, self-sufficient. I am a weak vessel. I badly need someone to share with. A small turn of the key in the lock, and the doors open. Bert, my dear Bertie it is impossible to reply to all this soul searching. Just reply to one thing. Am I nuts????

I never let anyone try to tell me one can't maintain contact through letters. If the bond is strong, of course it is possible. Because the medium of letters is more difficult than speech, when an inflection, a look, tells so much, if written contact is maintained, then in my mind the relationship is strengthened.

I now make you a promise. Never again will I destroy a letter to you, as I have done many times. Do you think you could say the same to me? Did someone say — love has many faces? Must have done, I couldn't make that up! One face is for you only, and, I feel, one of the most important faces.

My Love, and vaca con Dios. (Go with God) *B*

Barbara had fought through the 'casting couch' mentality and the unequal pay. Becoming bored with the politics of stage and film she took a chance on an adventure she had dreamt of since she was a child. The desert was calling. Barbara gave up everything she had in London to travel to Baghdad.

The story Barbara often told for her seemingly rash decision to leave everything behind in London, went back to her time as a theatre studio manager and her work with young actors. In 1949 she was sat with a group of young thespians who were moaning about the after effects of the war dragging on. How they were unable to get away from the struggle, even after winning the war. Barbara, disagreeing, saw the world as an oyster to be eaten and placed a bet there and then, travel was easy and she would prove it.

So, she set out one day and bought a second hand 1950 80" rag-top series I Land Rover, a demonstration model, from Henley's in Osnaburgh Street, London for £640. Having christened it 'Pollyanna' she was soon on her way to Bagdad.

Barbara had given it all up in a moment, naive or not, and struck out on her own, to travel using her wits, little money and without mechanical back up or a publisher paying her way. It was 1950, a time when there was no satnav, mobile phones or internet, just grit, determination and a growing need to prove to herself she could do it, and to do it alone. Having already travelled extensively through Europe on her honeymoon, Barbara decided to visit the deserts her father had told her about in her youth. She wanted to prove that nothing could stop her, that she could live a free life, unbound by convention, a belief that would make her unstoppable. She ignored many people who tried to tell her otherwise. At one point she was taken aside by a brigadier she'd met on the first stage of her trip, who thought he knew better, warning her that her ignorance would get her into trouble and calling her fool. A 'damn fool' for going it alone, hence the title of her first book. *A Fool on Wheels*.

Barbara collected maps, (most of which now housed at the Bodleian Library in Oxford), carnet de passage documents and set them in an ever-growing collection of things never to leave her side. She quotes a conversation with a bachelor 'friend', when trying to raise funds for the trip. The bachelor was Bertie, which she later confirms in her book *A Fool on Wheels*, describing how she persuade him her travel plans were sound. She told him her car would appreciate in cost after the trip and the Rover company would be more than pleased to help her service the car for nothing etc. She knew Bertie, as a business man, could not refuse a gamble, although along with it came unrest and worries for her older companion. She also knew he saw right through her explanation and it seems he knew better than to stop her.

Once leaving England, and while waiting in Gibraltar for the weather to improve across North Africa, she frequented a bar in her hotel. Anyone else would be discouraged by the brigadier at the bar, who felt compelled to point out again how *'silly'* he thought she was to attempt such a journey. The only reason she could give was just wanting to be there, his condemnation gave Barbara another reason to prove it possible. The brigadier may have had a point, the journey would take her from Gibraltar across Morocco, Algeria, Libya, Egypt, Cyprus to Lebanon, Syria, Jordan and Iraq. A woman alone.

Already delayed by flooding in Morocco and after choosing to alight in Tangier, Barbara was told to make her way as quick as possible across different parts of Morocco and Algeria, as she had mistakenly started her journey in the rainy season. She described leaving Morocco at 7am. on the first leg of her journey in the cold and rain, with a 'grandfather of a hangover'.

Having been re-routed Barbara was able to re-join her original path just outside Constantine, Algeria, as the weather improved. She had been warned of pick pockets, bandits and thieves, so Barbara was on her guard. She would face the crack of whips as young boys aimed at the windows of her car when she drove though small villages. Among the hills to Toukebeur and Chaouch was a place called the Longstop (so called as there were many bodies buried there). War had ravaged the area and armed bandits would patrol at dusk.

On leaving the town of Derna in North Eastern Libya, Barbara left the forest regions for what she described as the 'scruffy' desert, on her way through the Sahara, and to coastal town of Tobruk. She saw the area as 'bombed, devastated, isolated and unattractive.' The town had been liberated from the Italians by the Australian 'rats' (allied soldiers who had fought in the siege of Tobruk during WW II, on January 21st 1941). She met Greeks, Italians, Scots and Australians, as well as Arabs while there.

On her second visit to Libya in 1952, Pollyanna was shipped to Tripoli, after which Barbara would travel along the coastline to Traghen in the Fezzan and on to the Kufra Oasis. She worked with Herman Schultze-Dewitz, a former ADC to Field Marshal Rommel, helping him locate the bodies in the desert for the German War Grave Commission.

Barbara also took on deep sea diving to a wreckage off the coast of Bengazi, only a few weeks later, the wreckage she'd explored blew up. The accounts in her book *A Fool in the Desert*, saw Barbara take time out to rest among English RAF men and their wives, again in Tobruk, on the hot sand of Anzac Cove. She dozed and chatted with the R.A.F men and their wives from the desert station of El Adem. At one point they were disturbed by an Anson,[35] which swept low over the cove they were in. One of the men called the pilot dangerous and death defying as he rolled the plane above them. The bravado was seen as a necessary evil to the fighter pilot's mentality. It was a place where Barbara could revel in the heat and relax, describing a breeze as 'tasting like wine'.

Libya, on both visits, had seen difficult terrain with many police stops, sometimes the delays were caused by having to wait for the officials to return from a long lunch. The Libyan desert, known as one of the most inhospitable regions on Earth, saw temperatures vary during the winter months. Averaging 27° C (81°F) with night temperatures dropping anything up to -9°C (-16° F) below freezing.

When she stopped in Mersa Matruh, once known as the most beautiful sea resort in the world, having been reinvigorated after the first war, was in a

---

[35] **Anson**: a twin engine British-built multi-roll aircraft, used during the war.

sorry state as Barbara passed through in 1950 and 1952. It was here that Pollyanna lost her exhaust and while being repaired, Barbara was warned of unfavourable propaganda against the British. On speaking to an Arabic speaking American, she was advised, once again, not to go on alone. He told her of much Anti-British feeling in the area and warned of a hatred that would see her torn to pieces if she ran over a mere dog. Her guide from the area was more than happy to be with her, as an individual, explaining that the propaganda told of an idea. She vowed to be extra careful and continued on her way.

 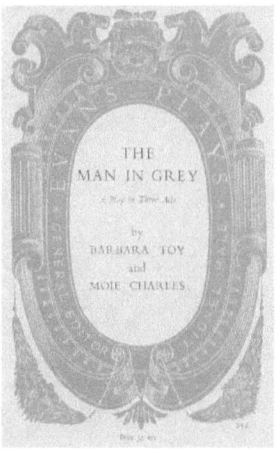

Fig 11

Three plays written and transcribed by Barbara.

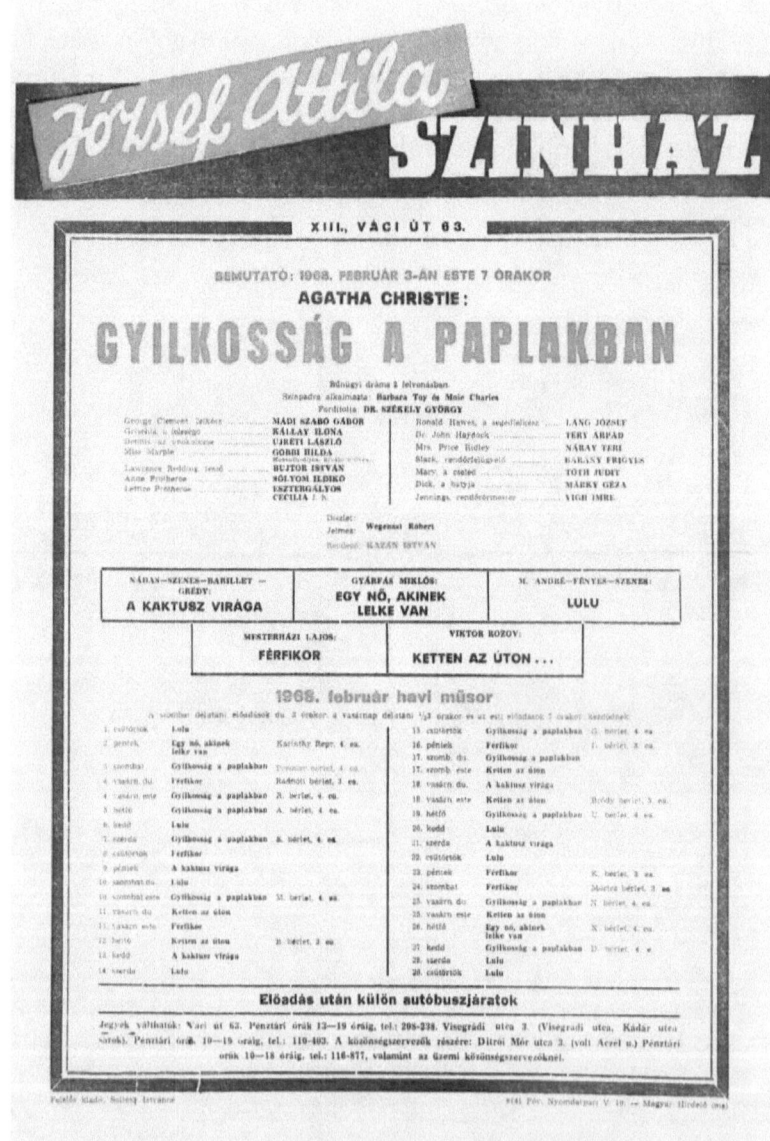

Polish poster for 'Murder at the Vicarage.'

A possible photo of Barbara's long term lover Billy. They would meet in Cagnes – sur – Mer where Billy lived with her husband Alfredo.

Fig 12

Barbara (left) from Honeymoon album,
possibly her first meeting with Billy.

Pollyanna embarking from Limassol, Cyprus.

Johnny, who Barbara met again in Tangier.

Spanish dancers at The Rock Hotel, Gibraltar.

Gibraltar

Gibraltar

Wadi towards a well, the Sahara.

On the way to Ghadames.

The old walls - Tebessa, Algeria

Algeria 1950

Main square in Tebessa, capitol city of the Tebessa Province, region of North Eastern Algeria.

Benghazi, Cyrenaica.

Benghazi children playing in the streets.

The officers Club, Derna.

Anzac Cove sunbathers

Towards the dunes of El Kneir, Libyan desert.

Pollyanna in Saudi Arabia

Sipahi, professional Cavalrymen, originally recruited by the French from indigenous tribes of Algeria.

Bedu horseman and Barbara.

Baghdad, Iraq. The Tigris from the terrace of the Zia Hotel.

Chapter 7
Bombs, bodies, bribes and babies.

When travelling the many miles to Algiers, Barbara met up with an old friend, a North African correspondent. She had wandered into a bar dishevelled and exhausted after hundreds of miles of travel. Her friend, calling her 'Ginger', was surprised to see her in such a state. They had met years before in Ceylon, while she was on her honeymoon. Their chance meeting had him question her motives for driving fifteen hundred miles through sleet, snow and ice, calling her ignorance abysmal. He stated Africa was a cold country but the sun was hot. She asked why no one had told her! He knew she would not have listened anyway and asked was she going to Bagdad on a commission? Barbara replied 'No, on a shoe string!'

She carried on despite all the advice her fellow male travellers had given her, despite bandits and officials asking for bribes, being shot at and feeling the wrath of boys with whips. Bombs and landmines littered areas of the desert, left from the war, with numerous graves of all nationalities. Sand storms, known as Ghibli's, would occur from nowhere at any time as they were not uncommon in the Sahara. Cold winds would blow in from the sea along the North Mediterranean shore of Africa meeting the hot dry winds of the South, together they could produce blinding storms that have been known to cover and suffocate entire tribes. Appearing without warning and with the possibility of last for days, they could bury her and the Land Rover and leave no clue that she was there at all.

At a point in her first trip across North Africa she was caught in such a sand storm, alone. Sand drifts were blocking the track she was travelling on, which she could avoid most of the time, as long as she drove at speed. Once stuck after a failed attempt to go around the drifting sand she had no choice but to dig herself out. As she opened the door the wind blew the door flat to the side if the car. Opening the back to find something to scoop away the sand the door swung into her face. With sand blowing into her mouth and eyes she managed to dig her way free only to find the car would not start. She needed to get out again and crank the engine.

Barbara later went on to say that her misery was compounded by breaking her best nail! A gentle reminder that she was a woman, brave robust and still feminine. In a later newspaper article in 1957, she described the ordeal of driving over large and unpredictable dunes, taking them at speed and at breath taking angles only to come to the other side and descend a treacherous downward drop to firmer land. The dunes were 'razor backed' and each was followed by another. She would have to use rugs and even her sleeping bag to give the wheels purchase once they had sunk into the sand, getting back into the car to do it all again at the next dune. Sometimes the sand storms would hinder her progress so much that she would only be able to travel a few miles a day.

When arriving at a border town, after such an ordeal, a crowd developed around her and were getting out of hand. A thin man, followed by a woman carrying a baby, pushed his way past the crowd, holding a very ill baby. He did not understand her pleas for him to take the baby to the hospital in Jefren. Barbara stated that this was the first of many similar incidents, there was an assumption that all European women were doctors. A tall man came towards her speaking English. She explained she had a letter from the Emir for the police officer in charge and that she had permission to travel from the King. The crowd dispersed and left her alone from then on. When she finally made it to the official's office, she was asked to pay to go any further. Barbara sternly refused to pay a bribe, taking her papers to the customs house herself. She then had to wait while the official had tea.

It wasn't long before Barbara had a hard roof fitted to 'Pollyanna' for security, the passenger door altered so that it could only be open by her once inside. Metal plates were secured to the usual open triangular access to the door handles and stronger glass was added to the side doors. At one point she had the canvas roof replaced with a hard wooden structure which became known to her mechanics as 'the chicken shed'.

I'd spent days transporting thousands of photographs, slides and films collected from Terri's garage, that now lay in my studio. I'd been worried she would throw them all away before I had time to look through them all. Sweetly, Terri had an area she'd piled up just for me. When I saw it was the largest in the garage my heart sank. So much unorganised and dusty tokens of Barbara's journeys, her life's work kept in uncoordinated heaps. But I had gone too far to give up now, I would find space and deal with it all later. The photographs were of faraway places, some with inscriptions on the back but a vast amount with nothing, no clues as to where they were taken or when. There was so much of Barbara's life before me, a beginning now placed in the evidence of her letters, tangled in her words and actions, the story of an unusual life lived. Each letter, each photograph had been laid out of order, sometimes without an explanation or reason for its existence; the jigsaw of Barbara would grow, from a time when the romance of travel was still a rare experience for most.

There were copious photos of sand dunes, crumbling stone walls of ancient fortresses, dirt roads and unkempt children. Over loaded trucks, sandscapes dotted with tribes' men, horses, camels and donkeys, hand carts and jeeps. Men and women lovingly portrayed despite some difficult circumstances. (Fig 13)

To realise the vastness of the regions and places Barbara visited meant relying on her books and hundreds of her maps. (Fig 14) I delved in and loved every minute. I felt as if I were travelling the roads with her, feeling her resilience and determination throughout, as mile upon mile of emptiness spread across the vast sheets of yellowing paper. Even with so many maps it was still hard going for her. She found most British maps were difficult to follow. Michelin Sahara maps were better on milage but The French Ministére du Travail Publique et du Transport map, dated 1944, only gave the positions of tracks made by lorries years before. Once she realised the maps were fond of 'filling in the gaps' of vast sections of desert, she was able to navigate with her compasses and wits.

Barbara would face exhaustion and fatigue on each of her trips, once describing herself as living in a mental haze as she travelled across the never-ending baron landscapes for hundreds of miles, along ribbon like roads. The vastness both awe-inspiring and relentless.

Knowing Barbara had travelled for so much of her life, I felt more like a land locked armchair traveller than ever. The routes she took then would be impossible now as war has torn the Middle East further apart. Ongoing wars between Israel and Palestine, Civil war in the Yemen. Earth quakes in Turkey and Morocco. War-torn Syria. Afghanistan, Iraq, Libya and the Lebanon. The feud of Saudi Arabia and Iran for control of the Middle East and the Arab spring uprising, oil playing a big part. Barbara once said, during a BBC radio interview, (possibly 'Women's Hour'):

> 'People go expecting it to be the same and it won't be the same, nothing is. Anyhow you are different aren't you, you have changed, and you are probably looking for other things. I just look back, for instance, on my time in Southern Arabia, it was an enchanted time and I really enjoyed it, bit of a lotus eater shall we say. I know it won't be the same, but that's okay. I think a lot has changed for the worst but that is politics really and we can't help that. And there is always, everywhere you go, a little group who are upsetting the whole scene, so to speak, but I don't feel as much can be changed by people as I used to.'

A sad observation of a traveller who clearly loved the regions of the Middle East. In a later book in the 'Fool' series, a *'A Fool Strikes Oil'* Barbara is even more aware of the fight to control the oil regions as the desert she loves becomes peppered with oil dogs:

What would she have made of it now?

"A Fool in the Desert"

The Motor. 2nd November 1958

The title refers to an admirable willingness to venture where perhaps angels would fear to tread, and not to any lack of sense on the part of the authoress, who shows in a well-told tale of travels in Libya in a Land Rover named "Pollyanna" that she is more intelligent and capable than most. To travel solo in a land of obscure, but nevertheless real, dangers, varying from left-over mine fields to natural hazards of sandstorms and poorly marked tracks, calls also for courage.

The reason for her journey is set down clearly: "It was the desert that drew me back to Libya. I wanted to cross the Sand Sea, the black hills...and visit the oases; above all, I wanted to meet the people who spend their lives wandering over these silent surfaces." This she does with entertaining results, varying from the rather macabre trip with a German War Graves Commission looking for bodies, to a brief Shangri-La existence in the depths of the Southern deserts. She traps the spirit of the desert with her pen: "As I drove towards the horizon, the world stretched ahead of me, uncluttered, empty, and the world pulsated under the avalanche of light..." and presents a timely piece of escapism from November in England.

H.B.C.

Fig 13

A Police Sergeant and his child bride, in the Fezzan.

Fig 13

A destitute child.

Some of Barbara's maps now housed at the Bodleian Library Oxford.

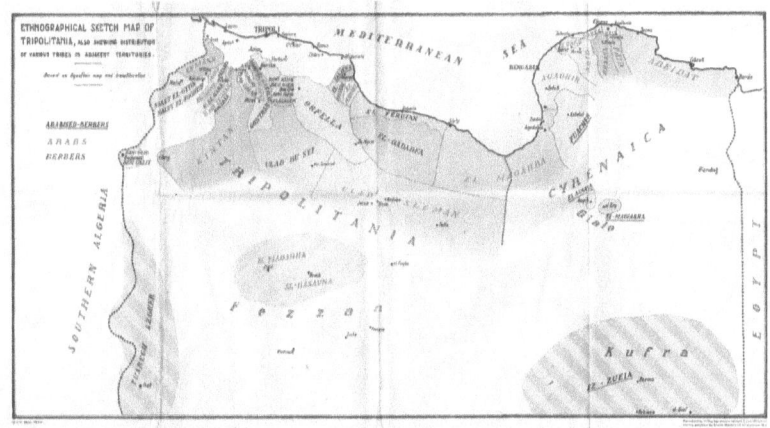

Fig 14

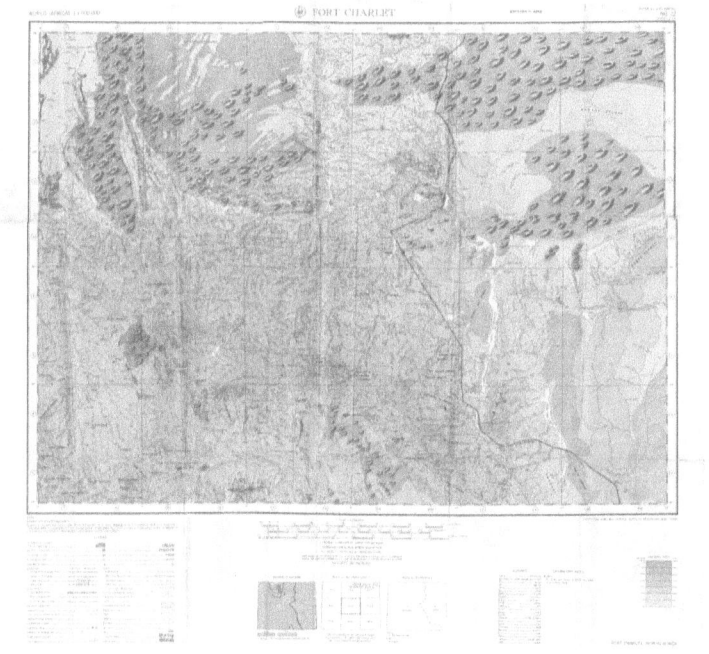

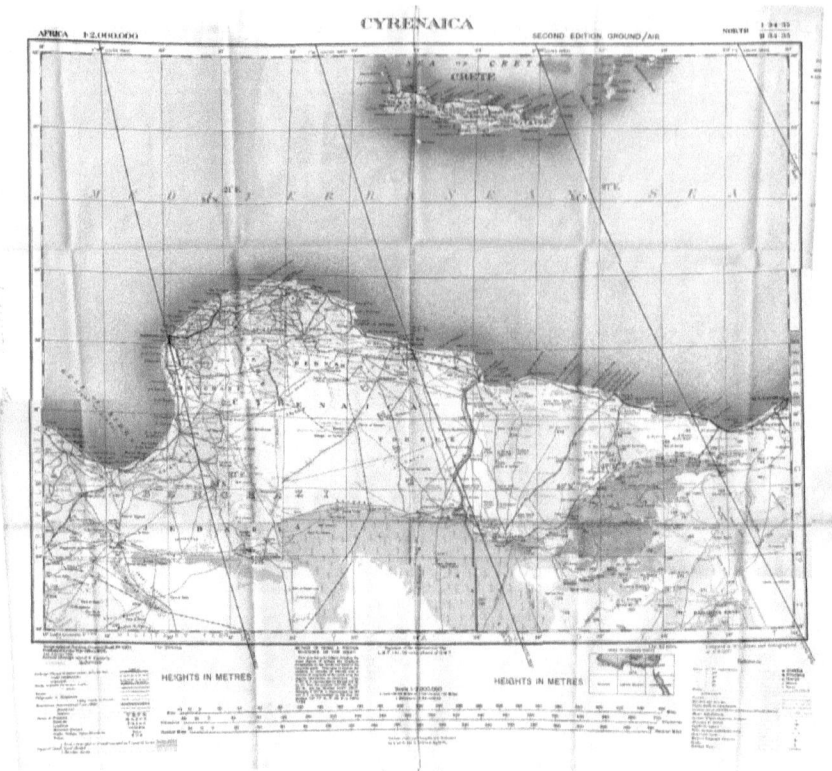

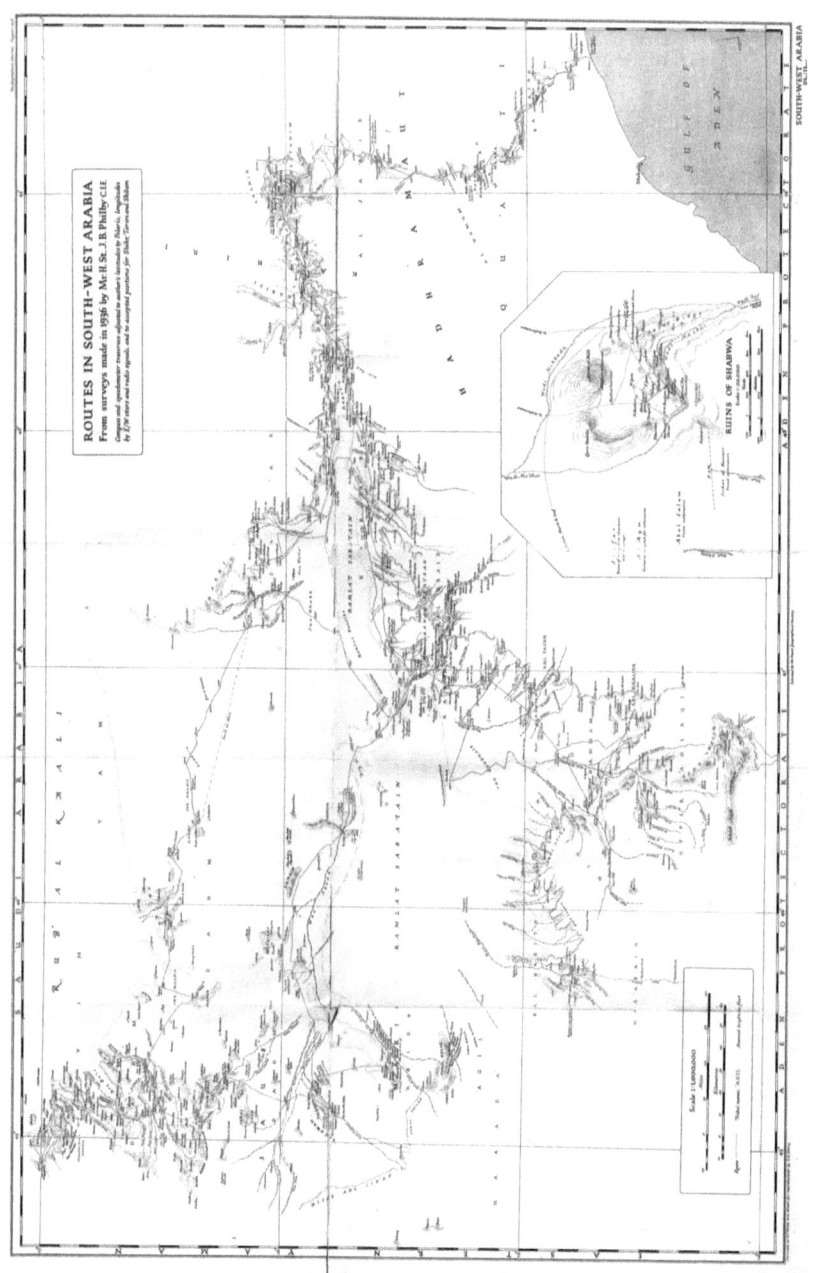

Bedouin woman and child.

Aboriginal children in Australia.

Fruit sellers in Tripoli.

Ngorongoro Crater, Tanganyika.
Barbara photographing Hippos.

Barbara and a Turkish journalist in Istanbul.

Barbara Toy

Barbara with her second Land Rover in the Fezzan

Barbara, 20th December 1952, Libya.

Camping in the Libyan desert

A foldable hand basin.

Barbara in the Arabian desert.

Libyan Desert tribe.

Oasis at Ghadames

Natural well in Libya

Family at the well, Libya, sometimes hostile.

War Salvage trucks, Tobruk

4 bodies found in the desert of Cyrenaica

World War II war graves

Chapter 8
The gold of black.

London
15th November 1951

Dear Mum,

So, you are off on holiday - you do seem to be getting around these days Altogether. I did like young Helen so very much, she is such fun and so good looking.

I've sent £50 off to you % Edward Street, I hope you get it before you leave. I thought you might buy a few things for yourself for Christmas. Unfortunately, I'm afraid I have missed the ordinary Christmas mail, I'm sorry, time just whisks by these days. I sent you a few books for Sadie's boys, I'm hoping they may get through, I do hope so.

I think I am letting the flat again, I have someone who wants it and London really, it is impossible to live here these days. I shall probably go to the cottage for a while and then abroad somewhere as it is much cheaper out of England. Toni will notice the difference with everything when she gets back.

I am struggling with my writing, its hell, don't seem to get down to it - it's maddening and of course, I'm like a bear with a sore head.

We have been having a beautiful Autumn, not really cold and many of the days sunny and mild, really lovely.

What is Ian going to do? Does he want to take up art as an artist plain and simple or some sort of commercial art. What a washout I am as an aunt, if only I'd 'married well' I could have a proper home and have him over here instead of living a life of a bum.

Love
      Barbara.

February, 1952 in accordance with King's death.

Beginning of letter missing...*second hand easy chair, I only have one!*
It has been very sad here since the King's Death. I was glad to be in England at the time, it is always a source of wonder to me, the love and affection and respect the people have for the King. It was remarkable too as although he died just before midnight the next morning every shop in the West End had their windows decorated in black, purple and white.

I have my dressing gown out and everyone is suggesting that if I don't have twins at least I ought to have???? - I can't say how I feel about this lovely gown. If you only knew, and that you should spend all that time making something for me. Well, I just can't get over it.

   Love darling,
    Barbara

London
18th July 1953

Dear Mum,

  I wrote to you about a week ago but have been really cross about Toni's sister, so I tore the letter up. Their people <u>will</u> barge in on me and I <u>have</u> a telephone, however don't mention it. I suppose such a person, being a 'relative' has a right to act the way she did!

  I'm off today on a cargo ship for some weeks. Tally was lucky to get the time off, I didn't think he would get away this year.

  Finances are very worrying but feel I *must* have this break to cope with it all. Have been having a hell of a lot of muscular rheumatism which has crippled my right hand, I hope the sun will clear it up. But naturally feel better with the prospect of fully leaving here.

No news still trying to finish my book.

  Love,
   Barbara

Bertie writes again, reassuring Barbara's mother:

Richmond
July 17th 1953

Dear Mrs. Toy,

I hasten to answer your letter to put your mind at rest. I am pleased to say Barbara is quite well and is in England until tomorrow. I have spoken to her since I had your letter, I have given her a 'dressing down' (but of course it is like water off a duck's back) for not writing to you more often. She tells me she has written several letters this year and maybe they have gone astray. But she will write you either before she sails or on the ship. Because tomorrow, Saturday, she is taking a cargo boat to the Mediterranean for a few weeks. The ship goes to Malta, Greece, Turkey etc. It should be an interesting trip for her. I have travelled on the ship myself and she is a comfortable Swedish boat with wood cabins, good Swedish food and carries passengers. 'Britta' 5,500 tons.

Barbara has been working very hard lately on her book of her travels and is taking this opportunity to finish it. It is purely on account of this that she has not written to you so often as she would have liked. Anyhow I know by now you will be relieved and don't worry about her and please always write to me if you want any news. Apart from anything else I am always glad to hear from you.

As Barbara and I saw the Coronation[36] *together as we had seats in an office of an old friend of mine. The weather however was appalling, it rained most of the day and with strong winds. It was such a shame as the people on the streets were drenched. Still, this is England and we have to put up with it.*

I do hope you are keeping well.

Yours,
Bertie Loch

---

[36] Eight days before **Coronation** Day, temperatures soared to 31.7°C in London, changing to torrential rain on the day.

London
Tuesday 9th December 1953

Dear Mum,

Many thanks for the two packs of stockings that arrived at Bertie's place. It was very kind of you but you really shouldn't, we can get all we want here now. It is difficult if you send parcels and letters care of Bertie as they are firstly quite likely to get lost as they stay in his letterbox all day. And also, my porter here at the moment is very often the only one who knows where I am when I am away, he forwards all my mail. But really Bertie has to ring him to get my address.

I'm sorry not to have written since I came back but as usual came back to a heap of trouble and work and just haven't had a minute. For goodness' sake stop thinking I might be ill, I haven't been over the last years so why should I now!

Christmas is almost on us again; it is always such a horrible thought over here but thank goodness most of the people I know ignore it completely.

Will write again before Christmas.

Love,
Barbara

London 1954

Dear Mum,

I am so glad to hear you are up with Sadie and feeling more cheerful. Very many thanks for your Christmas parcel which arrived and was duly appreciated and mostly eaten by friends. You shouldn't however have bothered as these things *can* be bought here now.

I don't know whether I have ever told you that while I was away on the trip to Turkey, they put a kitchen in my flat. I am now supposed to do my own cooking and as I can't afford the 'service' my own cleaning as well. As you can imagine, I really don't do either! However, when the dirt gets too much and Wei kicks up too much of a stink because he's hungry, then I do something about both.

We had quite a nice time in Paris but of course it was quiet. We really went as Bertie's brother-in-law had been terribly ill and I thought the idea of getting away and treating him as though he were perfectly well, would do him a lot of good, which it did. The four of us motored over and luckily enough we had good weather. We came back here to the most awful freeze up and now all of us are going round, looking our age, and muffled up in every woolly we have.

Wei burnt and blistered his nose propping it up on the electric fire. Everyone's pipes are bursting and the papers make the weather head line news.

I often think in amazement the fact that Sadie has two growing up sons, whom I have never seen, it is in a way such an important part of my life and yet I know nothing about them really at all. How I wish I had made good and was able to do something for them in some way. It's all very depressing.

Could you let me have the recipe for lamenting (I think that's the name) cake you used to make. It was covered in chocolate and coconut. When you send the recipe don't say 'a dash of this and a handful of that, I'm no cook and cannot be as carefree as that! Also, can you send me your recipe for your curry, which I tell everyone is the best I have ever tasted. I tried to make a Christmas cake but put Tide (soap flakes) instead of sugar into it. The first clue I had anything was wrong was when it began to creep into the sitting room. I guess one shouldn't try to learn to cook in middle age.

I wonder does the Queen [37] come up your way? You should see her if you can she is as rather marvellous person and looks very lovely in the flesh.

Would you thank Sadie for her letter and tell her I will write to her soon.

Love to all,

Barbara

---

[37] The newly crowned **Queen** Elisabeth II made an extensive tour of Australia in 1954

London
17th May 1954

Dear Mum,

Very many thanks for the lovely cookery book which is full of lovely food things. I don't do much cooking of course except when I have someone here, but it is nice to have if I do. Anyway, I use a pressure cooker a lot because as my flat is so small, I don't like the smell of cooking round for too long.

At long last I've finished the blasted book thank goodness. I nearly cracked up under it. Norman Lee who I wrote to you about edited it for me, but left before I'd finished which was maddening as it came when I was just about at the end of my tether.

We are now having awfully cold weather after having a couple of weeks of summer, which is probably all we will get!

I did a broadcast the other day, I do wish they would send it to Australia, but don't suppose they will. It was past eight minutes but I believe it was not bad.

Thanks again for the lovely book.

Love,
Barbara

London
11th September 1954

Dear Mum,

I've just received your letter as I am having a country night away because it's going to be awfully hectic in the next few weeks. Thank goodness the publishers accepted my book; of course, when they publish it will be another matter, but it does give me a publisher behind me which helps with facilities and visas. (Fig 15)

Re *my going away, firstly I am a good deal safer than I'd ever be here where one could easily be coshed on the way down the street to post a letter. Secondly, I can't afford to live here, and thirdly it is the only thing I want to do and life is much too short and uncertain to do anything else.*

Yes, people do make a lot on the radio in Australia I hear, they certainly don't here. I got £8 for my last broadcast and wasted about 2 weeks on it.

So glad you have a good time with the Rudds and that you've missed the worst of the winter. The weather has been bad here I believe but as I have been working, I am too far underground to see for myself. I have to take that information from others. I hope to see Helen before I go, when I have finished this work, although I rather think they are flying all over the place.

Shall write to you at Sadie's address before I leave.

Love,
Barbara

SS Armaniston
Newport
3rd November 1954

Dear Mum,

I do hope you are quite recovered now - I have been worrying about you as I haven't heard. I've been in a muddle and a medical I had before travelling, they have found some problem with my womb, rather like the time before. I think I had better have a baby to settle things down. Was whisked into hospital and had to cancel the boat, but got fed up with the hospital after four days. However, it is all over now. I am on board ship after the most awful rush and heading for the Persian Gulf.

I have let my flat to a woman luckily who let me stay a few weeks more so things can't be all that bad. I hope to finish my second book on the way out. Luckily the publishers liked the first draft of it so that's encouraging. I have dedicated the first one to you, I hope that is alright? Let me know how you are if you are able, send letters to

London it is safer, my porter is the only one who knows where to send mail on. I suppose you will be in charge of Christmas this year, that ought to be fun.

    Love,
      Barbara

A letter, of which there were few, from Barbara to Bertie:

Government Guest House
Kuwait
25th January 1955

Dear Bertie,
  I am sorry about not sending a cable but the fact is I've run out of sterling and cheques, I feel it's silly to use the others here, when I'll need them for Saudi Arabia etc.

  Yesterday I received a cable from the King of Saudi Arabia informing me that he would be away for ten days and to then come along, he sent a greeting welcoming me! I really think he must believe I am someone else. However, all these necessaries are underway, and I'm getting a full native costume made, in case I have an audience with him, which is going to knock me back a bit. But it is worth it and will come in handy later on, especially if I get to the Yemen. It's an elegant black affair embroidered with gold thread, a voluminous dress and cloak which goes over it. (Fig 16) They are working day and night, five of them, to finish it.

  I can't understand why you can't see Riyadh on the map as it is the capitol. You must have an extremely old atlas. It is about five hundred miles from here. I'm told by Colonel Dickson I will 'lose caste' by going in Pollyanna and alone, so I may have to hire someone in the way of a servant when I approach the city.

  I wouldn't write anymore to here; you could write care of the British Consul in Riyadh if you liked but don't send anything important as I am not all that certain there is a consul.

This is in haste as I am rather hectic having to go and get jerry cans etc.
  Love,
    Barbara

Royal Guest House
Ridayh
25th January 1955

Dear Bertie,

As you see I had arrived in Riyadh. I left Kuwait last Monday and took three days and two nights to get here. The track was frightful and Pollyanna's exhaust pipe gave way early on. The whole of Arabia must have heard us coming. We stayed the first night at the oasis of Jeria, where I stayed with the governor's wife as he was away in the desert shooting. The next night we slept in the desert and it was frightfully cold. We arrived here about four in the afternoon and I was brought here, causing quite a bit of commotion. It appears as far as I can see, that there are no European women here at all, just one German nurse. (Fig 17)

The first night I had an audience with his Majesty for a short while. He gave me an extremely nice gold watch and two rather magnificent gowns embroidered in gold. This is, I believe, the traditional thing to do. I then met members of his harem including two of his wives. They were all enchanting and looked quite magnificent in beautiful and fantastic clothes. Unfortunately, the King left next morning on a shooting trip so I may not see him again.

I now have the difficult task of trying to persuade them to let me continue to Jeddah. They naturally want me to go back to Kuwait as it is the nearest place, they were extremely shattered to see me arrive more or less alone and in old Pollyanna. Whatever happens, one thing is clear, I can't move an inch without the Kings blessing and even with that things aren't all that easy.

There are no consuls here, British or American, so if you send anything it will either get lost or sent to Jeddah. What I shall do, I haven't the slightest idea. I only hope I don't have to go East again as that will be extremely costly getting round to Aden again. However, they can't keep me here forever so something will happen.

I'll write again if there is any news, it's hard to write here really. The only way to contact me is by cable but there is not likely to be anything very important. I only hope this China[38] business doesn't blow up before I reach the coast.

Love,
Barbara

Two unaccredited newspaper cuttings from Barbara's archives:

'A Fool Strikes Oil' by Barbara Toy (John Murray 18s).

The latest instalment in the travel adventures of Miss Toy and it rakes her, in her old Land Rover, across the vast country of Saudi Arabia from Kuwait on the Persian Gulf, to Riyadh the capitol and then on to Jedda on the Red Sea. As the Guest of the King of Saudi she stayed at the royal palace where she was a guest of the ladies of the harem. She writes of the people she met, ordinary tribesmen as well as Emir, and of the places she visited. In an absorbing illustrated story, she tells how as a royal guest she saw wealth and glamour, but in her long trek across the country she saw the old Arabia, just stirring to the smell of oil.

---

[38] In 1955, The People's Republic of **China** and the Republic of China were at arms over a strategic island in the Taiwan Strait.

King Saud gave her a blessing

What a woman is Miss Barbara Toy! Still in her twenties, small and slim, she has done what few men would dare to do – crossed the great deserts of the Middle East... alone and for the love of it.

First, in her Land Rover, Pollyanna, she drove from Tangier to Baghdad. Then through Libya. Now, still with the faithful Pollyanna, this lone ranger has ventured through the vast wastes of Saudi Arabia, where thieves still get their hands cut off and where a stranger takes his life in his hands.

Locked up

As the guest of King Saud whom she met along with his ladies of the harem in his palace in Riyadh, Miss Toy was guaranteed a fairly safe journey. But even with the King's blessing and with a young Saudi guide-companion on the worst desert stretch, she ran risks. At one village she had to be locked up overnight in the local prison for her own safety and there were some awkward moments as she

skirted Mecca, the Moslems' Holy place which no infidel dare enters.

In all she travelled over 1000 miles from Kuwait to Jedda, seeing the Old Arabia and the new, stirring to the succulent smell of oil.

Yet, in *'A Fool Strikes Oil'* she writes of her trek as casually as if she had been travelling round Aberdeen. It is only on reflection that you appreciate what a remarkable woman she is.

Unknown newspaper.

Kandara Palace Hotel
Djedda
P.O. Box 473
Saudi Arabia
3rd March 1955

Dear Mum,

As you see I am now in Djedda. I came here from Kuwait, motoring all the way across the continent in Pollyanna, my Land Rover. I had quite an exciting time in the capital Riyadh for I met the King of Saudi Arabia and some of his wives. I am having a fine time for I am a guest of his majesty and was staying in the Royal guest house in Riyadh, and am now a guest at his hotel.

The city is most extraordinary, full of lovely old buildings which are now being pulled down and very modern ones are taking their place. Our British Embassy has been most helpful to me and I do find that having a book coming out does a great deal to help me along. It is impossible to write all about what I have seen and done, let's hope you will be able to read it in a book one day.

I received your letter about my dedicating my first book to you, who else would I want to dedicate it to? You are after all the first person in my life and you and Sadie are all I have. The fact that I don't see you for so long doesn't make any difference.

I will write you again when I reach Aden.

Love,
*   Barbara.*

The Assistant Adviser Northern Area
Seiyun
Via Aden.
24th June 1955

Dear Mum,

* Your letter of the 6th June was forwarded on to me here. I can't think why you haven't had a copy of the book, it was sent to you by the publishers ages ago. Any way you can buy it in Sydney it got quite good reviews, better, I thought, than it deserved and is selling reasonably well. By the way, in it I mention that my sister described Heslingfors and Fes to me. I meant my sister-in-law but didn't want to go into the whole business of marriage for its better from the book point of view that I am alone, as you will see when you read it.*

* I am still here and the weather is very hot, the place however is lovely. There is nowhere really to stay and although I stayed at the assistant advisor's place for a while, I have now taken a house.* (Fig 18) *It is a huge rambling place made of mud but you'd never know it as it is solid and all painted white. I pay the large sum of 80/- a month for it and have a boy who looks after me and does absolutely everything. My furniture consists of a camp bed, a canvas chair, a box for my typewriter and a mat. The furniture gets moved around to each of the rooms as I run away from the sun.*

* The house is set in palms and the dates are now ripening and a lovely golden-brown colour. The garden is full of the most fantastic birds and every morning at seven*

o'clock the schoolmaster comes and gives me an Arabic lesson – at which I am extremely dull.

I hope to go off on a trek into the desert soon and it's going to be b... hot.

I wonder did you see anymore of Norman Lee; I hear he's coming back to England soon; I may see him in Aden as he passes through.

You can either write direct here or to London when they will forward letters to me. I shall be here, I think, for some time as the monsoons are starting and I can't ship Pollyanna out until later in the summer, it's also a bit dangerous driving along the coast to Aden.

Talking about the Saudi King, the great man Ibn Saud but he is dead; it was his son[39] whose guest I was.

Fancy Sadie having a job with an accountant, she always was a better one than I was, I never could add.

Poor Ian, it must be hell just starting out, but no doubt he'll finds his own kind of friends in time, people do settle into their own groups after a while. Sadie must miss him terribly.

They seem to be having fun and games in England, one strike after another; by now I suppose the cost of living is so high it's impossible to do anything but exist.

I can see my schoolmaster coming across the millet field so I had better get something on.

My love to all,
    Barbara

Beyt Bakrani, Seiyun, Yemen
Via Aden

---

[39] **King Saud** was seen as the least competent of the previous Kings many sons. He opted for hostilities with the Egyptians and squandered the state treasury, driving their economy to the point of bankruptcy. He was deposed by his family in 1964 replaced by Crown Prince Faysal.

3rd August 1955

Dear Mum,

It was nice getting the last letter from you direct from home. It saved it having to go all the way to London and back again. I was thrilled you liked my book and I do hope it sells reasonably well in Australia. I was, however, shocked at the price. We think 16/- which is the English price, is bad enough. I am sure I wouldn't pay 25/- for it! The publishers have bought my second book, which is about my travels in the Libyan desert. Unfortunately, it needs some alterations, and I'm trying to do something about it, as well as concentrate on this place. Being a one-track minded person, I find this rather hell.

Funny you should mention Norman for he passes through Aden on Friday next the 6th on the Orantes on his way home. He wanted me to fly down and see him but the planes don't connect very well and I can't afford to stay in Aden for a whole week. He wants to do a book with me but we never seem to be in the same country at the same time. He is a very good friend to me and I certainly wouldn't have written the book if he hadn't boosted up my morale and kept me at it. I have many things to thank Norman for.

It still stays hot here but I love it and will be very unhappy to leave it all. My house is beautiful and I go away and come back liking it more and more each time. I have just been down to the holy city of Tarim (Yemen) *staying with the Italian doctor* (Fig 19) *and had a marvellous time going round seeing all his patients with him. I saw more in a few days of local life than I would otherwise in weeks. My journey, however, was cut short for he went out shooting with another guest and there was an accident, his toe was shot off! He is an enchanting person, in his early forties and has given his life over entirely to working here among these people.*

I shall probably be going home in September; I cannot go before because the monsoon has started and I can't ship Pollyanna out of Mukalla until it changes course or something; and as there is a bit of trouble in Bedouin[40]*, I can't go over land which is a pity. You've probably heard a bit about the trouble here and from time to time the road*

---

[40] An armed conflict occurred between Saudi Arabia and the tribe communities over oils fields.

gets cut which means we have no way out except by plane, and I've certainly no intention of leaving Pollyanna here.

I really am having great fun here, I am the only European woman with the exception of a German woman doctor, who is in another town, in the whole Wadi. The people therefore look after me very well and give me all the help I want.

Do let me know what sort of reviews they give the book in the local papers. I hope they are not too bad. Yes, some of the London ones are not too bad and the publishers tell me it is selling quite well.

My life isn't quite all beer and skittles as my book may suggest, one has to pay for everything in this world I think and I forfeit quite a lot to lead the life I do. Also having to do things with so little money, there are stretches of awful boredom and loneliness and I can't afford to move round much at certain times and in expensive places. However, it is a side that no one wants to hear about so I just don't write about it!

Am off today with some of the local agricultural people to go to another wadi and see some old excavated cities; so once again the packing begins.

Yes, it was Bertie I mentioned in the book, he is a dear and very good to me. He gets a bit fractious when I'm away so long but all the same he rather likes the things I do and is always thrilled when things turn out good for me. I'm very fond of all his family and his sister-in-law is one of my best friends.

Love to all,

Barbara

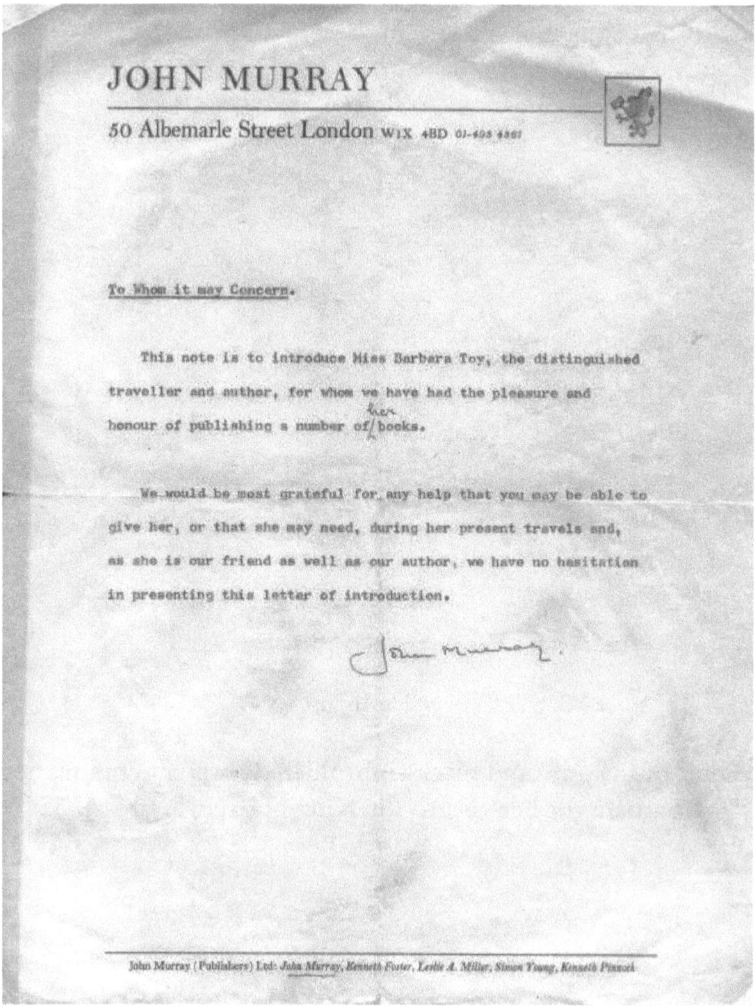

JOHN MURRAY

50 Albemarle Street London W1X 4BD 01-493 4361

To Whom it may Concern.

This note is to introduce Miss Barbara Toy, the distinguished traveller and author, for whom we have had the pleasure and honour of publishing a number of her books.

We would be most grateful for any help that you may be able to give her, or that she may need, during her present travels and, as she is our friend as well as our author, we have no hesitation in presenting this letter of introduction.

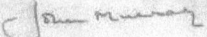

John Murray (Publishers) Ltd: *John Murray, Kenneth Foster, Leslie A. Miller, Simon Young, Kenneth Pinnock*

Fig 15

Fig 16

A section of the gold and black embroidered garment commissioned by Barbara for her visit to the King of Saudi Arabia 1955

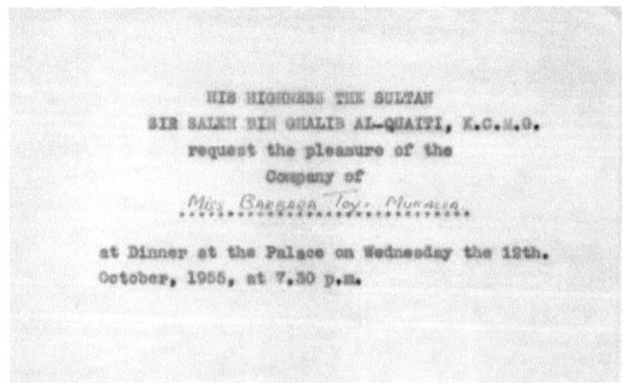

Invitation to appear at the Sultans Palace.

Fig 17

German nurse/Doctor

Fig 18

Barbara's sitting room at Seiyun, Hadhramaut, Yemen

Fig 19

Italian Doctor

Sultans Palace, Beyt Seiyun.

The sign says 'Beware of Mines.'

A Bedu in Wadi Lusar, East of Aden Protectorate.

Hadhramaut

Saudi Arabia desert tribe.

Barbara in Kuwait.

Detail of a red and gold embroidered dresses given to Barbara by King Saud.

Purple velvet and gold embroidered gown.

Barbara outside a tomb, Southern Arabia

Photograph by Gordon Le Masurier.

Barbara dictating a book in her St James' flat.

Chapter 9
The World

London S.W.1.
28th November 1955

Dear Mum,

    As you see I am back home. I've been meaning to write to you for ages but things are hectic here. Have to concentrate on the new book, as am in a jam, as usual, with money especially round the end of the year. They say it is a good Autumn but I find it terribly cold – have to spend most of the day having hot baths to get myself warm.

    Have been doing a bit of broadcasting and may be doing some television at which I will probably expire with fright.

    Bertie is very well and getting very fat although he gets furious when I say so. I've put on a lot of weight myself. I got dysentery badly and they pumped me with penicillin before I left Hadhramaut and it often does make one get a bit plump. Its working itself off pretty quickly now though. I had a lovely time on my way home, stayed with the Residency at Mukalla for ten days waiting for a ship, it was great fun. I've got an awful crush on the Colonel which is a scandal at my age. However, while there's life there is hope!

    How are you all, I haven't heard from you for age? And how are Sadie and the boys, will you get together for Christmas? I'll send you some of the photographs when I have them printed but it won't be for a while, I've too much on my plate.

    I sent you about £44 from Aden which I hope you will make use of at Christmas. It was what I had left and it seemed better to transfer it to you than send it here...this bloody typewriter runs everythingtogether.

    My love to you all and I hope you have a good Christmas

    Love,
        Barbara

London S.W.1.
8th December 1955.

Dear Mum,

Have just received a letter from you saying you received the money. I feel bad when you thank me so much, I do little for you and feel awful that I have never been able to do anything permanent for you. I'm afraid I have never been much of a success financially. However, perhaps someday I will sell some film rights and make some real money.

I went to have some drinks with some Australian friends of mine last night and met Carl's wife. What an attractive person she is and so full of life. I was amused to hear they have four children – last time I remember him he was a fair-haired boy Margo and I had to cart round with us.

I'm off on Wednesday to Libya for two weeks, the Libyan Government want me to go to get some up-to-date data for this book of mine. Which is probably a little dated, as I was there over two years ago.

I do hope you all have a good Christmas, for my part I'm pleased to be away as Christmas here is always dreary now that Wei's gone. Of course, I would love to hear from the aunts and would certainly answer. I never write to them as I feel they are as bad at writing as I am! I get a lot of letters from people in Australia who have read the book which is very nice. It is something to think that people enjoy it – or at least they say they do.

How is Ian getting on with his job? It will be nice when you are all with him.

I didn't get the Herald review but the Bulletin arrived, I enjoyed reading them and thought the criticism very good. Did Sadie do that as well?

Well, here's to a very Happy Christmas and I'll be thinking of you on Christmas day.

    My love,
        Barbara.

London S.W.1.
1st March 1956.

Dear Mum,

   I am so sorry love, not to have written before this but things have been very hectic. The weather to begin with has been so b… awful that no one who didn't have to, has left their house for weeks. From my window here, the house opposite has been covered with ice from burst pipes and my whole flat has been sealed up with sticky paper and I haven't had a window open for days! Now, thank goodness the thaw has set in and life is as normal as it ever was in this climate.

   Firstly, I've never thanked you for the lovely slip which I found when I returned from Tripoli. It was very lovely and thank you very much. I've got a good deal plumper and so it fits me well – I think it is middle age spread setting in although my face looks as scraggy as ever. I haven't a rag to my back, but haven't the time or the money to waste on clothes which is I suppose a pity for Bertie, he always gets so thrilled if I do buy anything. A friend of mine knitted me a lovely blue jumper, a sort of Italian design and I have got a new skirt to go with it, so what am I talking about?

   I've just sent my revised manuscript off to the publishers and feel as though I have laid a rather large egg. I think it is bad but then I'm always pessimistic about anything I do.

   Sorry they didn't broadcast our Younger Generation Question Time but as I keep getting odd guineas for re-broadcasts of it, it may come out some time out there. At the moment I am writing a few broadcasts, hoping they will be done and if so, I will let you know. In fact, I will go to the Australian people here and see if they won't do one or two. Do let me know if they get television over there, I shall be most interested. I will be sending you a couple of photos of me on the last trip to Arabia.

   I'm glad you had a good Christmas, I spent it three hundred miles down in the desert and slept in the new year!

   Bertie has had a bad cold; he gets a bit jittery about his health and retires to bed very easily, which is just as well as he works far too hard. He is over sixty now but certainly doesn't look it.

*How is Ian getting along in his new job, does he like it?
Give my love to Sadie and let me know about the panties.*

Love to you and look after yourself

    Love,
        Barbara

                                      London S.W.1.
                                      12th June 1956.

Dear Mum,

    I am so sorry it has been so long since I've written to you but things have been a bit hectic and I have had a bad attack of the flu. Also, I am in a panic trying to get my book finished and having to do other things to help us out as well....

    London is very full; this is the first summer I have spent here for years, and I find it tiresome. The shops are marvellous here these days, although I never worry much about clothes. Just anything can be bought from any country.

    I sent you couple of publicity photos; I don't know if you ever received them.

    My new book comes out at the end of August, it has been held up with the printers' strike, unfortunately. I designed the jacket myself so, what with the book, the photographs and the jacket, its rather a one man show!

    Do let me know if the photographs arrived.

    Love
        Barbara

London S.W.1.
20th August 1956.

Dear Mum,

Thank you for the lovely stockings which arrived for my birthday. It was sweet of you, but really you should not have bothered. Birthdays are best forgotten at my age. I had a very quiet one, was, in fact, working very hard. …section torn

…Enclosed is a slip about my next book. It comes out next month but of course with the printer's strike, has missed the bus a bit, as things are a bit different from when I wrote it.

I didn't want Ian to do anything special for me, I just wanted some odd sketches which I would look after and return if he wanted them back.

Norman Lee (Fig 20) is in Hobart, I think, but at the moment he's not writing to me, this probably means he's got a new girlfriend. I've seen him through a few marriages and will probably see him through a few more, he's a dear old thing and has always been a great friend to me.

Glad you received the money, I only wish it could have been more, but things go up and down with my finances as you can well imagine.

Give my love to Sadie and hope you are well.

Love,
Barbara

London
10th September 1956

Dear Mum,

This is a very hurried note as I am a bit hectic today. The book comes out this morning and the publishers have sent you a copy air freight, I think.

On Saturday a young Australian who is tied up with A.B.C. came and did a recorded interview with me. It sounded a bit silly when she played it back…I've had a bit of advanced publicity about the book which may help although it is coming out at rather a controversial time, with the Suez [41] business. Anyhow I've got one television programme out of it and another in the offing, which helps…

…Am off to have lunch with my publisher who has just read the next book so goodness knows what state I'll be in by the time I get home again. Have gone terribly dull on these two books, God knows I hate writing; I suppose it is that I am just not a writer. In any case, with the third one, if they don't like it I'm going to scrap it. I see no point in wearing myself out when I can make the same amount of money with the things I like doing.

A magazine called Britannia and Eve is doing an article of mine which I'll send you, I think it comes out in the October edition.

Excuse this hurried note but I wanted you to get the broadcast.

Love,
        Barbara.

Sorry I sounded so soppy in it. I was a bit nervous.

---

[41] 1956 The Egyptian Government seized control of the **Suez** Canal from a French Company.

Pakistan
No Date Given

Dear Mum,

Thought I would just drop you a note as it is Christmas day and rather a dry one as I haven't had a drink all day. One gets out of the habit in Muslim countries anyhow. It is ruled by a Wali [42] who has complete control.

He happens to be a very good man and sees the little state is very well. It is in a lovely valley surrounded by hills and quite unspoilt as it is miles from anywhere.

There is a dear little hotel very comfortable and well run and everyone, being unused to visitors, do all they can for one.

I suddenly realised it was Christmas and came up here from Peshawar where I had gone on my way to the Khyber Pass. Am off tomorrow back to Lahore and through Deli quite soon.

The proofs of my next book are waiting for me there and I have to go over them. They, the publishers, are rushing this next book through as they think it so topical. I hope they are right.

Unfortunately, I don't think you will have received the money I sent in time for Christmas. I'm so sorry, Lahore was my first real stopping place and my mail got all behind. I hope you and Sadie will buy some odd thing for yourselves with it.

It made me realise I was getting near home when it cost me double to send a cable to England, the one I sent to you.

Love,
Barbara

---

[42] **Wāli** of Swat was the official title of the leader of Swat, Princely state, and named after the Dynasty that ruled from 1926 to 1969.

Now on a world tour, Barbara travelled from London to Brussels, Germany, Austria, Yugoslavia, Turkey, India, Pakistan, Thailand, Singapore, Australia and the USA. Using the tour of Australia to visit her mother. Making notes for her book *Columbus was Right* 1958.

While travelling around the Australian outback Barbara was once again faced with the dry sand, this time of the riverbeds around Coen, driving over sharp banks with steep drops. After passing numerous, gigantic ant hills and the grey desolation of miles of track, she made it to where the sand turned red. The dipping sun turned the ant stacks into glistening statues. Flocks of wild birds, galahs and budgerigars, would swoop by her or move out of a tree as she passed. Kangaroos joined in the welcome as they passed over the track in front of her. She eventually came across good tempered Aboriginals and her presence was noted among the small community.

Coen
Cape York Peninsular
Australia
12th August 1957

Dear Mum,

Here I am at the Cape. (Fig 21) *The tracks are certainly pretty lousy; I don't really know how Pollyanna keeps going. I am waiting here to get permission to go further North to Weipa where the big bauxite*[43] *mines are.*

This is a one-horse town but great fun, it's the first town (one pub) for about three days travelling. Have passed and stayed at some of the stations, and last night camped besides three graves under a mango tree! I've passed cars in the last three days, so as you see, there are no traffic problems here.

There are, however, lots of wild pigs and crocodiles, the latter if you sit down on the bank are liable to come up and push you in if they are hungry. I camp up, well on high ground.

---

[43] **Bauxite** is an ore in the first step in the production of aluminium.

It's getting pretty hot now but I don't mind it and the nights are lovely. This is a hurried note as a plane has come in unexpectedly and I can get this letter off. Shall be back in Cairns probably next week, so you can write there.

Don't by the way, mention about Ewing outside the house. It is terribly important that you don't, as the papers would just like to catch on to that and undo all my weeks of sweat and toil. Not that you're likely to mention it, it isn't particularly important to anyone you know. But these things get round, get in the air if they are talked about. It is also important because of The People article.

    Love,
          Barbara

Alice Springs
Thursday
12th September 1967

Dear Mum,

I am off today for the South. May not go to Ayres Rock it's hundreds of miles off my track and a bad one. The place is full of tourists and they go everywhere.

Had a letter from Rex Battarbee [44] and when I got there, you'd think he was an ancient monument, the droves of people around.

You can probably catch me air mail in Port Augusta but it is probably not important...

Hope you did something about the flat and caravan, it is important.

    Love,
          Barbara

---

[44] **Reginald Ernest Battarbee** was an Australian artist painting landscapes of Central Australia.

Barbara writes in book *Columbus was Right* how she was plagued with car problems along the way, not helped by the high winds that battered her as she tried to change the tyres. Hand cranking the start while being pelted by the small stones the wind blew at her. At one point a truck slowed down and a young man leaned out giving her instructions as to how she should be starting the car. Furious she told to help or b…r off, at which point he left her to it. While travelling she still had to deal with her growing domestic problems at home.

Ewing had passed away and Barbara was in endless negotiations with American estate lawyers and his remaining family. She wrote to her sister:

Sydney
4th October 1957

Darling Sadie,

So many thanks for all you have done. I would just never have got this far and certainly not off next Tuesday without you. The whole scandalous business of the log book and registration is a long tiresome story of which I'll go into, when I am on the ship and have more time. It means that this last two weeks have been taken up with petty officialdom, worn me out completely, and given me absolutely no time to research or see anymore.

Also, many things for the lawyer's notes. Ewing was resident in California although the law, from what I could see in a law book here, is practically the same. There may, however, be a snag in the long separation. I don't know a lawyer personally here, as you mention, and indeed none of them seem to know much about American law. One I went to suggested that when I get to 'Frisco. I just engage one, to enquire of the lawyer who is dealing with it, and state what I can't afford to pay. As the Rootes Group are dealing with me (for Rover) and will probably meet me, I shall probably ask him for a good lawyer, in any case the lawyer said I am not jeopardising things by waiting until then. Eleanor has ceased to write after the letter stating I do not, after all, participate in any of the property.

There has been fun and games with the shipping company, I give them a cheque and then they give me one for 'articles and lecturing'. I hadn't that amount with me, after the fare, so I had to tell them to hold up mine until I had cleared theirs! Never a dull moment.

I have asked Qantas to fly me from New York to London if their new service is operating, I think they will. Only thing is of course, perhaps I should go with Pollyanna.

Gosh I'll be glad to get off and have a nice rest. Twenty days at sea will be lovely. I'll sleep and sleep.

Poor Mum is rather weepy and it's going to be hell on Tuesday when I leave, but of course there is nothing I can do.

I might not write again before I leave, but thank you darling for what you have done.

Love,
Barbara

At sea
Sunday 13th October 1957

Dear Mum,

There is a rather involved postal system on board, you have to post before a certain time and it catches some mail or other, but I have a feeling I am always just missing them.

We get to Suva (capitol of Fiji) *tomorrow morning and have a day, or at least until five in the evening there. The weather yesterday, which was spent at sea, was rough and cold but in the evening, it fined up and was marvellous.*

Had a nice day in Auckland which I liked when I eventually got away from the press which started at seven in the morning. Anyhow, I feel like I have 'sung for my supper' as far as the Orient Line goes. Did a broadcast, quite a nice one, about ten minutes with a nice old girl. It's a pretty place, isn't it? Isn't it the place where you used to be?

Have done nothing but sleep and rest and have not joined any of the sports contests, making my bad arm excuse. The ship is half empty and is a disappointment from the holidaymaker's point of view, although I must admit I like it. The sports manager is Viscount somebody or other, he's got a voice just like the man who talks in that record 'Oh darling dreaming of me?' Goodness he's funny.

There is a lovely but snobbish restaurant upstairs where you can go by paying a small extra fee. It's very nice and exclusive with lovely views through big glass windows out to the stern of the ship.

I spend most of the mornings at sea, when its fine, at the swimming pool so am getting quite a bit of colour. I am going out for the day tomorrow with some people to have a native lunch and look at a show of hibiscus. All very touristy for once!

Unfortunately, I can't use my Dictaphone on board because its DC, which is a nuisance. I seem doomed not to be able to get down to it.

There are quite a few children on board, all extremely well behaved and nice. I was able to get a rather nice table lighter and ash tray for Bertie in Auckland, which has eased my mind somewhat. Not as nice as a painting but still it's something.

I'll send you a cutting of the Auckland paper, when I write an ordinary letter. Maybe I'll have a note from you when we get to Suva ...

... Hope you are well...

Love,
Barbara

Vancouver
23th October 1957

Dear Mum,

We get into Vancouver tonight late, but can't go off until morning. It's raining, doggy and much cooler although not cold now the weather has changed. I'll be glad when the journey is over. I don't like board-ship life without the scenery.

I gave a long lecture yesterday, a bit nerve racking but I'm glad I did it. It's all good practice.

Viscount Grayson presented me with a sailor toy, and this morning I was presented with a diploma for 'services rendered'!!

Old sir Leslie Morshead [45] and his wife are on board, she is a dear, he's very old now but nice. There are two elderly ladies at my table, both from Brisbane and both very wealthy I should think, by looking at their minks and jewels. But they are both extremely nice and treat me as a kid.!

I bought you a little brooch and am trying to post it but it is not so easy, I will try in Vancouver. I am looking forward to seeing the city it looks a lovely place.

Had a cable from the Rover agents in New Zealand, who heard my broadcast and wanted to use story and photos for publicity, so it must have done reasonably well.

Love to you all,

Barbara

---

[45] Lieutenant General Sir **Leslie James Morshead**, KCB, KBE, CMG, DSO, ED was an Australian soldier, teacher, businessman, and farmer, whose military career spanned both world wars.

Hotel Maurice
Seven Sixty-one Post Street
San Francisco
California
23th October 1957

Dear Mum,

As you see, I am here at last. Today is exactly one year since I left England – one of the longest as far as all things I have done.

I love San Francisco, it's a lovely friendly place and the people so nice and kind to one. It's not nearly as high powered and slick as American propaganda leads one to believe. Lots of the people are rather homely and cosy.

Enclosed are two cuttings from the papers, it seems even here it is worth giving me a write up, although I was a little surprised.

I received a letter from you and one from the aunts, which I'll answer later. Yes, I forgot to bring the shorts, scarf etc but it doesn't matter now. I am sorry you have to send them on to England. I've sent a suitcase back to England via the Liner Orsova, so I am really down to the bone as far as clothes are concerned. It is going to be a bit of a problem as everyone wears such new clothes and the things in the shops are marvellous. In fact, everything is marvellous – all you need is money! The cost of things is funny. All the travelling and hotel things and food is expensive but the things I can't spend my money on, like clothes aren't too bad at all and furs seem very cheap, and absolutely lovely.

The city is very beautiful and the hills make it full of grand views with the lushest hotels I've ever seen. One hotel has a fabulous cocktail bar called Le Ronde and it has a small merry go round going slowly round. I went down and sat in one of the seats just to say I had and a very lush blonde waitress – almost nudist, came up (Ian would have loved her) and asked what I wanted. I said, nothing I've come for the ride. She was quite nice and gave me a glass of iced water. Later a man took me there and she greeted me like an old friend and we got the best service, he said he'd never had. There ain't no justice!

The weather is unseasonably warm and sunny and of course the building is all kept at sizzling point. I leave tomorrow for Los Angeles and shall have to go a little quicker than I thought because of the dollars. Had to pay $62 for insuring *Pollyanna* which was a blow. The drivers are rather frightening, except they get such a shock when they see her that they practically pile up along the road on top of each other, gaping.

Petrol, however, is not so expensive about 2/6 as far as I can work it out. I went to ask for petrol and they looked at me as if I was mad!

If you want to write, I think the best place would be Las Vegas, C/o the Post Office and put it to "wait arrival" for I don't think I will be all that long in Los Angeles. Whatever you do don't send anything important as my movements are a bit vague. The other towns would be Santa Fe, Houston, New Orleans, and C/o the British Embassy, New York eventually.

Thanks so much for the cutting which will be added to my others, I'm getting quite a few and it's a pity I haven't kept one book of them, I suppose, all along.

Everyone is most kind in this hotel, which isn't as lush as it looks, but it has a nice food bar where I eat all the time. Everyone is most chatty and this morning a man who had read one of the write ups insisted on paying for my breakfast. I protested but not all that hard.

There are some beautiful homes here and it's a fine place to live, I should think. It is surprising how many English people I have met here who had emigrated and settled.

Will write again from Los Angeles. In any town that has the American Express Tourist Agency, it would be better to write to them.

Hope you are quite well, and that poor Denny's finger is better.
My love and look after yourself my sweet.

Barbara

P.S I feel when I get home, we should look and see if I have any money left from my cottage that would help with your extension. It is not going to be enough for me anyhow.

Holbrook
Arizona.
15th November 1957

Dear Mum,

Sorry not to have written before but – once again – I am running away from the bad weather. Everywhere I go they say you'll have to hurry because the snows may block the roads soon. However, I'm more or less heading South for Santa Fe.

Received your letter at Las Vegas which was quite a mad house, worse than Los Angeles but well worth seeing. All those sorts of places, one needs money and good clothes, I'm just too dirty and travel worn to really enjoy it. They put so much store in appearances, it's quite childish really.

Surprised to hear Sadie might not keep the house on, it's such a good way of saving money, at least it always has been for me, I'd never had been able to get on without mine behind me, and it has stood me in good stead lately. Ian seems to me the last person who would want to be confined to the four walls of a flat. However, there it is. I shall sort out my finances when I get back to London and see how we stand.

Had a rather nerve-racking time in Los Angeles as that is where Ewing lived and died. The California law is that the wife cannot inherit a penny of any money which the husband hasn't actually earned, and as poor Ewing never earnt a penny in his life – that lets me out! However, the finding out of all this was nerve racking and I was glad, really to get away, I will be glad to get home and away from all that atmosphere.

I do hate the thought of you taking that pension, it makes me feel I shouldn't have spent the money I had on this trip, even though it will probably pay dividends in the long run. I've always been a gambler as far as money is concerned and it has paid off. But this business, I just don't like it.

Most of the roads are very good; they shoot out across the desert with billboards all along, I have to speed up when I come to a sign which says, "Drop your speed to 45 miles an hour"! Motels are everywhere and not all that expensive if you look around…. The people are always friendly but impersonal, although I had fun when I ran into a group who all had jeeps and were going off for three days across country, equipped with every kind of device for safety and armed with ice boxes galore. They call themselves the Memet Cavalcaders and presented me with a huge badge (Fig 22) for Pollyanna. Everyone came along, the wives, the kids. They seemed a breath of fresh air to me after Los Angeles.

I keep meaning to ask if Sadie wouldn't mind ringing the Police Station just in case someone handed in that Malayan badge which I lost off Pollyanna. She could post it back to London, surface mail, if they did. Pollyanna has been playing up a bit and is now tied up with many bits of insulating tape and is much better. Have had two punctures from huge nails, which seems funny in such a country.

Eleanor writes that she wanted me to go to Florida with her for thanksgiving but of course I won't make it there in time. In any case, I've hardly the clothes for Florida!

The sights are well organised here – too much so in fact, for someone like me and everywhere there are lectures on the place and everyone takes it all rather seriously.

I suppose it's beautiful and warm there now. Hope Denny's finger has quite recovered. I've been meaning to write to Ian but have got a thing about writing at the moment, and in any case, he'd probably think he'd have to answer it and I think he's as good at correspondence as his mother!

Will write again soon.

Barbara.

Still on her world tour, Barbara goes on to write in her book *Columbus was Right* as she makes it to America. She saw the Las Vegas desert as the most sophisticated in the world, surrounded by hills and uncompromisingly flat. The cheap hotels on the outskirts of the 'strip' soon turned into bizarre and fabulous luxury hotels. Neon coloured signs and hoarding on the road ahead announced the coming of Johnnie Ray, Eartha Ki, Celeste Holm and Sinatra. Unimpressed with Los Angeles, she describes it as an over blown business man about to have a heart attack.

Fig 20

Norman Lee (Photo from unaccredited source)
Wrote many books under the pseudonym of Mark Corrigan

Fig 21

Cape York, Australia.
Inscription reads, 'please bloody close the gate!'
it appears open.

Fig 22
Badge still on Pollyanna today.

Sydney Harbour Bridge, 1957

Las Vegas Nevada, USA

Whispering Rocks, Arizona. USA.

Turkey

India

On board an Indian Dow

A young person of Bangui, Central African Republic

Ghurkha Woman and girl, India

Thailand

Barbara, Bangkok.

Chapter 10
Pollyanna beats them all.

An Australian country magazine, wrote of Barbara's 23-year absence for her home country and how that time had been filled with experiences that could be read about in many of her books. They talk of her dynamo energy and restless spirit, that would see her travel from one place to another, always alone, but never lonely. They go on to mention the British brigadier she met in Gibraltar and his unwitting christening of her first run of three books. Calling her a fool for taking on such dangerous journeys. *A Fool on Wheels*, *A Fool in the Desert*, and *A fool Strikes Oil*.

The newspaper noted she was back in Australia for her family, as well as her desire to travel the deserts of her native country. At the time the interview was given, Barbara was in Brisbane, to have her beloved Land Rover Pollyanna serviced for the trip inland. Wowed by Barbara's resilience, intelligence, vitality and humour, the journalist seemed even more impressed, considering the tenacious redhead was a petite and dainty lady.

While honouring her ability to tell a tale as Australians do, he relayed how she told of the gift she received from a sheik of the ruling family in Kuwait. The gift, a sheep's eye, was surreptitiously placed on her plate, which was, of course, just another challenge to Barbara. Swearing the eye winked at her, she swallowed it down to the delight of over 100 pair of eyes watching her. She was rewarded by her host, who commented 'you are the son of your father', an esteemed compliment in that part of the country.

The newspaper also marvelled at her ability to cope with dangerous situations, but commented that not all the tales she divulged could be true… The torn newspaper ended there.

Another article in The Sydney Bulletin, reviews her life after the release of her book *A Fool on Wheels*. They mention her life in theatre, both in London and repertory around England, her work at the film studios, and her collaborations with Norman Lee on the plays; 'Life Line' and 'The Moon to Play With'. Going on to produce 'Spring Meetings' for the J. Arthur Rank organisation. It mentions her dramatising several plays for Agatha Christie, (there was only evidence of her transcribing one of Christie's in her archives, *Murder at the vicarage*). The article went on to say she drove an ambulance during the World War II, in others that she was an air raid warden. Barbara was only too pleased to give the interview while in Aden, after travelling the Persian Gulf for months, as her father was a former member of the literary staff of The Bulletin, before becoming the first editor of The Women's Mirror in Australia.

Greenville Motors
William Street
Sydney
4th June 1957

Dear Bertie,

As usual I seem to be in a hurry. Great to-do goings on, about me getting publicity for the new book. The press here is rather terrifying. They are only interested in leg shows and candid confessions. Now they want some photographs of me showing my legs! (Fig 23) *I've written to Mr. Bates asking him if he knows of some and may contact you. I think I am right in thinking; I left the box of my negatives – the one with the two drawers which you made for me – at your flat. If he should want it, do you think you could drop it over to his place one night, he lives, I think, near the factory…he is in the telephone book. …*

…I'm off today to do the television with Pollyanna, and am in a bit of a fluff, as one of the big papers is doing an article by me, which is rather tricky and they keep ringing me up checking what they – or I – have said. Everything they do seems a little off key to me, everything is sensationalism.

Then tomorrow, I leave for the Snowy Scheme [46] *for a few days. I forgot to mention, did Bates have that one in that bathing dress near the swimming pool. Could you ask him if he rings? Or have you a copy? It's a damn shame I haven't more casual photographs. You might ask him if he has any others of me in my shorts, or things like that. Sorry about this haste.*

Love,
Barbara.

Wednesday
28th August 1957

Dear Mum,

Received your note, I do hope Ian is feeling alright. It is a nasty business, and I suppose the doctor has told him to keep away from glaring light, it can affect the eyes.

Am off today for Tennant Creek.[47] You ask do I want any mail sent on. I had asked Sadie about it, but perhaps there isn't any. If anything does come when you receive this send it to:

% P.O. Box Alice Springs and then hold everything.

In haste

Love,
Barbara

---

[46] **Snowy Scheme:** The Snowy mountains hydro scheme in South East Australia. Australia largest engineering project.

[47] **Tennant Creek**, a hamlet on the main artery between Alice Springs and Darwin, gold mining, Aboriginal culture and cattle.

278

When I showed the tattered newspaper cutting to Terri, we had laughed at the suggestion that an Aussie would tell a yarn, having lived with an Australian for many years she was well aware. Ever protective of her beloved Ian, Terri defended Barbara's supposed actions as newspaper embroidery, "why should the truth get in the way of a good story!" Terri had a grin and twinkle in her eye, as she passed me another very strong coffee and a 'visitors' biscuits! Which were, as usual, delicious. When she didn't take one, she showed me a saucepan full of breakfast porridge, and making her excuses, she pushed the plate in front of me to take another.

Each newspaper article we looked at had differing details about Barbara, there was no way of knowing what was true and what was embellished.
'I'm not sure she would have told us either way,' Terri continued, 'makes no difference, she had ants in her pants, I just hope she was happy.'

I watched, as I had done many times, Terri scurry around the tiny kitchen and I was once again reminded of how similar Terri was to Barbara, energetic and continually on the move. Terri would walk miles each day rewarding herself with a pit stop at Marks & Spencer food hall on the way back through Chipping Norton. Or she would walk the Cotswold countryside with her friend Patrick and his dogs. She'd catch the bus to Oxford, an hour each way, just for a bag of coffee beans. She may not have travelled far and wide, but Terri rarely sat still, unless it was to knit a new garment. She never followed the instructions, did it all her own way, and made up her own colourways.

Terri was private and generous, as was Ian. Barbara was also a dichotomy of the longing for privacy and a need to be seen. Never happier than when alone, she still sought the limelight, appearing in many newspapers, on TV and in radio interviews.

Barbara's long-awaited return to Australia happened as part of her first world expedition in 1958-9, and was where she was asked by the Land Rover company to give up her beloved 'Pollyanna' for a newer model. She always thought Pollyanna was the best of them, having travelled in at least three different models. It wasn't until 1989 that Barbara heard of a man who had purchased Pollyanna and called her, wanting memorabilia he could present at shows. She asked to buy the Land Rover back, but he refused. Some six months later she was contacted by a relative of his, who informed her Pollyanna was for sale, as her then owner had passed away. A car that cost her £640 in 1950 now cost her £3,500. At the time, there was no garage to house the car at her cottage in Chipping Norton. It was later added by Ian.

Now the garage was long void of any vehicle, just rubbish bins, paint pots and the old kitchen cabinets. Terri had finally got her way with one room, the kitchen. The old, dark oak kitchen cupboards, were relegated to the walls of the garage, housing jars of nuts and bolts instead of jams and pickles. There was an old elaborate table, who's top tipped over revealing hand painted tigers and exotic flowers, dusty and unwanted now. Another with multiple compartments, each with their own lid. Artifacts Barbara had found in the desert, were strewn among the debris, along with a metal tin full of arrow heads.

A mix of old shoes, and carrier bags of mixed papers, having been decanted from the attic, sat alongside bills and newspaper cuttings, all huddled together in the corner. Ian's walking frame and slippers were tucked away near the door, ready to pass on to whoever needed such equipment next. The garage, had become a conduit to expel the unwanted collections of both Barbara and Ian. The more involved I became with the past life of Barbara who had owned such memorabilia, the more the empty garage seemed, despite the clutter it now held.

Ian, also a car enthusiast, had built the integral garage after inheriting the property, but there was only room for one at Snails, so Pollyanna had to go. It was around then that Pollyanna was housed with the Pickfords, a garage dedicated to the preservation of Land Rovers of the past. That is until Ian himself could no longer drive; his car now also gone, leaving more room for Barbara's banished things to wait in its dark corners, for disposal.

When I found Pollyanna's new owners, I was thrilled to be able sit in the driving seat of this tiny vehicle. I was shocked at her small size, her bare metal appearance and fabric top. There was no sign of any luxury inside, Pollyanna was sparse of room for luggage or supplies. The seats were small and lacked any cushioning, the dash was a metal rod that had, what looked like, a first aid kit tin bolted to it. Two gear sticks with worn handles nestled at the foot and the windows were scratched and worn. The smell of oil and exhaust lay over the metal work and once moving, the engine noise was as loud as the rattling bodywork. I couldn't imagine taking her on long journeys, it was definitely not a car built for comfort. What adventures this little car had seen, what history was imbedded in each squeak and rattle. Her new owner seemed as entranced by her history as I was. Barbara was closer than ever, her trust in this vehicle justified.

Writing to her mother Barbara shows the trust she had in Pollyanna, as she encounters ice while on her world tour:

Jacksonville
Florida
23rd November 1957

Dear Mum,

You'll probably be surprised to see I'm now in Florida. I had to come East rather quickly from Santa Fe as the weather broke, and I got into ice and snow, it really was dangerous, with Pollyanna's smooth tires and traffic whizzing past. I couldn't go up to Taos which is North of Santa Fe and was greatly disappointed, and also on going South found the roads impassable. So, I cut down into Texas, which I absolutely loved, the people are so very nice, and pottered across through Louisiana with its lovely old Plantation homes. They all looked a bit bedraggled, as it poured all the time, and I really couldn't see a foot ahead.

New Orleans was a lovely old town, and then suddenly very modern. Goodness these busy towns are hectic, you can't park anywhere, and you don't dare stop for a minute. It took me four hours to call at two places for my mail.

Today the sun came out for the first time in ages, and the television people came and took shots of me arriving on the Atlantic coast, and driving right through and onto the beach for that's where route 90, leads.

I would like to go South to the holiday part of Florida, but don't really think I have the money, it's silly really if one isn't properly dressed and holiday places are really just for holidays.

I'm getting quite an authority on motels, think I'd better open one myself when I get back. They are certainly very beautiful, but the trouble is, if you don't want to pay money then the next accommodation is really very sordid. There is an awful lot of poverty and the running cost of a family must be very high. You see an awful lot of old shacks, really bad ones, with big limousines outside. They seem to have their automobiles, even if they have to sleep in them.

Goodness, I wish I could go and see their caravans or trailers, as they call them. They are fifty feet long and very many people live in them, in small settlements. They are beautifully fitted up with fridges, washing machines, central heating, air conditioning and everything. Two or one bedroom.

Everyone is stirring for next week end which is Thanksgiving, when I suppose the nation will get into its cars and go madly from East to West, or from West to East.

Pollyanna just keeps rolling along. I've only got one piece of insulating tape on her at the moment, although her exhaust pipe sounds a bit like Frankie Lane. Hope you are well, you could write me C/O British Consulate, Park Lane New York.

Love,
Barbara

A bouquet is left on one of Barbara's Land Rovers:

'...I have an unknown admirer who sends me flowers (Fig 24) at each port. I do hope it isn't the Bosun who got knocked on the behind. Also, a doctor friend of mine in Equatorial writes, quite casually, to say he's probably sending a chimpanzee down to the ship at Dakar. I'll look nice with a one roomed flat and a chimp as big as myself....'

London
Thursday
14th March 1958

Dear mum,

Nice to get your letter, have not written I'm afraid as, as usual, their doesn't seem to be enough time to go round. Except for one or two breaks, I've been working eighteen hours a day without a stop. I press on, but the book stinks. Just don't want to write this one, that's all there is to it. However, it's probably good discipline, a kind of Lent penance. In any case it's got to be done.

Pollyanna is in the Piccadilly Showroom window looking a bit daft amongst the slick new cars, but she's causing a lot of interest as you can imagine.

Do thank Denny for his letter, he is a dear little kid, has he any idea what he wants to do? He ought to win a scholarship to Oxford or Cambridge and come over here.

What was the trouble with Tal's (Sadie's husband) *eyes you never told me? I don't hear from Sadie of course, but then I've got another five and half years to wait until my letter quota comes round!*

Do you know if Darli McCourt is coming over? You might telephone, if you want, to give her any messages, unfortunately she can't bring my seal. However, it's best left there at the moment, as I don't want it broken, and it seems it is the only thing I have left in Australia.

I am living on a diet of veginin coffee and cheese but, as reported, its evidently agreeing with me. I think sitting at my desk day after day is a kind of rest, I just haven't time to worry about my other problems. The business in America gets vaguer and it seems to be that any money will be eaten up by the lawyer's fees. Anyway, something I hear must come out, it may mean at least payment of rent and give me, perhaps, a chance to work on things I really want to. But I don't like legal complications and refuse to let it bother me.

Hope you are well and that the weather is better

Love, Barbara

Barbara writing again to her sister-in law after the death of her husband Ewing.

73 St. James Street
London SW1

Dear Eleanor,

Goodness what a lot of trouble. Why didn't they go into all of this when I was in New York?

Your cable arrived well ahead of the letter so I was completely confused and now wait for the one you mention in the cable as evidently its important.

Now I have to go to this awful Rover Company and have to go to Birmingham. I am one of the guests of honour, speeches, demonstrations, all very frightening. By that time the letter will have come from you.

How silly that all this should have blown up after all these months; after all the trouble you have had. I can't think why it wasn't settled while I was there.
Am off for the train, which I hate.

Love,
Barbara

73 St. James Street
Monday

Dear Eleanor,

Today. At last, after a letter and then a cable, John Orr replied stating facts and I've sent off the letter you wished me to sign.

Your letters have shattered me and it's difficult to write.

Dear Eleanor, firstly no one knows the true story of Ewing and me; they'll probably not even go into my autobiography! You suggested I married him for his money, well, he had none in Australia, only debts as you know. Things were much worse for me; I was disinherited on my marriage and would have otherwise been the owner of a fine art and bookshop which was to have been my career. Also, would I have refused the money from your mother had I been only after the money? Over the years I had nothing, and some of them, the war ones, weren't very easy.

I'm not a particularly good person but I have a set of standards, unorthodox perhaps but they make it possible for ME to live with MYSELF. I had felt that you knew these things instinctively. If you feel all that you can't like me much. I've always had a great feeling for you – and admiration.

And the last accusation that I was not appreciative of all you did for me in New York. Perhaps I should try and explain. Firstly, it was the end of a long journey; I was exhausted and depressed; more on the mental side than the physical. Your cable about Ewing, the will etc. and the subsequent cancellation of the most important part of my journey, made the trip in Australia rather disastrous in many ways. I hate waste especially money as there are so many worthwhile things to be done with it. That journey was to have been the main part of my book.

Maybe I'm not very demonstrative, maybe I didn't say 'thank you' properly but I felt it and still do, dear Eleanor, and I hope I've shown it in other things than words.

Oh dear! I had to say all that because I felt a bit bleak. Now it's off my chest!

Love,
Barbara

Barbara's book *Columbus was Right* was dedicated to her sister-in-law Eleanor Rixson Cannon. As Barbara and Ewing never divorced, it took many letters and lawyers to resolve issues after his death.

73 St James Street
London S.W.1.
17th April 1958

Dear Mr Orr,

My sister-in-law will probably have spoken to you about the letter I wrote her yesterday.

My lawyer here feels that, 'for my files' I should have a statement of the Trust made by my mother-in-law Mrs Mary Rixson from which I am entitled to part of the principal. Also, please let me have a letter which Mrs Cannon wishes me to sign in connection with the other trust.

Although I know exactly what I want to do in these matters my lawyer, quite rightly I'm sure, feels that there should be statements from you about business and transactions of the estate.

I was so sorry not to meet when I was in New York.

Yours sincerely,

Barbara Toy Rixson.

London
Tuesday

Dear Mum,

Will you thank Sadie for her letter? I'll answer it soon and thanks for the information. It also made me laugh a lot (the letter I mean) Unfortunately I can't do anything with the information at the moment as I am laid low with a bad attack of shingles which, I believe, you had a little while ago. I feel lousy and have been told by the doctor to forget work, lawyers etc. That's a horse laugh. However, the worst is over and now I am beginning to itch! I'd evidently been staggering around with it and it was Darli and Peter (I had dinner with them) who suddenly said 'you've got shingles. I wondered why I felt so awful and looked exactly as Masie would have described me! She, poor old thing, to ring up with a 'last will and testament' tone in her voice to enquire how I am and then proceed for an hour about her troubles! It's a great pity she doesn't go home, I think, but I suppose her pride won't let her at the moment.

Re the last parcel, no good worrying now. It is the luck of the game and I am always philosophical about such things. My porter Bridges, this end is always meticulous about collecting stuff.

Greta Morrison has been really extraordinary about helping me. She is a dear and I do so like her very much.

Thank God the publishers have rung up to say the like the what they have seen of the book so far. But being of a suspicious nature I'm wondering if they are just saying that as they are worrying about my being ill. Colin Simpson [48] *is here, but of course I couldn't see him. He's off to the continent to write a book about it.*

We are having marvellous weather I am told although I don't see it in here, will write again soon.

Love,
Barbara

London
Sunday

Dear Mum,

So sorry not to have written before but I have been in a state. The bloody book really is off my chest at last. It is a stinker and I should have scrapped it ages ago, it's just my cussedness at not getting a book out of the journey that made me go ahead. They've been subjecting me to a kind of Chinese torture and messing me about. Now I am flattened

---

[48] **Colin Simpson was** a journalist for The Daily Telegraph and the Sun. A travel writer working on documentaries for ABC television.

out completely. All my ordinary work and business has piled up, so for the next week shall be doing business letters etc.

You haven't said what the pillows cost, I want to know as should find out what it cost to send things and if it is worth it. Also, what's the point of a present if it costs money; I know that sort of thing myself!

Had a letter from the aunts and will answer it later, also Sadie's. Give my regards to the cleaner woman I thought her rather nice. Guess I like widows, being one myself! My shingles have cleared up which surprised my doctor who was quite certain, considering how much I'm working that I was going to collapse again. But I just look like Mamie says I do and feel a bit deflated. I fact, definitely look my age. (At this time Barbara was 50yrs old)

The weather is awful at the moment, raining buckets. Have seen something of Darli but I am really no good to anyone at the moment and feel guilty as I can't do more for her. Just can't cope with organising things at the moment.

I'm sending a few snaps, I took a lovely one of Wootie, but will keep it as I don't feel you have the affection for the gentleman that I have. Do you want that coloured one of us back again?

Old Sir John (Murray) who read my book and liked it, surprisingly enough, said… 'but my dear, your spelling is rather unusual.' I said you ought to see it when I was young and produced the letter you sent me that I sent to Santa.

Yes, Mamie has bought a house here and moved in, I gather. She's not going to find it easy to live here on her allowance but that's her own affair and people must find these things out for themselves. People from warm climates don't realise the steady cost of keeping warm here.

The business of Ewing's affairs still goes on, and I feel sick in the stomach whenever I think about it. I'm no good at legal affairs and business and thank goodness until now, I've never had to worry about such things. One advantage of living on one's wits!

   Will write again soon.
   Barbara

73 St James Street
London S.W.1.
28th April 1958

Dear Mr. Orr,

 Thank you for your letter dated 22n April 1958 which I received today. Thank you also for the information and facts about the two trusts now clearly set out.

 I hereby enclose the letter which my sister-in-law Mrs Eleanor Cannon wishes me to sign relinquishing my rights in the 1929 Trust created by Mrs. Rixson.

Yours sincerely,

 Barbara Toy Rixson.

73. St James's Street
London S.W.1.
April 1958

Dear Eleanor,

 Since I wrote to you, both the photostat of your mother's letter and your last letter have arrived. The photostat didn't alter things as I'd thought by your first cable. From today's cable I gather you mean court action between us. I would never go to court against you.

 As I see things though, it is that the 1932 Trust was the one from which your mother wanted to give me an income when we were in New York and when I said 'no' she transferred it to Ewing. Wish I had it now! Five months later she changed her mind about having the principal from the 1929 Trust; but there is no law about changing one's mind!

 The only thing is, the letter you yourself sent me to sign is a bit vague. As it has not yet been specifically stated which Trust I am entitled to, I think the bank should write directly to me stating all this so that the lawyers here have a record of it. I don't want to find we've worded it so that I've signed away the whole, or the wrong lot!

Although it is nothing to do with the bank or you, there has been surprise here about the will and the fact of their having established residency in California and for this reason I do see, in the future, we should have things recorded properly.

Do let me know what you paid for the duty on the clock and the ring. A present, no matter how small, shouldn't have to be paid for.

Pollyanna behaved magnificently in the countryside and was photographed from every angle. She is now doing a tour of the provinces. But I'm the one who has to stay and 'get on with it!'

I'll drop a line to Mr Orr, but perhaps you'd speak to him also.

My Love,
    Barbara

Cagliari
Venice
21st August. 1958

Dear Mum,

This old ship seems to be the original 'slow boat to China'; it's been going on and on but I leave it soon. Feel very much rested although had an awful 'to-do' about the proof of my book ('Columbus was Right') *which messed me up, so don't know how much they will have corrected.*

It's very hot here as it always is at this time of year, but cloudy. Venice is full of tourists and one has to get off the beaten track to enjoy it. It's completely spoiled now really, as they come in their millions and the motor boats have almost completely taken the place of the gondolas.

So sorry to hear Sadie had a bad cold, they are miserable; hope she is better now. I suppose spring will be on its way out here so that will be better.

Goodness knows what's happening at home I haven't had any mail but as there seems to be nothing but trouble there, perhaps it's all to the good!

Am glad you have kept all those old letters as, I may want them someday, although I never was a good letter writer, but they would help me to place dates etc. Don't want them now though.

I must owe you for the pillows and the boys' presents, will fix it up when I get back to London.

I found, after I'd sent the photographs, that I had another of myself but will send it later.

No, the Rixson estate is completely held up through the 'female' line and all I can say is, thank goodness I didn't count on it and get myself involved financially. I've always had a funny feeling about the whole thing, and in any case, money never comes to me if I treat it seriously, so I'm laughing like hell!

Love to all,

Barbara

Barbara seemed consumed at times by her late husband's affairs, although stoical about the outcome. She was still travelling and getting ready for her next trip across the Sahara, from Libya to Ethiopia, The Congo to Lake Victoria and the Nile River. Going on to Khartoum in Sudan and Kenya. Adventures contained in her next book *In Search of Sheba*, 1961.

The attic held more to do, and I had placed to one side several large film cannisters, one of which had the word Congo written on a scruffy label. I had managed to prise one of the tins open, and was met full in the face by the strong smell of chemicals and rusty metal. Gently opening out the film, I looked carefully at one of the reels. It was difficult to see any images until further into the reel, it felt delicate, I didn't want to chance damaging the stock.

I had a film documentary producer coming over from Los Angeles, as she had heard through a friend about Barbara Toy and was excited to see the content of the films. In a whirlwind of expectation, I had put all the cannisters into a suit case and trundled off to London on the train. We were able to open up each of them, taking a look on the Steenbeck editing machine at the BFI. (Fig 25) It soon became clear that the small lengths of film and the grainy uninteresting sections, were the outtakes and edits Barbara herself had performed. It begged the question as to where the actual footage had gone. As the film producer left, sadly she came to the conclusion that there was not enough to contribute to a documentary of Barbara Toys travels. Gutted, I assured her I would let her know if I ever found out what happened to the rest of the films.

London
Thursday 12th September 1958

Dear Mum,

I always seem in such a rush. But am having fun as a friend has lent me a film cutter and projector and I'm going through all my film, cutting out the dud bits and also sorting out a bit for Darli, who wants it for T.V. when they review the book. It's great fun, and one of the jobs I'd have liked to do, film cutting. As usual if you want things done you have to do it yourself, so I'm going ahead and trying to make up the programme myself. Even if I make a b… of it, I'll at least have learnt something.

I hear the executrix has signed the release of the Trust at last. She couldn't really hold off forever as it was to do with her, as my mother-in-law made it. And this reminds me of something that has been on my mind for some time.

There are a couple of things I want to do when I know this is behind me, and the first one is getting your place fixed. It doesn't look like you are going to get that money back for some time and I want you to go ahead with the alterations, I'll pay for them. You know what you want to do, but I was wondering, as you spend so much time at the aunt's place, whether you would rather spend the money adding to their place. That's if everyone is agreeable. Anyhow, that is for you to decide. There is an alternative that Sadie sells her place and with the extra money, buys a larger one that has the right sort of accommodation for you.

But if you decide to go ahead as you originally planned, perhaps you'd better get Jamie to advice, he always seems such an enthusiastic go-ahead person, so as long as he doesn't have you living in a large bowl on top of an umbrella! At least he'd know the snags of local councils etc. I'm writing this now as you should really get on with it.

Am starting having interviews about the new book already and have a feeling it may go better than the others. It'll either go better or be a large, or rather larger raspberry here.

My sister-in-law is rather anxious that I go live in America, but because of the currency it would mean immigrating there and the money wouldn't be enough or me to live on. And as I haven't connections, I might not be able to make the extra.

It is getting much cooler and the sun has gone – for good I should think, until next year. I hear you have been having it very cold over there lately.

In haste, as usual.
Love,
  Barbara.

London
3rd December 1958

Dear Mum,

As I don't seem to be getting an answer from you about this, I am enclosing a cheque for you to cash, if you can put it in your account. It's the money for the repairs or whatever you want to do with it, also the £17 I owe you, and £50 Sterling which is £62.10 that I should have sent. That makes £1329. Don't worry about this anymore, I can't re-invest it now as the market is at the top.

My other finances as regard to the Trust, bring me in a reasonably steady income, if things keep stable here, it makes it possible for me to clear up my rather muddled way of living and finances; for although it isn't bringing in any more, it makes me independent, even if I don't write anymore plays. However, it's not enough to stop me working which is a good thing.

Am sorry I have been so bad about Christmas but am rushing trying to get away. Anyhow I just don't approve of Christmas, except for kids, and thank goodness none of my friends do anything about it here. I've just sent the boys some books.

London is like some awful Irish stew, with me in the centre bubbling up at the moment. However, the letting of the flat is hanging fire which is a nuisance as I can't go until it is let.

The book is going very well despite the fact that there are many books out there at this time.

Do, darling, get yourself something you want with the enclosed. Something to give you some comfort or enjoyment, if you don't put it towards the building.

Would love to get something for Sadie, just can't think. If you thought of something, could you possibly get it and let me know the cost? Had thought about something like a clothes hoist, which she seems to want badly, but it is so mundane and really part of the house.

Will write again when things look a little clearer.

My love, look after yourself, you're all I've got.

Drop me a line that you received cheque.

Barbara

(Fig 23)

Barbara at the baths, Saudi Arabia. Her 'legs' photograph.

(Fig 24)

Pollyanna with newly fitted light reflecting hard top. In 1960. A bouquet left on her Land Rover window.

Fig 25

Barbara's film canisters

Fig 25

Steenbeck machine at the British Film Institute.

Barbara at the wheel of the Diesel Land Rover in Australia.

Fellow travellers on the road to Baghdad, 'Pollyanna' fitted with a new roof for security, known by Pollyanna's restorers as the 'chicken coop.'

Barbara was lent a new Land Rover in an effort to get a reluctant Australia interested in a diesel version.

Series II Land Rover.

Barbara in her 80s, reunited with her beloved 'Pollyanna'. Inscribed on the back of the photo in Barbara's hand

'Returned to owner, Pollyanna with a face lift.' 1989.

Guy and Tom Pickford, Pollyanna's restorers, and present owners. 2023

'Pollyanna was to be used in the spirit in which Miss Toy would have liked. We still take her on long journeys as well as shows.'

Tom Pickford 2023

Pollyanna's lucky red boots

First aid box from a motorbike and the truncheon given to her by a Moroccan policeman for her safety.

Sadie, Barbara's sister, with Ian and baby Dennis.

Chapter 11
All roads lead from London.

In 1959, Barbara set off on her fifth expedition, this time across the Libyan desert, the Sahara, the Tibesti mountains and the Republic of Central Africa. Onward South through the Congo and Uganda, along the river Nile to Khartoum in the Sudan, and finally to Ethiopia. A journey that became the inspiration for her book *'In Search of Sheba'* 1961.

She was to drive a new Land Rover, having been persuaded to part from her trusted 'Pollyanna', despite the vehicle seeing Barbara over 210, 000 miles. The brand-new Series II Land-Rover had everything she could possibly want for her proposed journey across the Sahara and East to Ethiopia. The roof was painted white, and attached to both sides of the body were two light weight sand-channels, in specially prepared sockets. Unlike the jagged pieces of the old oil drums, used previously for this purpose, which had bumped around in the back of Pollyanna. Two jerry cans, also in sockets, stood on the front bumper bar, there was an extra petrol tank under the near-side front seat. Above the dashboard the air vents had been screened with wire to keep insects out, and in front of them were two petrol pumps, one for each tank, placed there to catch the breeze. Barbara would later comment that they had worked very well, and during the entire journey the car never once over-heated.

Behind the front seats there was a 'deck' similar to Pollyanna's which covered the entire back; and the interior 'below deck' was lined with Dunlopillo which made packing easier and ensured the safety of breakable things. There had been extras and refinements added to Pollyanna, the standard vehicle, since Barbara first bought her. Firstly, the engine being 2 1/4 litre, gave considerably more power; dashboard pockets and well sprung seats had been added to the interior. A list Barbara would recount as reasons to keep her going.

As her equipment was being transferred from one vehicle to another, Barbara described the young man at the handover as having a slightly brusque manner, and wondered if he knew what she was feeling at that moment. Pollyanna was to remain at the technical college in Chesterfield as a demonstration car, allowing young boys to work on her, taking her out for the odd trip. Barbara was to leave Pollyanna, her companion and partner for over 10 years, in which time they had ventured where women were forbidden to go, survived treacherous terrain, and returned safely each time. As she drove away in a newer Land Rover model, her view was obscured with tears.

London
Wednesday
December 1958

Dear Mum,

Oh dear! Oh dear! I really can't see why you aren't allowed to be given a present. What would happen if you won a thousand on the lottery? However, I am enclosing a cheque for £200 and I'll send the other as you want it. If you are dead set on not doing the building, then if you are going to buy a television, or a car, or a fridge, just let me know the firms name and I will send you a cheque for them. Perhaps the alterations would be difficult and expensive, although I wouldn't want you <u>not</u> to do it because it costs more, we could pay over time. I could send the builders the cheque. However, maybe we'll wait and when I come out, we will buy a little place somewhere.

Darlin, I am at a dead loss, have sent you nothing for Christmas and now you haven't even this money. <u>Do</u> hope you bought something for Sadie from me. But things are awfully rushed and I want to be out of London for Christmas, it's a horrid time and full of memories. Won't be leaving for some time though, maybe the middle of January.

Better destroy large cheque as bank won't do both cheques.

Love,
    Barbara

St, John Hotel
Solihull
7th January 1959

Dear Mum,

As you can see, I am up in Coventry. I had sent Pollyanna home by ship from Tripoli, and she docked at Liverpool where the Rover Company bought her down. Now I am stuck here in one of the worst fogs I have ever seen.

Thank you very much for the stockings, which arrived just before Christmas. I was down to my last pair, as most of my clothes had been left in the car.

As you know I don't like Christmas, and the nicest thing about it is the fact that it is over. I stayed in London and went to friends most days. People will never let one do what one wants to and just stay home!

I was given a Siamese kitten who was perfectly enchanting, but I really couldn't keep him as his loud meows disturbed everyone. I was sorry to take him back and miss him badly.

I have been having awful trouble with my knee, it has been very painful, I haven't been able to walk on it at all. Now it has suddenly cleared up and I really think it was mostly nerves, because of all the awful Christmas rush and bustle. Luckily it wasn't weak just painful, I was reminded of you in Florence coming down sideways from the Uffizi Palace!

Thank Denny for his letter, I'll write to him soon. This is a very old-fashioned hotel and very cold, even though it is only 8.15p.m., I will have to go to bed to keep warm.

Will write again when I get home, and again many thanks for the stockings.

Love,
Barbara

London
Thursday

Dear Mum,

It was nice to get your letter I've not written I'm afraid as, as usual, there just isn't enough time to go round. Except for one or two breaks, I've been working eighteen hours a day... rest of letter missing.

London
12th January 1959

Dear Mum,

I am awful not to have written but things pile up on me, I've been up at Birmingham getting the new Land Rover and taking a three-day mechanics course, so that now I'm thoroughly confused as to what goes on under the bonnet.

Many, many thanks for the Christmas present, which arrived in a box enough to carry a dog kennel. My friends have appreciated them very much, as you know I can't eat much sweet things, but what I could was a fine. You shouldn't do these things; I know you think of me and when all's said and done, I'm generally not here, and it just sits round waiting for me.

Having had a lot of arranging to do, special permission for the journey and putting down deposits, in case they have to dig me out! Spent three hours, finally at the French Embassy today for the French Equatorial Africa visa and permits. Now there is all the business of getting petrol dropped off for me. If I don't get off soon my visas will begin to run out and I'll have to start all over again! Am very anxious to do this journey, as it will be the last really long one for me to do.

The book is going extremely well, much better than I thought, and for some reason my name has become more established. I suppose it is that old English thing of if you keep going long enough, they wake up and notice you.

It's deadly cold and snowy, I came back from Birmingham in a blinding snowstorm with the new car. Had an awful pang leaving poor old Pollyanna, but the new one is quite terrific and so very comfortable. Glad you had a nice Christmas, it is always so funny to think of it as warm. Am still trying to let the flat, can't really understand what's happened here these days, it seems as though no one wants to commit themselves. Anyhow, it must get let soon, but of course, its worrying. Gosh I shall be glad to get away, I'm so tired and nothing now will do any good, but as soon as I'm off and behind the wheel I'll feel different.

If you really do decide to build, I hope its enough money or if its more, we could pay at the end, if you want to spend it on anything else, don't think you can't because I mentioned the building. I know you want a television, and I am always trying to persuade the A.B.C. to take some of my material and pay me with a TV set, as money over there would be complicated. It's a pity really that I didn't know and see more of May Carnel here, because she could really have taken you one, they are so very cheap here.

Do hope Tal has quite recovered, poor old boy, there is nothing worse than being ill, especially when one isn't used to it.

Am having navigation lessons, the car will be bristling with compasses of every kind. My instructor, a wing commander and young enough to be my son, has an awful crush on me, confidentially, so I never really know if he's concentrating on me or the stars.

I've had a good old clean sweep of the flat, given everything portable away and just kept a few clothes I like, so now I've practically nothing to pack and could go off tomorrow if need be. It's not easy to write because the biting wind has made all out fingers crack and they are very sore, it really is b... awful weather.

When May Carnel comes back, ask her to write to me. I'd like her to drop a line, I liked her so much.

What's happening with Dennis, is he going to university?

Lots of love,
Barbara

Among the items given to me by Terri, were two battered and flaking leather suit cases, now sitting at the 'Barbara end' of my studio. One smaller than the other, they have sadly had their travel labels ripped off, leaving the leather hide underneath fluffy and pale. On top sits two wooden boxes with red stencilled lettering.

DELICATE INTRUMENT
TO BE HANDLED WITH
GREAT CARE TYPE P10
EXAMINED MANCHESTER 25 JAN 1944

ASTRONIMICAL COMPASS MKII
EXAMINED Dunstable 1st March 1943

Two rusted swing clasps on the larger, had long since loosened, no longer holding fast to their housing on the lid. The wood had darkened with age, only a glimpse of its former glory could be seen where scratches and scuffs had dented and removed a few small sections. Each corner of the heavy thick panelled box, was held with dove joints and rusted nails, green baize wedges secured the metal circular compass inside, which measured 7 inches across and 4 inches deep. Opening the box caused the array of needles to wobble. On seeing the glass of the compass, (Fig 27) the directional orange lines were obscured, wishing I knew how to use this fascinating object, a film, of what I thought was dust, sat over the glass. Wiping it with my fingers, I was stunned, there was the gritty sensation of sand still clinging to it, a remnant of Barbara's last journey perhaps.

The other compass (Fig 28) had a wooden housing painted an army green. Similar rusted hooks, that once crooked over nails to keep the lid shut. This one, the fastenings, were more difficult to move. The wear and tear of the instrument inside was more obvious, the design of it was much more complicated. It lay sideways in its bespoke housing, green baize wedges gripping on this one too. Complicated sets of dials and magnified sights, made the wanting to know how to use it even more of a yearning; I could see why Barbara needed navigation lessons. On the inside of the lid a scrap of yellowing paper says:

PACKING
SET COURSE TO "S" AND
LAT TO "9" AND PLACE
IN BOX WITH LEVELS DOWN.

How long these instruments must have spent going nowhere, hidden among the attic studio chaos. They'd sat pointed motionless at a continual one way, at their journey's end, latterly used to prop up a damaged table, or as a step to higher shelf.

Sebha, The Fezzan
23rd February 1959

Dear Mum,

  Sorry I haven't written in ages but have been on the move, lots of things happening. Am stuck here for some days, as had a bit of spring trouble. Have to take on 70 gallons of petrol for the long trek across from here to French Equatorial Africa. From then on, it's not too bad.

  It's terribly cold at night, but warms up during the day. This place has changed a lot since I was here last – new buildings and the Foreign Legionnaires have all gone. It's not nearly as colourful.

  Was very unlucky to be held up here because two bloody Frenchmen have attached themselves to me, saying they can't go alone; they have got a silly little Citroen so it will mean going very slowly and spending most of the time pulling them through the sand. Couldn't be more unfortunate, and it's impossible to explain that I want to go alone and in a way it's my job. It's been a bad start and I'm very disappointed, now the police know and won't let anyone go alone.

  Not much news, and I will write when I get to the other side. If you want to write, send the letter to London and Sidney will forward them on.

  Lots of love,
    Barbara

Barbara's new Land Rover had not been fitted with reinforced springs and when she arrived in Sebha, she was in need of help. Although she had been given permission by Chief of Police, Brigadier-General Bardi, to use government workshops, it meant a trip back to Tripoli.

Her French companion was less than pleased at the delay, and did his best to persuade her to continue. Barbara knew better. As a seasoned traveller of the desert, she knew this would be a mistake and refused. With over 70 gallons of petrol loaded, the car would sink like a stone, and with no definite way forward across the ever-changing sands, Barbara stood firm. The repairs took over 3 days.

As predicted, the route took them through a large sand mass before reaching the plains. Even with no landmarks to gauge the height and size if the dunes, the French insisted on going before her in their Citroen, despite her offering to find firm sand for them.

As Barbara followed, the Citroen was sinking deeper as the driver spun the wheels. Many hours were spent digging the car out of its sandy grave, time Barbara was unhappy to waste.

The White Nile
7th April 1959

Dear Mum,

As you can see, I am on the way down the Nile, that is, from its source to Khartoum. Have always wanted to do the trip and came up from Uganda. I put the car on the steamer, but because of her weight, they thought she wouldn't go on the steamer and moved her on a barge with two large lorries - out in the blazing sun. It's an odd arrangement. The steamer with the engine has four barges attached to it, two in front and one each side and they push them along.

The current is so strong that the whole thing goes bang into the banks, first one side and then the other.

Well, it appears that my barge was too heavy and we bashed into each bank with extra vigour, the whole thing ran away with them - and then to make matters worse one engine packed up, so in the end they had to leave my barge by the bank and come on without it. So, the baring seen to, God knows when I'll see it again.

This is a fabulous country, and for ten days we have been going through Sudd, which is a kind of swamp, almost a floating island, made from the centuries of waste washed down from the beginning of the Nile. The few people one sees are very primitive and mostly only wear a string of beads and carry a spear. They are fine looking, very black and tall. They stand for hours just on one leg. There are very many fine cattle with large horns, which they never sell, as they don't use money. This seems to infuriate the more so-called 'moderners' further North. They live almost entirely on blood from the cattle and milk, which seems a very adequate diet, judging from their appearance.

They are one or two smart Alec students on board, who try to stop one photo snapping, which is maddening considering it is the main reason I came. The natives themselves don't mind, but the students work on them.

LATER:

Still no sign of my barge. I have about 1200 ft of film in the car which will be ruined. Also, the battery will have died.

Poste Restante
Fort Archambault
French Equatorial Africa
11 September 1959

Dear Mum,

This is, as usual, in great rush. Am off tomorrow because of the rains, which were all wrong and the weather, as usual, is 'most unusual'. I should have stayed longer, for my back and head are really very bad. The very easy journey from Nairobi here, left me with a hell of a backache. However, I've been drugged to the hilt and now I know why people do take drugs; I've been going round in a lovely haze not bothering about anything- and no hangover!

Darli writes that the little article I sent *Woman's Day* is coming out soon. It is just a little bit and they didn't want any photographs, which seems a pity, as I have some good ones. I suppose they have evidently bought some at another time and want to use them up...

...I've been a bit worried about your place. You say Jimmy hasn't started yet, damn it all, it should have been finished by now. One thing is quite certain that when Jimmy gets paid, you hustle him on. I think they get a percentage of the cost. Also, what is he making you, and I hope you are not stinting on the money (after all, I can always write some more of these frightful articles!) Is the room big enough, and is he building a kind of porch, so that with open windows you have a good space? Also, you must have your own bathroom, this is most important. Even if it costs more, this really is important. I don't seem to have Jimmy's address or I'd write to him. If he is too busy, get another person to do it. My goodness, he's not building the thing himself, he can get them to hustle surely. It's been months.

Will write a longer letter on the way, the above address may catch me, it all depends on how I get held up with the weather, but don't write or send anything important, otherwise write to London.

...I suppose the bathroom will cost more, but do it anyway.

Love,
Barbara

Nigeria
26th October 1959

Dear Mum,

Time goes so quickly and I find I haven't written to you for ages. When I was coming through the French Equatorial Africa, I was so short of francs that I couldn't even write letters!

I do hope the drum arrived and you didn't have much trouble, I got them to put the value down, but let me know what the duty was, one shouldn't have to pay for presents. They use them for coffee tables, but perhaps it is too easily knocked over unless attached to a stand. I thought they were fun and couldn't leave Africa without getting a drum, but of course my flat is far too small for such things.

I'm off tomorrow for Fort Lamy, (Chad) *and a last bid to do the Tibesti, Sahara trip again. If they won't let me, I'll retrace my steps and go across the Sahara the ordinary Hoggar route.*

I am feeling much better, and my headaches have almost gone, you will be pleased, I have put on weight.

This is a beautiful country and I have some good photographs. Darli sent the article to me, I'm a bit cross as they put their own photograph in. It was supposed to be a small village of three houses and huts, and the one they put in, I'm sure, is one of the concentration camps [49] *in Kenya!*

Will write again soon.
        Love,
              Barbara

Unable to travel alone due to the occupying French rule, Barbara travelled in convoy with a guide, her wish to do this alone was rejected. The 600 miles from Tripoli to Sebha, Fezzan, was followed by a further 200 miles South across the Libyan desert to the oasis of Gatrun. From there was an unchartered wasteland of sand to Zouar in the Tibesti Mountains. A land she reports to be devoid of people, animals and birds. It took a further 600 miles and over five days to reach Gatrun.

---

[49] **Concentration camps** were designed by the British to control the Mau Mau in Africa. Known as the Pipeline these camps were renowned for their brutality. The uprising was against the British unfair labour practices and resettlement programs. Thousands of black Kenyans lost their lives.

(Fig 26)

Photograph by David Sim at Photowide.

Barbara posing with Pollyanna
outside Land Rovers Piccadilly Showroom.

Fig 27

A sand filled compass from The Barbara Toy archives.

Fig 28

Astrological compass from the Barbara Toy archives.

Inside Pollyanna. 2023

Life on the Dhow

Rice seller along the Nile.

Barbara with a captive leopard, Kenya 1959

Kenya

Young African mother.

Congolese tribes

South African family

Egyptian beach at Mersa Matruh.

Colonel LeBlanc[50], Barbara, Mohammed the Sudanese cook, Stanley Johnson, engineer and driver, and Habbib Alla, civil servant.

Barbara's travelling convoy members across the Sahara Desert.

---

[50] In 1949, just a year into the production of the Land rover, explorer **Colonel LeBlanc** drove his Land Rover from England to what is now Ethiopia, arguably inventing the automotive overland expedition.

Chapter 12
A night alone

A BORD *Si-Kiang*
Le *15th February 1960*

Dear Mum,

I received your letter here, and I can't remember if I told you I was coming by this ship. I let the flat very well and this fitted in, so that I'm more in pocket than out of it. Have been working quite well since I got on board, as there weren't any other passengers, but today, I gather four more get on here at Marseilles. I shall try to post this letter here but it's the one thing that's really difficult.

I received Sadie's letter also, for which many thanks! However, I can't really make out her plan, don't know what she means by 'stove' and 'sink' in your room, which seems 'L' shaped. Haven't you at least a wash basin in your room? I would have thought that even a shower with an immersion heater wouldn't have meant many pipes and things. And in any case, I still think it should have been bigger. However, I'm sure I don't know what I'm talking about, and you'll do as you please!

Darling, I didn't say you weren't practical, I said, in my letter to Sadie, that it was practical to put a bathroom in, even if it was much more, because it increased the value of their place. etc. etc. I know only too well that any practicality I have comes from you. For which thank <u>you</u> very much!

My knee, it appeared has a strained muscle or something, accentuated by the cold weather, but I was amused at your saying I have rheumatism, I'm riddled with it and have treatment all the time in humid and wet weather. I had an overhaul before I left with regard to the bash on my head. Re my back and eyes, the Doctor was pleased I was coming away, as he couldn't do anything until I'd had a rest after the desert struggle, which did knock me out rather. My eyes, since I've rested on ship and also been working in daylight, (which I can't do in England) have been much better, thank goodness. They are not so strained. In fact, it's probably nothing but old age! The things of the spirit are far more difficult to cope with always, than the flesh.

Am enclosing a list of ports we go to also a list of agents' names, so if you want you can write me to these ports.

Tell Sadie I'll write her soon, and thank her for the letter and plan, I know she's busy, bless her. I hope her back is better now. All my friends seem to have back or knee trouble, I think a lot to do with it is the tension people live in these days.

If Ian gets a scholarship, what does that entitle him to?

Will have to get hold of the pilot now, and see if I can get this taken ashore.

My love,
    Barbara

Dar Es Salaam
East Africa
4th march 1960

Dear Mum,

The letter you sent to London has just caught up with me. Here it is very humid, the first really hot weather we have had. And as the rainy season is just about to start, the humidity is at its worst.

Have been going into the business of that drum I sent you, the people here are livid with the authorities and said they had no right to destroy it. It really is just the same high-hat treatment I get with the car all the time. They are taking it up, so if you hear anything you will know what it is about. They're scared I think I'll write it up, although what's the use. The only thing is, as they say, they could have sent it to London. Liberties have hundreds of them, they'd no right to say they weren't allowed in England.

This really isn't any travel in the ordinary sense, I'm just in the ship to write the book and working very hard. I let the flat, I think I told you, at a good rent and so this is just about balancing out. From here we go South and round the Cape, but I think I sent you an itinerary.

Some of these places are very lovely, and the houses modern and most attractive. There is a small rail strike here and the Europeans and Asians are manning the derricks as volunteers, just anything could happen. One of them knocked our Bo-sun on the behind with a Renault car, and for about half an hour there was chaos, everyone told everyone else just what they thought of them. It would still be going on now I think, but there was a sudden downpour and everyone dived for cover.

I was a bit upset to read you'd bothered to buy one of my books, I'll get Murray's to send you some....

Love,
   Barbara.

Si-Kiang
Durban
South Africa
16th March 1960

Dear Mum,

Your letter was waiting for me when I arrived here. Now it's getting a little cooler, thank goodness, as it's been awfully humid the last three ports. I didn't actually go ashore properly at Beira, S.A. as was working rather well and didn't want to break into it.

This seems to be a very noisy, busy city, the kind I don't like and has sky scrapers all along the front. We stayed six days, I believe and the Rover Agents will lend me a car if I want it.

You will be amused to hear that the Rover people cabled me, wanting to buy the car back and leave the credit if I want one later. I had said I'd like to sell as was never very keen on it, but of course I can't ask for the money as they gave it to me! In any case it's an unnecessary expense when I am in London, as one can't use it much as the parking restrictions are getting hopeless. The Rover Company will always lend me a car for odd weeks if I want it. The car is now on its way with a journalist from the 'Daily Mail' to North Africa....

...We took on an English passenger at Lorenzo just near to here, he was a commercial traveller so knew the country very well. Otherwise, it now looks as though we wouldn't have any passengers until Cape town, which is as well, from my point of view.

Have been working on deck and look very brown and freckled, my hair has bleached an odd honey colour, so I really look a bit of a guy.

Do let me know what the extra money the room is costing and <u>answer</u> this! Also, what do you do about Jim?

The book progresses very slowly and I'm having the same trouble I had with the last one, in that I tried to do too much, especially having four cameras to cope with. In any case, I'm always a bit bored with the whole thing when it is over, and from my point of view, it's already in the past....

...This is a very scrappy letter I am afraid; I've got such a large mail today and seem to have been writing for hours. My mail seems to get bigger and bigger and one is always fighting someone, either the landlords or the Income Tax people. Or bills one knows ones paid and they swear one hasn't. I have a friend who burns all letters and I really think she's got something there.

Greta Morrison, I see her when I'm in London, she pushes me on, gives me a dig or shames me by telling all the other authors work really hard.

Hope you are all quite well.

    Love,
        Barbara

Barbara would work on one of her books, describing one journey as she travelled on another. On her fifth expedition in 1959 (written about in her book *In Search of Sheba* 1961) saw her time eaten up by the pressure of publishing, and the organization it took to complete sometimes difficult and unusual events. On one such occasion, Barbara decided to visit what was known as the Princess/Prince Mountain, Wahni, in an Ethiopian park. By this time, she had already travelled through Libya, The Central Republic of Africa, The Congo, Tanganyika and the Sudan. The mountain, locals named Wehni Amba, was a place known to have imprisoned the brothers and sisters of the heirs to the throne centuries earlier. The Princes of the Blood were said to have lived in extreme discomfort, with little food and clothing. Barbara wanted to be the first human to spent the night there in over two hundred years, saying her American market loved to read of firsts. Barbara persuaded a local French helicopter pilot to drop her as near as he could to the top of the mountain, a sharp sided finger like projection with no landing site. As they drew near Barbara had to jump to the crumbling ridge, it took three attempts get her back. She describes the return journey in a small article:

> 'He brought the helicopter slowly in towards the ledge. I watched the top rotor arm come perilously near to the mountain above me as I crouched on the rocks. The engine was racing furiously as Jean tried to counteract the wind and the near side skid moved in over the ledge and began bouncing up and down. I grabbed the wine jug, my cameras and the spoor which I collected for later identification, and jumping over the skid, placed them on the seat. I had to make three trips before I was able to climb in finally, and immediately we were off. It had been much more difficult to board the helicopter than to than to leave it, for by now I realised what the whole operation entailed, and how hazardous it was.
>
> We circled the mountain again. It looked so different to me now. I knew it all – the half shell of the church and the crosses of tufa, the fallen junipers and the

olive tree where I had slept and finally the great door of the guardhouse swinging open over the precipice to the valley below. As we turned towards the plateau, I wished we had not come away. The vultures were settling back again, the only sign of life on the Wahni, (Fig 30) and of the animals there was no sign.

The Cornhill (Fig 31) No. 1027. Spring 1961. 'Wahni, the Princes Prison Mountain.' Barbara Toy. Pg.30 John Murray Pub.

A small scrap of an unknown newspaper review:

She finally persuaded a French pilot to take and spend 24hours alone among the prison ruins on the Peak. As usual she was armed only with her truncheon.

Films she took there were later shown on the British television and she wrote a book *In Search of Sheba* about her experiences.

On her return trip across the desert, she had an Arab guide who spoke no English. They nearly came to grief when the Land Rover's half shaft broke early in the journey.

It took her 90 days to cover 460 miles of desert pulled only by the car's front wheels. At one point it took three days to cover ten yards of soft sand.

A letter dated the 8th July 1959 stated that as Barbara, purporting to be a correspondent to the BBC, would benefit from subsequent publications of the event and therefore she was to pay for her own helicopter flight. She received, from the flight control at TAR, a bill of £415.00 rounded off to £125 per hour. There was no evidence in her archives that she was ever a BBC correspondent.

Cape Town
South Africa
28th March 1960

Dear Mum,

Your letter has just arrived, it was lucky because we were supposed to sail yesterday evening and are held up with strikes; otherwise, I would have missed it. This is a beautiful city but there is a lot of native trouble, and it looks as though the balloon may go right up. We shall all be glad to get away.

Now we take on other passengers and it will be a little full, however it is the home stretch, and I must work terribly hard, as I am very much behind with the book.

Am terribly thrilled to hear about Ian and his scholarship. How many more years has he got of study? It's such fun always, to hear of people doing what they really want.

It has been cold and windy here but today is perfect, it is difficult to stick to the work. I return home on Easter week end, which couldn't be worse as it is always a mad house trying to cross the channel at such a time.

Give my love to Sadie, I am always meaning to write but time goes so fast these days and there is so little of it.!

My love and look after yourself.

Barbara

London
18th August 1960

Dear Mum,

You will think me the end, not having written for so long, but I am so hectic and bogged down with work, that I just don't get round to writing until the late hours and then just drop into bed quite tired.

I also find I didn't send the photographs to you, so will send them airmail in a day or two. Had quite a surprise when Dorothy Scott walked in on me the other day. She is making her way round the world by ship and coach, I gather, looking terribly well and so nice. I've got her horribly on my conscience, as I haven't got in touch again. It's a bit of a difficult life having not only to work, but to look after one's private life as well. Really must marry a pansy who likes housework, it would take that off my shoulders at least.

They seem to be having a bad summer here, but from my point of view it doesn't really matter, as when the weather is nice one wants to get out, now there's not much temptation.

Will write again in a day or two, when I have sorted things out.

Many thanks for the lovely hankies.

Love,
Barbara

(Fig 29)

Barbara with helicopter pilot Jean Massot.

Fig 30

The Wahni ridge where Barbara landed, with vultures circling.

Ruins of the church on the Wahni mountain.

From the top of the Peak at 19,000ft

Cooking for one.

THE CORNHILL MAGAZINE

No. 1027 Spring 1961

	PAGE
BIOGRAPHICAL NOTES	v
THE GOLDEN DOMES OF IRAQ AND IRAN (*Illustrated*) by Freya Stark	1
THE NOBLE CAT OF ESTEPONA (A Story) by John D. Stewart	9
WAHNI, THE PRINCES' PRISON MOUNTAIN (*Illustrated*) by Barbara Toy	16
THIS MORNING, THIS EVENING, SO SOON (A Story) by James Baldwin	32
THE MODERN BUDDHA (A Poem) by Mary Lomer	74
AFTER DEBASEMENT IN MANY PLACES (A Poem) by Peter Green	75
INTIMATIONS OF IMMORTALITY (A Story) by St. Clair de la Mare	76

JOHN MURRAY, 50 ALBEMARLE STREET, LONDON, W.1

Fig 31

A phallic sign, Mali

Barbara sunbathing on deck on her way to a long-deserved break on the Cote d'Azur.

Barbara on way to Lalibela, Ethiopia.

Tukul houses, Ethiopia.

A girl from Harar. Ethiopia

Ethiopian drummer

Chapter 13
The Riviera blues.

After an unusually long break, Barbara took off again on her 6th expedition, leaving the Riviera and most important to her, the sun.

London
22nd September 1960

Dear Mum,

I'm sorry I haven't written for so long but things have been hectic – which seems to be a natural state for me when I am in England. In any case, it has been a disastrous year for me in many ways.; however, everything passes. Hope you are all well and looking forward to the summer; for our part it is well on the way to Autumn and rather coolish.

Have been very worried about the Congo[51] as I still can't get news from my friends there. I send a copy of the London Evening News to you. It has some photographs and bits from my trip in Ethiopia.

London's traffic gets more and more chaotic, they have now put parking meters in all the most improbable places, one right across our door! I think I have told you, I sold my car, as it is impossible to use it in London anymore and shall wait until my next trip.

I meant to send the enclosed ages ago but time went on, sorry about it. Also, been tied to the desk with this work, my letter writing has to be done really at the end of a long day.

---

[51] Congo: Nationalist uprising in 1960 to 1965 was to overcome colonial rule.

Have been having a long to do list about my old cottage, the one that was left with tenants in it. No one would buy it because they couldn't get vacant possession and now, they have come down on me to re-roof it. This would cost between £400 and £500 and as I only have 25/- a week for it, it was going to take a long time to get my money back! However, I think I've persuaded the tenants to buy it, I won't get much, but at least it will be off my hands. I am keeping my fingers crossed that the deal will go through.

There is very little news here, except that the whole of London seems to be rebuilding; the buildings to the South and West of me are being pulled down and office buildings are going up. There is an awful lot of speculation going on and prices are up to the most ridiculous level.

Love,
    Barbara

London
29th July 1960

Dear Mum,

I'm so terribly sorry that it has been so long since I've written to you. I've been horribly busy and with a hell of a lot on my mind. I am working endlessly on some film, which incidentally, you may see some time on TV. But it's very concentrated work and my eyes get very bad with the strain.

Glad you like the article in 'Cornhill', it is taken from the new book and now I hear it is also going to be done in an American magazine called 'Mam'selle'. I'm thrilled about this, as I've always wanted to get into the USA market. They of course love everything that is 'the only one in the world' type of thing.

I laughed about you saying I was timid child, I still am about some things, especially people, I'd rather be dropped on a hundred mountains, than walk into any cocktail party, the only difference being that I <u>now can</u> walk in without anyone knowing how I feel! I think I have the place in France, but I am not quite certain. It has been a packet of trouble financially; the whole thing may yet be dropped. I want it so I can let this place, which is too expensive and go down there. It is in a tiny village clustering round an eleventh century castle built by Grimaldi. It has become a little 'touristy' now and was *first discovered because Renoir lived there. Later, people like Simone, Collette and Picasso have, at different times, lived there. I also thought it would be a place for Ian to go when he finishes his studying and wants to wander a bit – felt that what was good enough for Renoir would be good enough for our Ian! Shall send you photos of it if it ever eventuates. It is really just a part of the old castle ramparts, and the whole thing will fall down with the first nail that's put into the wall.*

A couple of American friends of mine, women, a doctor of philosophy and another a professor of something or other are, motoring through to Australia and I've given them your address. I'd love you to see them sometime, although they won't be there for some months. They work at a University in New York state and are great fun. They are very appreciative of anything that's done for them, and I'd be most grateful if you would have them over for tea or something. They are quite good value and you'll find them fun.

Mamie Marks turned up one day looking fine and full of beans, seemed to be on a whirlwind trip round the world, from what I could make out.

I see quite a lot of Minna Schuler who has a beautiful place about twenty-five miles from London. She's got a lovely garden and two nice cats. We're having a fine summer, it's very difficult to stick at one's desk.

There is an exodus this week end, when just everyone who can, goes away for the first two weeks in August, and London is quiet as a tomb. I rather enjoy it as it's the only time you can get any service in a restaurant.

Everyone is in the doldrums here at the moment, because of the financial situation and we are in for a bad slump. Inflation is really upon us, and there is going to be bad trouble. One gets so bored with the incessant talk of lack of money – they've put 2/- on whiskey and gin which is bad enough, and cigarettes have gone up also. I don't smoke myself and I'm always surprised at the money people spend on smokes, often when they can't afford it.

This is just to let you know I am still alive and I'll write again soon.

Love,
        Barbara.

This time in a more modern Land Rover, Barbara's third, a 109" series II Dormobile, registration 5751 WD, she drove from Timbuktu to Tripoli, crossing the Sahara diagonally from Algeria, the Niger River to Libya, taking in the rock paintings near the oasis of Djanet. Later to described in her book *'The Way of the Chariots.'* 1964.

Postcard

Tombouctou
Republique Soudanaise
23rd January 1962

Finally arrived here across the desert, got a bit off track and didn't turn up until the dead of night. It's fun to be here, lovely place. No mail at all as I think they only know their own spelling. Letters would reach me c/o British High Commission, Accra, Ghana.

Love,
         Barbara

Tamale
Northern Ghana
25th February 1962

Dear Mum,

As you see I am in Northern Ghana and on my back across the Sahara. Was very lucky to get my return visa so soon, as now the crossing won't be all that hot. I hope to go diagonally across and into Libya, whether it is possible remains to be seen.

Have loved this place, and find Ghanaians very nice and friendly and such a change after the suspicious people of Mali, who nearly sent me round the bend. This won't be all that long a trip, and I hope to spend sometime in the South of France, as I have let my London flat till September.

Got into a bit of a muddle as the bank sent me £250 in travellers' cheques for the trip, to Timbuktu, and they never turned up so have been trying to make do with very little. Shall get the money back eventually but it takes time.

Thanks for the cutting about me, my bit of the rampart, what is always called so grandly an apartment isn't near Cagnes, a few miles from Nice.

Was surprised to hear Ian had left home, has he finished his studies? I always wonder about him and what he wants to do, but he never writes at all. I gather he wants to go it alone the whole time. Perhaps Sadie would write me about him. I could help if he wants to come abroad but I gathered his work at the school wasn't finished yet. I never really know what any of you are doing.

It won't be easy to contact me on this trip, although a letter Poste Restante, Tamanrasset, Hoggar Mountains, French Sahara, may find me or finally c/o British Embassy, Tripoli, Libya. (To await arrival) but if I do get there, I shall be very pleased.

Hope you are well.

Love,
Barbara

Barbara was very often greeted by officials as both a difficult anomaly and an inconvenience. A foreigner, and a woman alone, was both a responsibility and a burden. Although Barbara had all her permits in place, officials would regularly scrutinise her passport and papers, keeping her waiting. On her way to Timbuktu the Chief of Police questioned why indeed, she would need to go at all? Often, she would keep any information vague, not committing to times and dates. She was also unsure of how to explain her fascination with the desert. How could she help them understand her romance with faraway places, and the pull she felt to push beyond the known, to get to the ends of the earth? Their concerns may have been justified.

As she journeyed further, the Land Rover side window was shattered. A bullet had narrowly missed her chest. The car had been climbing through and area of thick undergrowth. She had disregarded the soldiers at the last post, and found herself in what had been cannibal country. Seeing herself as skinny and tough to eat, she carried on with wind whistling through the hole in the window and shards of glass falling around her. Barbara decided, had she been wounded, or died there, no one would have been able to find her.

Again, she longed for the wide-open spaces of the desert. Even though once there, she faced the prospect of the sand storms, that would cover the car for hours. Prepared, she had an old wooden tucker box that kept the sand from her cameras and note books. It also housed an old compass given to her by Sir Francis Chichester, who she describes as a fine traveller in her book *The Way of the Chariots* 1964.

Barbara later wrote in 1967, a letter to her mother with a slightly less glowing account of him:

…. There was quite a reception for Fran Chichester (Fig 32) *when he returned as you probably saw on T.V. I think the whole thing has been overdone and the public are getting rather tired of it.*

Terri had handed me the leather-bound compass as gently as a thin-skinned egg. 'This was from Francis Chichester,' she informed me, she seemed pleased; someone she had heard of at last. I looked at her as my hand cupped the leather cased compass. I went to give it back but she waved me away, her arms high in the air, as if the gesture had annoyed her. More for the pile I thought, overwhelmed by having another part of Barbara's story in my hands, and equally terrified of the responsibility. What was I to do, if I was to ever tell her story, would I do her justice?

Terri hadn't ventured into the room for some time, leaving me to file some papers and carefully place Ian's newspaper drawings in folders. I'd been worried she would find the scraps of paper that Ian would draw on after they had argued. Unflattering comments and cartoon depictions of whatever the problem was. Terri knew of them, but seeing them would be something else. The studio was changing as the black bags of rubbish were collected. The paintings of Ian's sold, the light was allowed in, now the unused art boards had gone. I had spent so much time there absorbed in two worlds, one with the artist, and one with the explorer. The outside world seemed dull as I was finding myself slowing down to make the experience last longer. When Terri finally appeared, she was suddenly feverishly looking through the remaining old tins and boxes.

'What are you looking for?' I asked Terri.

'Barbara had a small gold necklace that was a miniature book of the Quran, but I can't find it. She was searching you know, for herself, I guess, she kept an open mind on everything, religion too.' 'Yes', I chuckled, 'she never seemed that keen on Christmas!'

Barbara had many religious texts in her library, her searching not solely land based. On a trip to Tamanrasset in 1963, she kindly gave a local priest a lift. In her book *The Way of the Chariots* 1964, she describes him as a man of the land, his colour blending with his surroundings. They agreed they were both looking for something, for her it was as much about the people as it was about the wide open and empty places. The kindness of the tribe's people she had met in her beloved desert, and solitude and oneness with the earth, that made her feel whole. Both agreed it was the things found in unexpected moments, that held their fascination and trust.

The esteemed travel writer Laurens van der Post, described Barbara's journeys, as a profound inner search in the most inhospitable place. He wrote a review of her book *The Way of the Chariots*, 1964 for which she received from the Long-Distance Land-Rover Association, the trophy only once before awarded.'

London
12th June 1962

Dear Mum,

As you see I am back in England – cold and rainy most of the time. As I have let my flat until the end of the year, I shall be going back to France to write the book, and hope to get away about the 25th of this month. However, I've a hell of a lot of work here and it remains to be seen whether I can make it by then.

London gets more and more ghastly, I think I have almost come to the time when I don't want to live in the hustle and bustle anymore; it is like a madhouse, and the traffic problem overshadows everything else.

At the moment I am in Bertie's flat, as he is away in Yugoslavia but comes back at the end of the week, when I'll probably go to a hotel, or down to Minna's place. The servant problem being what it is, she, Minna, was forced to take an 'unmarried mother and baby' to get any domestic help at all.

You say in your last letter that if you won a lottery you'd come over. Well, I really don't see why you shouldn't come over if you want to. I'll certainly sell some shares and send the money, and you can fly to Nice (seven miles from my place) and spend the last summer there with me. I shall be working, but it has a nice terrace. The only thing against the flat, is that it is rather a lot of steps, but we could get over that.

Why don't you come, I would love it, and you may as well, what with atomic bomb, I'm all for doing what one wants, now; goodness knows what the politicians have in store for us.

Another thing, I would love to have one of Ian's paintings, but do <u>not</u> want him to give me one, I would like to buy it. Probably he'll say 'What does the silly old… want to buy something she's never seen.' But there it is, I can't very well see them from this distance, and I'd love to have one that he, himself, likes. Anyhow ask him, he can only say 'no' at worst.

Let me know about coming over and I'll arrange it.

I'm taking a girlfriend down to France for a few weeks, but will then be alone working.

Love to you all,
    Barbara

London
23rd June 1962

Dear Mum,

Just received your letter, don't be b… silly, if you want to come over, then come. I have the money, and even if I didn't, I'd steal it! I've never let the lack of money stop me doing anything I wanted. In any case, I've told everyone you're coming, so there it is. Although I didn't get all the money from Ewing's estate, as you know I wouldn't fight it, – I got enough, and after paying my numerous debts, I invested quite well. At the moment things are bad in that line, but they will recover. It's bad having all one's eggs in one basket, but there it is.

If you feel you don't want to come, then that's another thing, I shall be working very hard but hope to get the worst of the book underway, also the alterations to the flat, before you come.

I leave tomorrow with my old friend Migs (Minna), for France taking everything but the kitchen sink in the Land Rover.

This in haste, darling, as I'm a bit rushed parking.

My love to you all,

    Barbara

22 Rue Paissobran
Cagnes – sur – Mer
A.M. France
27th July 1962

Dear Mum,

Have just got your letter, very correctly addressed.

I shall certainly come over for Christmas, if that is what you <u>really</u> want. If, because of the bad steps here, you would rather wait to come to London, then that's okay. However, London these days is rather chaotic and I have a parking meter right outside the door, which means I can't even keep a car in London. Also, my flat is tiny and dark and one has to keep the lights on, practically all day. But I don't want you not to come if you'd like the jaunt. Otherwise, I'll come out, and this means I should have the book in its final stages, giving me something to hurray for.

I'm going potty here with the builders, who are awfully slapdash and vague and it's difficult to work in such a mess. However, things will sort out and I'll let it, if I can, for the winter to help with the repair bills. Everyone does that here, although really it can be just as cold there in winter as it is in England. I shall bring some colour photographs of it so you can see, and they are generally much better than the original.

I wasn't cross about Ian not writing, it's a fee country he can do as he likes, but that is why I didn't write him personally.

Love to all,

Barbara

22 Rue Paissobran
Cagnes – sur – Mer
A.M. France
20th August 1962

Dear Mum,

Am at last able to get down to my typewriter, and to thank you for the lovely stockings, and for the cable which arrived on my birthday. You shouldn't have bothered to do these things, though it is nice to be remembered. I would have written earlier but I have been laid low with the most awful cold, almost flu, which got a second chill on it as I was camping amongst the cement bags upstairs. I don't think the old nine-hundred-year-old disturbed dust helped matters. However, I have now come out of it, feeling a bit washed out, but recovered. Funnily enough, everyone has a cold at the moment, even though the weather hasn't changed much.

At long last my alterations to the bedroom, with its little bathroom, is more of less finished. An awful lot of fuss for such a tiny room, with washbasin and bidet. I was going to have a tiny bath, but we found it meant getting extra gas meters and wasn't, I felt, worth the expense. Anyhow, what I have got is what the locals have, and who am I to change the customs.

I hope to stay and finish the book, but it looks like I will have to go back to London at the end of September, for two reasons, firstly they won't insure my car for Europe another month (very high hat of them!). Secondly, my flay becomes vacant so I'll get back and work hard on the book and re-let the flat, leaving the car with the Rover people. It's really not easy to work here, I don't discipline myself enough and get distractions, not least the good weather. It's fun my coming over to Australia, for it will mean that I have four summers in a row.

On the 7th, 8th and 9th of September, we have the Kermesse Heroique (Fig 33) here, which is a time when all the people dress up in Medieval costume and do a kind of tableau on the ramparts of the chateau. It ought to be fun, very picturesque.

I got Sadie's lovely hankies and card, I'll write her in a day or two, I am terribly behind with my letters as you can imagine.

By the sounds that are going on upstairs, you'd think the electrician and the mason were killing each other. They sound as though they are having a hell of an argument, but probably agreeing that the 'English Miss' below is mad, that she spend all the sunny days typing.

Sorry about this disjointed note, but I keep being called away.

Will write again later.

    Love,
        Barbara

P.S. had such a nice letter from Ian, it's a pity he doesn't like writing letters, he writes such good ones – and also, what is prosperity going to do with no collection of letters by the famous artist! He got it all wrong though, for he thanked <u>me</u> for £50. I didn't give it to him he won it with his premium bonds.

Cagnes - sur- Mer
10th November 1962

Dear Mum,

I'm enclosing this letter to London, although I have written all this news in a letter, I've posted to you direct. Sometimes letters sent to London arrive earlier. As I have said, I am held up with a bad back and leave from Rome on the 18th, where I connect with the Qantas plane, arriving Sydney 20th in the morning, I think the flight number is 732.

In the other letter, I have sent a cheque for £25 hoping Sadie would buy a bird of some sort and some bubbly. So sorry about all this, but I sprained my back cranking the Land Rover, and it has got bad carrying all the heavy suitcases around.

Difficult to write as I am lying down.

    See you soon.
        Love, Barbara.

Richmond Hill Hotel
Richmond
20th may 1963

Dear Mum,

Was terribly shattered to hear from Sadie, that you'd broken your wrist. What an awful thing to have happened. Oh dear, oh dear, who do you think you are – Tarzan or something – shinning up and down those steps. I suppose it is not easy now either, to keep you in bed for any length of time. Sadie said you were going to the aunts for a little while, that ought to be much better and you will have company all day long. Not so good for Denny [52] though.

We had a chaotic arrival, late in the evening, bad dock, could not land or get proper customs men, the only bright spot was that they had sent my Land Rover down to meet me.

We got off the next morning, and certainly had a time getting settled. I thought I would go mad; I have never been so tired. However, Ian will have told you, he seems to like London, so he might even come round on the English!

We have had a couple of lovely warmish and sunny days, but now we are back to normal with cold and showers again. Ian is going to stay with Mina Dyason for a week or more, and I am off about a job, which came through a very dear young friend, bless him, so thoughtful, it will certainly be lovely to see him again.

No news really, things are difficult for me, as I am not in my flat, and yet to clear everything up, so things must pile up until I return.

Look after yourself, darling.

Love to all,
Barbara

---

[52] **'Denny'** Dennis, Barbara's second nephew, children of her sister Sadie.

73 St, James's Street
London S.W.1.
1ˢᵗ July 1963

Dear Mum,

Have been back here some days, but am working hard. Found your notes waiting for me. I am very thrilled to find your wrist is progressing so well. What a long business it is for you, the whole thing so maddening. I wrote you from Italy, but I think it went surface mail so it won't arrive for some time. You ask about the job, it was nothing very exciting, just a lot of hard work with a cheque at the end of it – such is life!

I haven't contacted Minna or Ian, he hasn't a telephone, so I don't know what he is up to. He is a lucky person that Minna was so kind; she knows everyone in this world and can do far more for him than I ever could. Let's hope that he has gone off to Italy or Greece, or Spain, as the weather here is frightful and quite cold.

No news, just working hard.

Love to the family and look after yourself.

   Love,
     Barbara.

73 St, James's Street
London S.W.1.
1ˢᵗ July 1963

Dear Mum,

Glad to see you are back in your home again. There is nothing like one's own little corner. Do be careful! Have been meaning to write but as usual in England, have been busy.

I sent off a cable for your birthday, a day early, as I don't think they deliver on Sundays. Hope you get it. Also sent off a little gift, but what with the rushed mail, I'm afraid it may arrive late. Do hope you have a good birthday and don't get too 'squiffy'.

As you will probably have heard, Ian is going off with John Sandford Smith to Quetta. It is a nice trip, and they'll more or less be following a route I took; though of course, they will have company. He's lucky to have the chance. It's a good thing for him to see as much as he can quickly, as at twenty-six, it must be different to start again to earn your living.

After quite a struggle, I've let the flat as last, thank goodness, and am in the throes of packing. Had given up hope of doing it before Christmas, now things have worked out nicely. London, of course, is chaos because of this stupid Christmas business. None of us keep it up here, it's just a hold up for anything that has to be done.

Shall be going to Paris to meet a friend I think, though not certain, and wanted to go down to Cagnes, but my tenants, I hear, are still in it. Am waiting to hear. In any case, as it is too small to have anyone else stay.... we shall see.

Sorry, this is a much-hurried note, I have many last-minute things to do and not having any maid now, have to leave the place clean after I have packed.

Have already broken two nails!

Love,
Barbara

Terri would still pop a cuppa into the attic studio, to help wash the dust from my throat. The small bulbous cup would teeter on one of my dwindling piling systems of papers and drawings. Standing near to me she stroked a once hidden painting of Ian's. Her fingers hovered over the beautifully rendered depiction of a length of patterned material, and the tears began to well. I placed a hand on her shoulder.

'Come and sit with me for a while, no need to go charging off.'
She perched on the only chair, and I sat before her on the floor, her sadness all too evident.

'Where did you meet him?' I asked, both curious and in an effort to have her know I cared deeply about her husband, not just the artist and his work. She smiled as a treasured memory returned.

'He had been to Pakistan to help in an eye hospital, really to be able to paint, but he helped in the makeshift wards too. Barbara helped him with who she knew, he needed to be out of Australia. He wanted to be an artist, something his father didn't understand, he thought there would be no money in it, and he should concentrate on the commercial side of things.

He became quite ill when he was in Pakistan,' she continued, 'and had to come back to London. I was a district nurse at the time and was sent to see him every day. I was to administer a daily injection, so you could say, I met him bum first!' We both laughed loudly and clinked tea mugs.

Over the next year of our visits, I could see she was struggling. I made the effort to talk of him as often as I could, she seemed to light up whenever we did.

'He seemed to have a bond with Barbara,' she told me one day. 'I think she loved the thought that he would be a famous artist. I don't know if she ever helped him financially, she was never in one place for long, so ...' she shrugged. 'Of course, that tailed off as she got older,' Terri pondered for a moment. 'Not sure she was on her best behaviour when she wasn't travelling, then again, no clue what she was like when she was!'

Terri was up again in an instant and collecting the tea I hadn't finished, slipping out of the room and down the stairs as if floating. Alone again, our talks brief but important, spurred on past the doubts of my own ability to save the remnants of a slowly reducing family. Collating the letters, a narrative was forming, nothing was lost in the letters of Barbara, her strengths sat along her doubts, her frustrations at aging and her never ending need to move, all flowed in the natural way of things, as with anyone. Was she lost or was she found, were there answers or more questions?
Through it all, her roots were Australian, her mother the anchor.

London
16th September 1964

Dear Mum,

Many thanks for the lovely stockings – it was very sweet of you to remember my birthday, but birthdays are rather out of place these days, they come so quickly. Sorry not to have written earlier but I have been away.

I think my publishers have sent you a copy of my book, it came out a couple of days ago. I was very fortunate in that Laurens van der Post, whom I admire, had written a very nice appreciation of it.

Here in England the weather has been marvellous and we have had a lot of sun, thank goodness.

There isn't much news, I have been negotiating the sale of Minna's house. Not really for myself and it has to be a great deal of trouble and expense during that time.

There is a lot of uncertainty here about the coming election, and if the Socialists get in, life will be very, very difficult – there won't be any place for anyone who doesn't work and things will be rather dreary, I think.

Hope you are well and looking forward to the summer.

My love to all,

Barbara

London
14th November 1964

Dear Mum,

Wonder how you're getting on, now that the summer is coming your way. Let us hope that you have as good a one as we did. The good weather had gone on and on here and the Autumn was wonderful. Now at last, the wind and rain are with us and, what with the Christmas rush having started already, London is the <u>end</u>.

I hope to leave in about two- or three-weeks' time and am having the usual round of injections, procuring of visas, etc. I don't know why it always seems to happen that all this has to be done, when it's getting near to Christmas. Couldn't be worse. Have also had the business of letting the flat etc. But things are falling well into shape and as it is just a matter of getting everything done in the time.

Can't type as much as the Cholera injections have, and are, giving me hell.

I do hope the copy of my book turns up at last, can't think what has happened to them. It is all going very well and because of the nice cover, is being used in most book shops windows. I shouldn't think there will be much done about it in Australia, as the publishers have lost Darli, their publicity girl, who was so good.

The Land Rover has been in the Piccadilly showroom window this week, quite a good display and it has sold quite a lot of copies of the book.

Hope you are well.

*Love,
Barbara*

73 St, James's Street
London S.W.1.
15th December 1966

Dear Mum,

Hope you got my cable today and something from David Jones. And I also hope you are having a better day than we are here! Many Happy Returns.

There seems to have been a lot of excitement about Francis Chichester arriving in Sydney, he certainly got a lot of publicity this end. He's a marvellous little man.

Your letter must have crossed my other one. I am sorry I have taken so long to write, when one is on the typewriter all day and every day, letter writing comes a good second I'm afraid. Of course, I love to get letters from you and to hear your news.

I sent some money to you which I should have sent at the end of September but things are in a bit of a muddle here at the moment as you must know. I shall send some more at the end of December.

It looks as though I shall be asked to do a radio play in a bit of a rush, so that will keep me on the old typewriter once again! I'm thrilled to do it though, if they <u>do</u> ask me.

Hope you all have a nice Christmas.

Love,

Barbara

It wasn't long before Barbara took to the road again in 1967/8. Her travels, this time, were captured in her seventh book *The Highway of the Three Kings*, and spanned her journey across the Yemen.[53] War was raging in Yemen at the time. She travelled across Saudi Arabia, Jordan and Lebanon, following the old incense route to Damascus. Joining the train of pilgrims on route to Mecca, on the way, she would marvel at the thousands of people on the move in overloaded trucks, and at the seamless erection of open-ended tents. Here, the travellers would be served a spicy stew while seated at long benches and tables, or on the floor. She also noted the large amounts of debris left behind when the camp moved on, listing Coke bottles, old tyres, plastic bottles and broken sandals, discarded truck parts left in pools of oil. An unwelcome aftermath of this wave of migration, once the tents were folded away, and the lumbering pilgrimage continued. The nearer they were to Mecca the more the Muslims naturally united and unified in their shared experience.

Barbara understood the Arab nomads need to keep moving, questioning if such religious pilgrimage would benefit the Christian faith.

Tiredness would soon hound her, as she returned to her solo journey. Single tracks that spread for miles, played tricks on her as she drove, at times, through the night. Unusual fantasy trees would emerge in her mind, closing in around her, even though she was certain to be travelling along an open plain. The morning light releasing the car from the strangling imagined branches.

---

[53] The British authorities left Southern **Yemen** in 1967 as a result of terrorist insurgence. North Yemen already had independence.

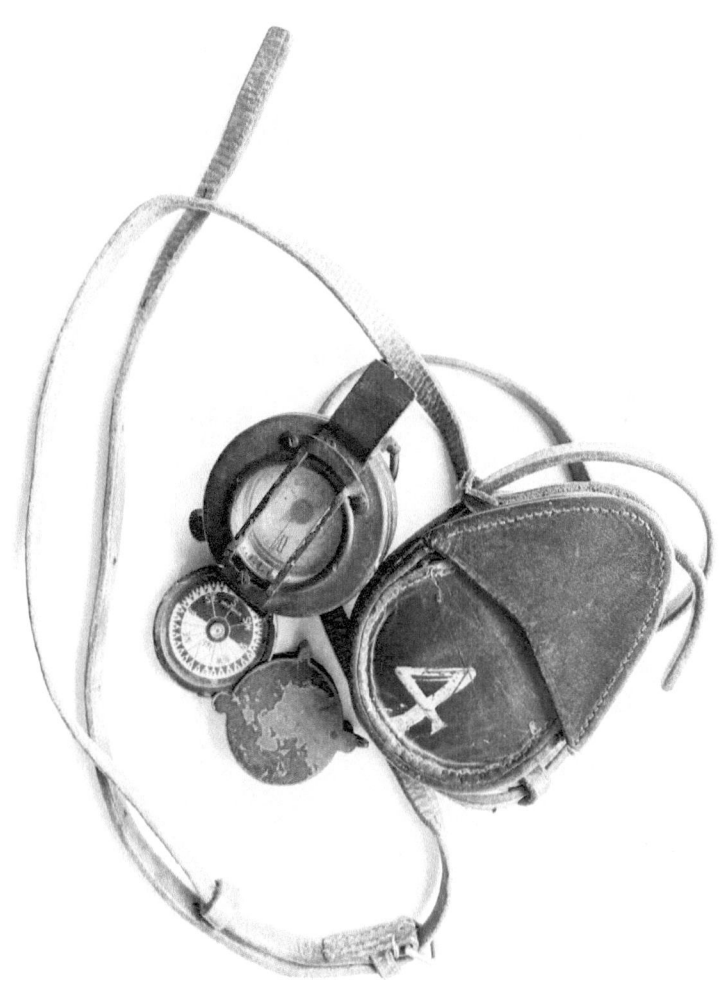

Fig 32

Small compasses from the Barbara Toy archives.

Fig 33

Kermesse Medievale poster.

Barbara near the Yemen border. Looking very pleased to be back in her favourite country.

Pilgrims from the Hajj to Mecca.

Barbara's house in Sey'un, Southern Arabia.

'Fatima, the water - girl, who supplied all the drinking water of my house every day, and swept the rooms with a palm leaf brush.'
(Barbara's quote from the reverse of photo)

'Salih, his wife and donkey making their interminable journey up and down the ramp from the well. Salih's wife plaited strips of palm leaf as she walked.'
Seyuin, Yemen.
(Barbara's quote from the reverse of photo.)

Kanaga Dancer, Songhai, Mali.

Tibu woman, central Sahara

Ghadames, Libya

Rock Paintings, Djaret, French Sahara

Barbara standing beneath the cave of rock paintings

Chapter 14
Wear and tear

St. James
London
8th January 1967

Dear Mum,

So many thanks for the Christmas presents, which arrived before the day, it was sweet of you but really, as you know I do not 'keep up' Christmas at all. I am glad you had a good time, and that the weather hasn't been that trying. Here, we have a cold spell but it is the first this year and the winter is being rather nice.

I am terribly upset that you did not receive the money which I sent off from Lloyd's bank on the 12th December, as you had said previously, that it was better that it went direct into your bank at Northridge, that is what happened. Perhaps they have received it and just not let you know? However, I have telephoned my bank and told them to confirm that it arrived, and to let you know about this. And as I said, I am sending another lot this month but haven't got round to it, for in the usual way, I am meeting a deadline with some work and until the end of this month, am concentrating rather a lot.

Shall write Sadie and Tal in a day or two. Sorry about this funny typewriter but my own has broken down, so I am having to use one which jumps all over the place.

I do hope that 1967 is a good one for you, and that the garden grows well but not too vigorously.

Love,
    Barbara

British High Commission, Aden
Federation of Southern Arabia
Mukalla 9am.

Dear Mum,

As you can see, I am once again in Mukalla, which I visited ten years ago on my Saudi trip. Have come overland from Aden after some trouble and leave today for Hadhramaut valley in the interior.

There is a lot of trouble in Aden [54] *but it is quiet enough here and very pleasant. I am hoping to go further North into the Saudi Arabian parts, but this is in the lap of the Gods!*

I hope you are all well. Have had a letter from Sadie and shall answer it from Seyuin. I am confused to hear Ian will go to England. He has no sympathy with their way of life, however, one's life is one's own and he knows what he wants to do. Most people are getting out of Europe these days

Love,
Barbara

Hope you can read this, writing it in the Land Rover

British Embassy
Jeddah, Saudi Arabia
19th April 1967

Dear Mum,

As you see I have arrived in Jeddah, having come North through the Royalist part of Yemen. Had to travel mostly at night because of the bombing, which was rather a

---

[54] The 'Radfan Uprising' began in 1963 against British forces, hastening the end of British rule in 1967, and the People's Republic of Yemen took control.

nuisance as I couldn't see so much. However, it was an experience, even if I did lose nearly half a stone on the journey.

    I ran into the hideout headquarters of the Royalists in the mountains, and had quite a time with them; but you will read all about it in my next book.

    I am sending this letter home in the bag from the Embassy, as it is the only way they reach their destination at present. The Hajj to Mecca has just finished, there is a pile up of five days mail. The city is very crowded as the pilgrims, almost a million of them, all seem to be trying to leave the country. I have been lent an apartment in the British Embassy, so I am living in luxury and having some privacy and quiet. Just as well, as the hotels are asking up to £30 a night for a room.

    From here, I go North to Jordan on the last lap of the old route I am following. It isn't all that easy, as I am the only woman driving a vehicle in this country, for the ban on women drivers still holds. Luckily, I got on very well with the Emir Prince Khalid at the border town of Najran, who gave me a letter, asking everyone to help me en route to Jeddah. And I have been given VIP treatment all the way. But, my progress from here is now in the lap of the Gods.

    I have let my place until the end of the year, and shall stay away working. It is easier that way, as people who don't work much, seem to resent one's capacity or getting down to it and working nonstop; as I well know to my sorrow!

    Jeddah has grown since I saw it last, they are still pulling down all the lovely old houses and putting up modern atrocities in their place, inevitable I suppose, but in the meantime the city looks a mess. It is, however, much more cosmopolitan than it was and there are many signs of the European invasion. There about 50 ships standing by to take the pilgrims home, they are decorated with lights at night and look heavenly.

    Ian seems to be taking his time, an awful pity if he has talent, he should get down to work soon. I suppose it was unsettling his going away right after finishing his training, and before he had settled on a pattern of work. Both Minna and Derek Smart, had great experiences with young artists and their beginnings, said quite independently of each other, that he should go back to Australia and establish himself. Europe as they say, is a graveyard of talent, where people all talk endlessly and sip wine in cafes. However, it is Ian's own life, and it is his own business entirely what he does with it.

I hear rumours, that our last budget in England has put the final lid on the value of the pound, so it looks as though it may be devalued, which will I suppose, level it up with the Australian pound. We seem to be getting into a terrible mess with this government, and certainly have made things difficult for business men abroad.

It is better to write to be c/o St. James Street, as Sidney is the only person, very often, who knows where I am. It is pure luck if Bertie happens to know.

Am off to try and see the new King, if he can't give me a letter to take North with me, nobody can.

Hope you are well, including the kitten who must be quite a cat by now.

My love,
*   Barbara*

As Barbara approached the district of Jauf, wanting to visit the circular tombs, she was advised to stay away. The ruins of the Ma'in were said to be some of the most spectacular in Arabia, but her guide, Aytha, refused to take her. It was well known that Republican bandits would not be far away, even the pilgrims of the Hajj would divert their journey away from the area.

While hearing this news, there was a bustle of nearby men. Pilgrims were moving away to nearby rocks, her pensive guide moved Barbara, asking her to stay low between two boulders. As she stood unsure of what was happening a plane descended at great speed. Pollyanna had been stood under the overhanging branches of the trees that lined the wadi, Barbara was concerned she would be a fine target. A bomber plane, turned to fly low over the wadi, where all were hiding. Barbara was once again facing the possibility of death, her guide, Aytha, watched in admiration at her steadfast attitude and self-containment. It was a containment, that was soon short lived.

Tiredness overtook her, the convoy had moved through the night with only a one-hour break and two hours' sleep. Barbara's temper snapped and she raged at her guide Aytha, telling him the journey had become futile without proper rest and food for all of the pilgrims, and she would not go on. The effect had stunned all those around her, the scene was electric, as trucks full of people watched.

Her travels were beginning to tell on her body and mind, once back in London the mundanities of that life caught up with her too:

73 St, James's Street
London S.W.1.
1st November 1967

Dear Mum,

A second letter sent before the first one, arrived today. It has been following me around. I am sure my porter forwards all my letters; it is just that they sometimes miss me, and take time to catch up.

I had, in fact, a letter from Ian, saying he had called and I had missed him. As I was going to Cornwall, after I got back to London, I did run into him, briefly, on the tube.

My porters keep my actual whereabouts from people who call or telephone, because I have fans – some of them real crackpots, who have been known to follow me into the country.

I was away this time, because of the trouble I had on the last journey, I have curvature of the spine and was trying to have it fixed. It was made worse by the fact that I had to travel by night as well the day in the Yemen, because of the bombing. I am very sorry if Ian was upset, it is naturally difficult for him to understand, for anyone for that matter, except my few intimates. Ian was going to telephone again but I gather he has a pal with him.

When I spoke about this credit squeeze here, I wasn't meaning myself, I'm certainly able to work if necessary, but it affects the whole set up and I'm sorry for all those people on fixed incomes, who have retired.

I haven't seen much of Bertie, he's rather involved and, in any case, haven't been going out hardly at all since, I got back to London.

Hope you are all well, and looking forward to the warmer weather. We've had the most marvellous Autumn, fine and sunny most of the time, though because of the number of red berries on the holly, and the fact that the squirrels are collecting more nuts than usual, we are told we are in for a hard winter!

Love,
Barbara

73 St, James's Street
London S.W.1.
6th November 1967

Dear Mum,

Have been meaning to write for ages, but have been rather under the weather, as I strained my tummy and it affected my kidneys. A nuisance, as I am on a job. Now, however, I seem to be okay thank goodness.

I suppose you are enjoying the warmer weather and, if I remember, it doesn't get too hot until after Christmas. Here, it is a bit cold but not too frightful, but everyone is running around about this stupid Christmas, so the traffic has almost come to a standstill. Someday it will seize up altogether. Christmas doesn't bother me, except for the crowds, as I always work over the holidays to let those who do celebrate, have a break.

There is never any news from me in England, as life is mostly work and an effort to get away again. Have been held up badly because of necessary extra jobs, and now this Rhodesian[55] *fiasco is going to have a very worrying effect on everything. Poor old England, it about puts the last nail in her coffin.*

---

[55] **Rhodesian** and British governments were engaged in prolonged discussions over Independence. Culminating in Rhodesia becoming independent Zimbabwe, April 1980.

The unemployment is now reaching awful heights, and it looks as though the common wealth people will have to go home to make room for the locals; nice if we are all tipped out!

Hope you are well.

   Love,
     Barbara

73 St, James's Street
London S.W.1.
19th January 1968

Dear Mum,

  Your lovely shoes-slippers arrived last Saturday, they are certainly warm and cosy, thank you very much. We need them here at the moment. Silly though, to send me anything, as you know I don't keep up Christmas. Hope you had a good time and many thanks for your note. You certainly keep up with your letter writing.

  There is a lot of fuss going on here about the weather, every time we have some ice and snow, we then get power cuts and floods etc, they never seem to learn.

  Ian telephoned before Christmas, didn't think he would, but I sent him a note. He was going to a friend for Christmas, which was just as well, for I was on call for the Red Cross, and think, in the end, I had cheese and biscuits on Christmas day. Some benighted friend sent me a small turkey on Christmas eve, luckily enough, the woman who is doing my research was here and cooked it.

  Thank Sadie and Tal for the fine bag, I'll write them in a day or two.

   Love,
     Barbara

73 St, James's Street
London S.W.1.
21st May 1968

Dear Mum,

Sorry I haven't answered your last letter earlier but was, as usual, caught up with lots of things, mostly work of course.

The weather here has been dire, with lots of rain and quite cold, it seems we had our three days of summer back in March!

How are you now? I hope alright, and how is the garden? Tomorrow is Chelsea Flower Show, which is always pretty marvellous, that is if one can get in early before the crush, the last time I went I couldn't see a thing.

I have been re hashing one of my old plays they may want to do on TV, but these things blow up and down and it could turn out to be a lot of work for nothing.

Also, I may go to Cyprus on a job but that would be quite nice, I have always liked the Island.

I saw Ian the other day and he looked well and sunburnt, so I don't think you'll have anything to worry about, one always gets 'bugs' in the East and often in the end, it makes one much more immune.

No more news – the world seems to be in a b…mess at the moment!

Love,
Barbara

73 St, James's Street
London S.W.1.
4th August 1968

Dear Mum,

Have been meaning to write to you. Naturally, we have all been busy since the awful Middle East Crisis, [56] *so many people thrown into awful circumstances.*

We are having a beautiful summer and it would have been nice to get away, but we can't all belong to the idle classes! The city is full of tourists, it's nice for them to have such lovely weather. The parks are looking fine and the sun even penetrates into my matchbox of a flat.

I hope you are better now and not doing too much. I gather Sadie's boss is off galivanting again.
Love to the family and yourself.

Barbara

Barbara was commissioned by John Murray publishing, to travel and write about Cyprus. This was her final book for her then publishers, and she felt somewhat confined by the relatively small Island, despite her love of the country. The book became known as *Rendezvous in Cyprus*.

On arrival, she was immediately struck by the unspoken rules of separation between the Turkish Cypriots and the Greeks. A companion, assigned to help, her went with her to collect the Land Rover at the port. Once reaching the gates of the town from the port, he informed her, he could go no further. Embarrassed, he waved to a large building, saying she would get another agent there. One section of the Island's people would go to school and work

---

[56] **The Middle East Crisis**, known as the Six Day War saw disputes between Israel and Egypt regarding the shipping rights of Israel to pass through the Suez Canal and the Red Sea.

with each other, but they were not permitted to live in each other's designated areas. Barbara, whose understanding of religious and ethnic backgrounds, perhaps more than most, found this practice astonishing.

C/o Ledra Palace Hotel
Nicosia
Cyprus
23rd April 1968

Dear Mum,

I have collected my mail from Nicosia, and got your letter. It is lovely to have news from you, but don't bother to write, as it must be tiring and just a card occasionally is nice to have – just the contact.

The enclosed can be useful, it is to hang on the wall and holds a tray, a useful way of getting it out of the way. Sorry, when I got it home, I found that one side of the material was faded, it must have been in the window or something. However, if you put it round the other way it won't notice, and if you don't want it, give it to one of your cronies.

Talking of cronies, how is your old pal the Pekinese, called Bamboo?

I just couldn't shake off my Asian flu, and kept getting up then having to go to bed again; all the time having a strange pain over my eyes, most unusual for me. So, in the end I was packed off up to the Karpas, which is a very unspoilt part of Cyprus, the long thin bit to the East, which is known here as the 'pan handle'. I was given a fisherman's hut in a little cove and did nothing but sleep and walk and a little swimming. The air was lovely and fresh and I felt much better quite soon and now have completely recovered. But the whole thing was such a waste of time, as you can imagine.

I am just back and very behind and with so many things, especially my letter answering but I shall write to Sadie right away.

By now the weather must be cooling off and this must make you feel better.

All my love, Darling.

Barbara

While trying to get to the Ledra Palace Hotel, beyond the Kyrenia Gate, Barbara was stopped again. A blockade of oil drums and barbed wire forced her to stop. A Cypriot police office, at a UN Observation Post, explained she would be entering the Turkish sector and seemed surprised she should wish to do so. Explaining she was from England, not sure if this would be a light to the touch paper, she was eventually let through. She was not as ruffled as she could have been, as she was taken by the officer's handsome looks, comparing him to a young Laurence Olivier.

Famagusta, Cyprus
12th June 1968

Dear Mum,

I hope you can read this, as I am writing it on my lap. I am down at the docks and sail this morning (I hope.) Have had you on my mind for the last few days, and hope you are well. Am wondering if you are home again now?

You would not like it here, the weather is really too hot, and terribly humid. I shall be glad to get away. Shall write to you as soon as I get to England, where I must be for a short while.

The situation here looks a little easier, thank goodness, it's about time, and the place is now showing improvement. I had a long chat with President Denktas [57] *who is quite a character.*

Some feral cats were very funny when I was packing, climbing into each suitcase as I filled it, sitting on top when it was closed. It is the one thing I miss in my wandering life, not being able to have animals.

Well darling, look after yourself.

Love, Barbara

Newspaper report of her trip to Cyprus (Unknown source) 9 Sep 1970

Change

It is the wild mountainous area, out of reach of the main roads but ideal for a traveller like Miss Barbara Toy, equipped with a Land Rover to explore.

But even now the places that so delighted her for their simplicity and isolation from the commercialism that is rapidly taking over, so much of the rest of the country may have changed.

If the plans to build a large holiday village with chalets, communal shops and restaurants goes through, lots of people will benefit no doubt, but with it's coming will go the world of Pol Pavlos and the flute playing shepherd; and the great fraternity.

---

[57] Rauf Raif Denktas was a Turkish Cypriot politician, barrister and jurist who served as the founding President of Northern Cyprus. He was eventually banned from retuning to Cyprus after visiting Turkey for negotiations and being associated with the Turkish Resistance Organisation.

Perhaps I am too optimistic, but I don't believe the Cypriot character, so deeply formed over the centuries, will change so much.

I like to think there will always be a generosity, the enthusiasm and the pride in their homeland for the sensitive traveller like Miss Toy to find. Though they would be hard put to recapture these qualities and the island's atmosphere as completely and delicately as she has.

Barbara with her travel companions in the Sahara,

Barbara collecting plant samples for Royal Botanic Gardens.

A house in Sey'un, Sothern Arabia.
'My garden was irrigated daily from the water from the swimming pool inside the house. (Barbara's quote from the reverse of photo)

Hadhramaut, East Central Yemen

Sultans Palace, Hadhramaut, East Central Yemen with 'Pollyanna' to the left.

Surrounding Streets

Saudi Arabia

A small boy in Jeddah

Barbara on route from Tibesti to Zouar, Chad.

Children of Tarim, Hadhramaut

Pollyanna embarking for Limassol, Cyprus.

Port of Limassol. 1968

Port Kyrenia, Cyprus, Harbour from the castle ramparts, the old lighthouse.

Priests sheltering from the sun under gold embroidered umbrellas

Photograph by Gordon Le Masurier

Barbara in her flat in St. James, London organising the pages of her book *The Highway of the Three Kings.*

Chapter 15
The next Rendezvous

73 St, James's Street
London S.W.1.
16th July 1968

Dear Mum,

... I had a lot of trouble coming back to England, as my Land-Rover had a bad breakdown, I had to wait in Italy whilst the spare part was sent over from England. A great nuisance as I was in the middle of a job and was absolutely stuck there. The poor old car is getting very old, she has to be coddled in order to keep her going. As I was so late in arriving, I had to whisk straight away up North and so didn't get your letter, nor Sadie's either. Now that I am back, there is a hell of a lot of sorting out to do, because things pile up when one has been away for so many months.

How are you, I wonder? Was amazed to here from Sadie that you had been doing the garden, and that it looked so much better for all the work you had put in. You certainly are a wonder.

Am rushing this off, as you must be wondering why I hadn't written, and shall write again.

Look after yourself,

Barbara

73 St, James's Street
London S.W.1.
26th August 1968

Darling Mum,

What a lovely surprise to have a gift token for my birthday. I was thrilled and have been waiting, and waiting until I had some time to go and find myself a present – which I have now done – before writing to you.

I am the proud possessor of a fine pair of new slippers, blue, comfortable and very elegant, and far too extravagant really, but then they were a gift. I wish you could see them. It certainly was about time I had them, as I looked at my old ones and found, despite the fact that I only wear the in the flat, that the rubber sole had word completely through, so that tells you how old they are. Thank you, my pet, very much. You must have gone to a lot of trouble to arrange all that.

London is very empty except for the tourist during this month, I can't help wondering where the locals go to for their holidays, as they can't go abroad very much now. It's nice for us stay-at-homes anyhow, as the streets are reasonably empty and the traffic not so much at the stand still, as it is other seasons. The weather is dire, dull and rainy, but this doesn't worry me much, as there is no distraction, and feeling it would be nice to get out instead of working.

I slipped and cracked a rib the other day. I am always doing it as my doctor says my ribs are like paper, but this one wouldn't heal and looks like I will have to have it bound up, which is a nuisance. I noticed it was more painful than usual, but didn't realise it was flapping about broken! I wish the National Health would issue me with a set of steel ribs, to save all this trouble.

Once before, about fifteen years ago, I asked you for the recipe for Lamington cake and I've lost it. Do you by any chance remember it? Or would any sponge recipe do?

I hope darling that you are feeling better and not working too hard in the garden! I hope to hop out again today and buy something with Sadie's gift, so shall write her after that.

Look after yourself.

Love to all,
Barbara.

73 St, James's Street
London S.W.1.
8th October 1968

Mum darling,

I suppose it must be getting towards spring over there; here we are having quite a good October so far, or at least, although wet of course, it isn't cold. As well as my book, I've been working on an old play again. The book progresses slowly, as there is a lot of research and this takes up so much time, spending hours in public libraries and wandering around museum libraries, sorting things out.

It looked for a while that I'd have to go to Biafra[58] *but now it seems unnecessary and, in any case, the young ones are better in such a place. Thank goodness things seem to be resolving themselves there.*

You shouldn't go on saying that I have done anything for Ian. I merely gave him a bit of money which, if one has it, is an easy thing to do; one can give that sort of a 'push', but the rest is up to them. Long experience has taught me not to do more, as it is resented, if only subconsciously. Anything Ian had done or will do, is by his own initiative.

---

[58] The Nigerian government, with British help, blockaded **Biafra** in order to starve its population. Between 1966 and 1970 more than two million Igbo people were murdered in Biafra.

One of my best friends has had a very bad operation, and I'm flying down to Nice today to drive back with her. Am rather looking forward to a couple of days break.

Look after yourself, darling.

Love,
Barbara

73 St, James's Street
London S.W.1.
25th January 1969

Dear mum,

Thank you very much for the money for Christmas, which I spent right away on a book I have been wanting for ages. I have been borrowing it from the library all the time, so thought it was a good idea to <u>own</u> it. For which many, many thanks.

I hope you had a good Christmas, and certainly the weather would have been better than here, where we had a bit of a freeze-up. Now, luckily, it is very mild and quite pleasant. I was rather unsettled over Christmas, as I was 'on tap' to go off and do a job and so couldn't really do much. But then I never do celebrate Christmas, as you know. Am always so terribly thankful when it is over.

It was a disappointment that you didn't hear the radio request, and gramophone record. I wrote to the A.B.C. and asked then to play a record for your birthday, and gave them a message to transmit and also asked them to telephone you about it. I didn't like to mention it, in case they couldn't do it.

What a pity! Anyhow I shall write and thank them for doing it. The reason was, that I may have been en route somewhere on that date and nowhere near a cable office, but as it was this didn't eventuate.

Goodness knows when you will receive this, as we are on the brink of a big postal and telegraph strike, which is likely to cripple everything for a long time. We are hoping *it won't go on for too long, but in any case, next Thursday is a complete close down of everything, including cables, telephone and all postal services. As though we haven't enough troubles here without this! They should put the military in.*

I have been surrounded by illness lately, firstly my best friend had a very bad operation, then my agent had another bad one, and also and old woman friend. I am becoming quite efficient at hospital visiting, although not very good at coping of course.

Your air letter, cards are very gay these days, I love the bouquet of Australian wild flowers, I had forgotten the flannel flowers, which I always loved so much.

I am trying to find more of those heavy pens I sent you, they don't seem to be here in England, I have sent a little friend of mine off to try and find some.

Am sorry not to have written earlier, but things have been rather disjointed and I have been away quite a bit.

Look after yourself and I do hope the weather isn't too hot, as I know you don't like it very much.

All my love,

Barbara

Barbara's mother's eyesight was failing, eventually her carers would read Barbara's letters aloud to her. They were always much anticipated.

73 St. James St,
London S.W.1.
15/4/69

Dear Mum, perhaps you can read this letter?
Sorry I have not written but have been away on a job.
There isn't much new here either — just a lot of work and bad weather except for Easter which was fine but windy — not that one sees much weather here.
Today is budget day when they will try to scrape a bit more out of the barrel. Shall try and post a couple of pens to you, not so thick as this one.

So glad you are well and, I suppose, happy that the cooler months are coming

Love

[signature]

Transcript:

73 St, James's St.
London S.W.1.
15th April 1969

Dear Mum,

Perhaps you can read this letter? Sorry I have not written, but have been away on a job.

There isn't much news here either – just a lot of work, and bad weather, except for Easter which was fine but windy – not that one sees much weather here.

Today is budget day, when they will try to scrape a bit more out of THE BARREL!

Shall try and post a couple of pens to you. Not so thick as this one. So glad you are well, and I suppose happy that the cooler months, coming.

Love,
Barbara

Ever mindful of her mother's health cost, Barbara's mother was now 91, she sold some of her jewellery to help with the financial burden of her mother's care. Her sister Sadie would report how things were going, and how pleased their mother was when Barbara sent gifts from her travels, on her returned to London.

Barbara, then 62, was still trying to bring some of her plays to the stage and arranging further trips.

By the 1970s, Barbara was seeing less and less of Bertie, but would still send heart felt letters to him when her loneliness returned. She wrote to him when she was on her world trip, while in Australia staying with her mother Nellie. She also confesses about another man in her life named Dick, who is not previously mentioned anywhere in her archives.

No date given

Dearest Bert,

You are a dear to write to me the day before leaving for Turkey, am longing to know the incredible circs. Don't forget to tell me. I'll haunt you if you don't, never whet my appetite and leave me up in the air.

First, family news... Nellie has made a simply amazing recovery, but I repeat she is in her 90s. Jess took Nellie up to Gordon for a few weeks, but they are home now. I am going up to no. 26 tomorrow to look after Nellie while Jess goes out. Strictly entre nous...I do think Sadie and Tal deserve some time to themselves.

Sadie had one hell of a bad cold, and was unwell for some time but she is over it now. Tal is well, and Den is a ball of muscle, literally, as he goes to the gym, twice weekly. Old Dudley dithers along, entirely supported by Sadie's efforts. Not mad on him. He has grown such an old, old man, not his fault I know! but is so indolent. Darling, I really feel you want me to always give you a true picture of home, so don't spill any beans you shouldn't.

Briefly, had two Swiss girls staying here. Had to ask them to leave. Slayed me to see the money go, but impossible, Nellie agreed on this. Lazy, would not learn English, growled about everything, stayed out all night a couple of times, would not go to work. Not pleasant for either of us. I have learned since, that they were, in fact, sacked as they never turned up for work. Hoping for someone else soon, as we are finding it hard to manage with only one in the house. I have worries about the place. The fence blew down in a gale, wonder if the landlord will put the rent up because of it. Also, this has been made an eight-story area. Much panic in the street, rates and rents up. Petition against it worked, danke Gott. Get bouts of worrying about what will happen to me when my dear old landlord dies. Must learn to wait, until I come to that bridge.

Joe arrived one night with the most beautiful Chinese girl; he had flown down, just for one night to see her. Dear old Joe, sweet of him to spend a few hours here, he never forgets to keep in touch, He's lost weight, suits him.... He flew home non-stop through the states, and was very wrecked.

I tried to tell you how I valued your last long letter, what it meant to me, couldn't find the words. Perhaps, like many of us, I am somewhat starved, and at times my expression of feelings becomes a little land locked, as it were.

Can you bear with me in a story? Will you remember writing me about a brief interlude, in Cornwall, I think. A lonely woman? I too had a chance, brief interlude, which seems to have unlocked me. With household and financial worries, plus being a little let down by ones I thought friends, now I will not turn on a party at the drop of a hat. I have rather knotted up inside with a ball of self-defence. I wish you could tell what the matter is with me. Why does a woman of my age still hope to share moments of magic? You, and only you, know what I mean by this. The quality of a day, a night, a certain light, a time of day, Autumn trees, anything that gives that sudden lift of heart. This brief interlude has helped unlock me a little, yet – it has also served to let me know how much I miss you. How much I need someone to share such moments with.

How lucky I have been. I shared with my dear Dick. I ballsed that by being too afraid to divorce and marry him. He died.

I have shared much with you, and now this little episode. A thought comes to me, I have had magic alone, shared it with children, or a man, you and Dick. Never with a woman. I wonder why? Here is my little story, written to you, the only person who will understand it. I hope that I can give you the feeling that the whole night was an enchanted one.

The following was a type written section included with the letter.

```
'The two half Spanish children of a young cousin,
were spending the evening with me; their parents
were going out. Timmy, five, Mark ten. Adorable
children.

 After early dinner, to fill in the evening, I
suggested a walk to the wharf, home by bus. Good
idea. Cold, a light mist. An exciting walk down
by the back roads, dark steps, the torch being
```

used to spot lurking pirates. Could we go over on the ferry, another good idea. A quality of unreality. The ferry creeping out of the mist. Outside, upstairs, you very much in my thoughts. At the quay, Timmy will thank 'the driver' (Pilot) for bringing us over. He'd never been on the ferry before. Up the steps to the wheel house. We found we had twenty-five minutes to wait for the return trip. Time for a cool drink. Better still the Oriana was berthed, we had time to look at her. Running ahead of us Timmy collided with the legs of a very tall handsome man. (Thirty-eight or nine) in uniform. We picked Timmy up, no damage. 'Taking the boys to see the Oriana?' 'Yes, between ferries.' 'Would you like to take them aboard?' Wild excitement. Introductions, Ron a customs man. Had been at sea, needed for personal reasons to come ashore.

Adorable with the boys, down on his haunches to talk to them, not being a big man, coming to them. 'What happens if a ship hits a rock?' Explanations about a second hull, water tight compartments. 'To me- perhaps it would be well if we could organise out lives this way.' Some talk on these lines. Walking and talking. I, a little tired lean on the rail. Ron joined me. Both together, 'its… You tell me first Ron.' 'It's an enchanted evening, I…, it's a fairy tale night.

The sails of the opera house rising from the light mist like a fairy barque, everything slightly unreal. 'You know Nancy, it is rare for two people to respond to beauty in the same way at the same moment. I, trying to be practical. 'Oh, I don't know Ron, we all respond to it, in our own way.'

But not to put a point where one could cry, which I promptly did. A light touch on my hand, and we just stood a while, until the boys joined us. Were the boys mine? No, could well be my youngest's grandchildren. I wanted no misunderstanding. I am not to mention age again, I had done it before. I am enjoying companionship I have rarely found, leave it that way.

On a passing ferry a band was playing, I could have danced all night. We danced on the deserted deck. Walked and talked. 'The pursuer is a friend of mine; may I go and ask him for champagne?' Only two glasses each and overboard with the glasses. Coke for the boys, their paper cups had to go over too. Not for a moment did I resent the boys being there, they were part of the picture. Ron told us he had to board another ship later, and time for the boys to be home. His ship was moving towards the bridge at Pyrmont. 'Time for one more dance, please tell me again your second name.' 'Just Nancy Ron, come on boys we'll take a taxi home.' On the way to the taxi, once more about my name, still just Nancy. 'I have never met a woman like you Nancy, we all have out problems, and you have helped me tonight more than you will ever know. I know you started just for a walk to the wharf, have you enough money for the cab?' 'Oh yes, yes thank you'.

I now digress to show you how the spell lasted all the way home.

I the cab I find he had slipped Mark two dollars in spite of what I said.' You be the man and pay Mark, add ten cents for the tip.' At my place. 'How much?' to the driver. 'A dollar ten. 'Make it a dollar twenty. Mark was handed a dollar change. 'You are all so happy it will be a pleasure to drive you, leave it a dollar.'

Timmy got in the front with the driver, Mark in the back then I. I held my hand out through the window and said 'Thank you Ron, the boys have had a wonderful night.' He opened the door, 'please get out. And you, Nancy, have you had a wonderful night? Nancy, I shan't forget you.' He took my face in his hands and kissed me.

The story she tells…could they be Sadie's boys? The wharf and the ferry, those she frequented as a child in Shell Grove? She continues:

I know where to contact him, but have no intention of doing it. This was an enchanted evening, but he was only about thirty-eight, and I am not seeking to become involved, nor make a fool of myself, and be hurt. I may be odd, Country – Clarish etc. but am no fool, and know a young man can be sincere, as I know he was, but that was just one evening. What it has done for me has shown me how deeply lonely I am (in the sense of true sharing) and makes me wonder why I never find anything like this with a man 'of suitable age.' I find them hideous old bores. Does the spark of dreams wear out quicker in men? I suppose, given the chance, I could marry for a lot of money, but I would be very conscious of what I was doing. I don't expect a lot out of life now. I would love a tiny perfect home, security, and someone with whom to share, that once in a while an uplift of the heart and soul.

I am sure you will understand me when I repeat, this brief encounter has unlocked me, to thank you, with a heart full of love and gratitude for all the past, and your continued love and friendship. I remember walking in Orange Park at dusk, you held out your hand to me. I was trying then, not to be soppy with a young boy.

I remember a yacht in Mosman Bay. I wished the others to Hades, so I could sail the seas with you. I remember everything.

This is the third time I have written this letter to you; I destroyed the other two. This one I will send.

I ask you to forgive about writing such a long letter about myself. When I say I am lonely, I know you will understand this too, not in just the sense of someone to natter to, plenty of that. I don't actively want to remarry. Just the little home, and someone 'on the side' to share a little with.

<u>Next day.</u>
Many thanks for the second letter. Wolves in Turkey, really? I didn't know or am I being taken for a ride? Anyway, if you meet them, I can tell you all about them, have just read a book. Very nice animals. In the winter they can live on mice, don't laff, its true. The female is monogamous, if the old boy does, that's it. Handy piece of info? I can also tell you how to protect the bounds of your camp. In the same way as the wolf marks its bounds. Stoke up well by drinking plenty of liquid, then all run around and do drops on all the rocks and trees etc. Laff again if you want, also true, well it worked for this man who wrote the book. Let me know about any other animals or birds, no doubt I can dredge up further info, which may be of help. Now won't it just be funny if there <u>are</u> wolves and, following my instructions, you make the camp safe from them. I will have saved your lives, but don't worry, they are not half as blood thirsty as they are made out.

Did I mention, at some stage, or make the comment, that I felt a sense of having been, in a measure, unlocked? British understatement. I could write and write to you. The reason is, to me anyhow, quite obvious. I am not, I stress, self-sufficient. I am a weak vessel. I badly need someone to share with. A small turn of the key in the lock and the door opens. Bert, dear Bert, it is impossible for you to reply to all this soul searching. Just reply to one thing. Am I nuts????.

Never let anyone tell me, that one can't maintain contact by letters. If the bond is strong enough, of course it is possible. Because the medium of letters is more difficult than speech, when an inflection, a look tells so much. If full contact is maintained, then, to my mind, it is strengthened. I now make you a promise. Never again will, I destroy a letter to you, which I have done many times. Do you think you could say the same to me? Did someone say - love has many faces? Must have done, I couldn't make it up. One face is for you only, and, I feel, one of the most important faces.

My love, and vaya con Dios (go with God).

Barbara

With conflicting needs, Barbara as she aged, began to feel more alone, ironically something she'd craved for in her early travelling days. Her little home, sadly for Barbara, would have been no turning of the key. Bertie and Barbara never saw each other again.

Still planning and searching for new expeditions, Barbara writes to an undisclosed friend:

…Sorry about the paper, such is the state of my finances! Returned after quite an exacting trip, the heat was unbelievable, but the trip was worth doing. Your 'letter to hand'.

Sorry I started the fracas about hotel Serai, as probably had it correct in the first place. It is in all the tourist books of Cyprus, and is either Serai or Serea, definitely not with an I. The quotation came – I think – from a book called 'A Traveller Journey is Done' - I think – Dilys Powell, about her first husband who was drowned near Greece.

So, you are off for the giddy heights of Bruges, goodness knows when we will see you again.

By the way, the map you looked up is a little cock – eyed; there is a fine road to Tindouf, and after that nothing but a few mines, and the remains of the Imperial Dakar Highway of fifty years ago. There isn't anything more until one reaches Bir Mograin, and joins the route South from the Spanish Sahara. Then, there are a few lorry tracks to follow. The Canaries are the Cote D'Azure of this part of the world, so naturally planes are much in use.

It would be useful to be in Ben Ezra [59] before the winter, if I want to sell. Can't hope to sell it in the winter. Am hectic at the moment, trying to arrange to fly East and get lorries back.

Have at last found a Mauritanian who knows something about the country, bit of luck. Also ran into U.N. FAO [60] head, on the last trip, who seems to be a fan of mine and this is useful. Very nice man naturally! If I can do this next trip, it will be fun. Just the chance of a camel trek this end but mostly too late. However, my Mauritanian had given me all the dope about the routes, and how to go about it on the way North when I may catch a late camel train.

As it is, the chariot has taken a bit of a beating, but I want to get her home without a break, so I am saving her as much possible. I cabled Sidney for mail when I knew I was coming back, so have to stay for it in any case. Cable cost me more than £5! NO room at any hotel, was lucky enough to get one of the mining company's apartments, which is nice.

Your letter sent to Dakar just arrived, don't know who you mean Mrs. L? when in a rush, can't interpret these abbreviations. Glad the films were okay, as it links an old reel from Cyprus days.

Am off tomorrow at 6a.m. (If I can wake up.) Searching for famous residences, which probably means a hard floor, and tracking down some old places. Am taking your lie low.

Love, B

---

[59] **Ben Ezra** was the name of a large cottage left to Barbara by her girlfriend Minna Dyason.

[60] **U.N. FAO**, United Nations Food and Agriculture Organization.

London
20th October 1970

Dear Mum,

Just a short note to enclose one of the reviews about the Cyprus book, which I don't think I have sent you yet. Also, a photograph – flattering as usual – of me taken in Mauritania. There is a great disadvantage about taking such good photographs, because when people see me, they always say 'Goodness, it must have been taken years ago!'

I am sending a parcel for your birthday by surface mail, and hope it arrives alright. It won't be much use at this time of year, but will do for the winter.

I hope you are continuing to progress and that summer doesn't prove too hot.

We were very shocked at the awful bridge[61] disaster in Melbourne, what an awful thing to have happened.

My love, Barbara.

73 St. James's St.
London S.W.1.
3rd July 1971

Dear Mum,

It was lovely to hear from you. Yes, I could read your letter alright. I have certainly written since Christmas, but everything was thrown out because of the postal strike here, and really, I think the huge piles of mail got so out of hand, that we begin to think that some of it just got lost. So many letters just haven't turned up.

The work I was doing up North has finished, and so when in London I'd be able to be contacted there, although I spent a lot of time in Africa, and likely to spend a

---

[61] **The Melbourne West Gate bridge** collapsed on the 15th October 1970; two spans of the Westgate bridge collapsed leaving 35 dead.

lot more in the future. I am off tomorrow for a couple of weeks to Spain, where a journalist friend is helping me with some research.

Dennis seems a nice straightforward young man, which is refreshing these days.

We have hot weather at the moment and it is nice for those interested in Wimbledon tennis, it was a great triumph for the little Australian Goolagong, who certainly seems to have captured the public's hearts.

Tell Sadie to always let me know if money doesn't turn up, as things are very erratic in this computer age.

Hope you are well pet; I hear from others that you are marvellous.

All my love,
Barbara

73 St, James's St.
London S.W.1.
5th December 1972

Dear Mum,

The other day I sent off a scarf, as a sort of birthday gift. I sent it surface mail; I do hope you got it.

As I said before, I haven't written as I am waiting to spend the money you sent me for my birthday, and I'm now off to buy it. – a bedspread, as the one I have got torn badly.

We are having the direst weather, wind and rain all the time, and the poor Christmas shoppers look more harassed than usual. I suppose you are at the beginning of summer now. We heard about the new elections and your change of Government, I hope it is okay.

There is not much news here as I seem to do little except work, which makes me rather dull for other folk.

I hope you are well darling, and that you have a good Christmas.

 Love,
  Barbara

73 St, James's St.
London S.W.1.
14th January 1973

Dear Mum,

 Lovely to hear from you - your letter was quite easy to read.

 Also thanks a lot for my Christmas present, which I spent immediately. I happened to be going through Harrods and caught site of my poor old face and decided then and there, to give it a little help. So, went and bought a good jar of 'night cream.' I don't know if the old face isn't really beyond repair, but at least it made me feel good.

 I have the most unexpected Christmas present, for I was going to Brussels in the track of a job, and met some friends there who insisted I stay, which was fine. A little early, but Christmas celebrations, are a thing I never do, as a rule.

 Sorry to hear you have been having a heat wave, as I know how exhausting it can be for you. We have been having the most unexpected winter, with practically no snow so far. We just had a big snarl up over the new year, when the fogs closed the airports for some days. Now it is warmish and sunny again.

 I am glad Bart sent you a card. He seems to be very well although I don't see an awful lot of him these days. He still works and carries a lot of lazy relatives on his shoulders.

Am still trying to arrange to go away, but have been held up, as I had to do some alterations on my last book and, of course, the hundred and one things that have to be done, seem to get more and more difficult.

Look after yourself and I hope things go well for you in 1973.

Fondest love,
Barbara

In an effort to continue travelling, Barbara writes to the Land Rover company looking for support and information, she was planning to travel to Russia, Mongolia, China, Korea and Japan. Barbara was now 65yrs old:

73 St, James's St.
London S.W.1.
15th February 1973

Keith Kent Esq.,
Public Relations Manager,
The Rover Company Limited,
Solihull.

Dear Keith Kent,

You will be more than glad when I finally cease to disrupt the world of motor manufacture; but in the meantime, I am scheduled to take off again next month. It is a new and interesting project for me and I would like to ask your advice. Would it be possible to fit in the time next week when I could – return the compliment – and take you and Clive Currie to lunch at your 'local'. In this way no time would be wasted.

After all my efforts with the Chinese, who have been very helpful up to a point, they suddenly put their foot down about allowing a private vehicle into the country, and I can't budge them on this. As I wouldn't want to do such a journey in that way, it has been shelved for the time being. Having geared myself for the departure, we had to switch right away, and I am crossing Russia by the trans-Siberian railway, going on to Japan, as the publishers want a book on that country. I would like to talk to you about this trip, as I do want to use a Land Rover rather than any other vehicle. Also, there is talk of me visiting Korea and Outer Mongolia, and it would be interesting to have any information you may have about these countries.

If you could spare the time, I could come up any day except Monday.

I can't say how sorry I am, to read of all the Company's troubles.

Yours sincerely,

Barbara Toy.

73 St, James's St.
London S.W.1
21st February 1973

Juul chin
Ulan – bater,
Mongolian People's Republic.

Dear Sirs,

I have read many times about Mongolian People's Republic, and about the great improvements that are happening there.

For this reason, I would like to visit your country this spring, and am writing to ask if you will give me a visa, so that I may do so? I have travelled in many countries over the years, and can give you references to show that I have enough money to make the journey, and am of good character. I have an Australian (British) passport and I live permanently here in London.

Any further information you might need about me, I shall gladly send you.

I am enclosing some international stamps for your reply.

Yours sincerely,

Barbara

A newspaper report from October 1969 shows Barbara had been planning such a trip for some time. It describes how she had been longing to take the ancient silk route from China. She had hoped to travel with the Arabist St John Philby as he had spent many years living in the Middle East, they had planned to travel together across the hostile Rub el Khali, Arabia's Empty Quarter. He had unfortunately died before this could be achieved.

Physically fit and determined, after travelling 250,000 miles over 20 years, Barbara still regarded herself as a tough old ox, but the usual taxing job of gaining permissions and papers for travel, was becoming more complicated.

CABLE:

Zhuulchin
Ulan-Bator
Mongolia

March 12th 1973

Dear Miss Toy,
We have received your letter Feb. 21st, 73 regarding your visit to our country. In this connection, we are sending some information. During your stay in Mongolia, you can visit such places as Gobi Desert, Hujurt/Kara korum - the ancient Mongolian capitol. In Ulan-Bator you will visit the national museums, theatre, Gandan monastery, and see the national folk dances and

songs. A cost of complex services for tourist per day, per person is 52, 50 US dollars. This price is based of course on the Mongolian Tugrik. Any changes, of course, in US dollars should be in the final payment. This price includes: A room with a bath in Ulan-Bator hotel and accommodation in a Mongolian Ger, (a traditional Mongolian home) in the countryside, three meals a day and the 8hr service of a guide - interpreter. If tourists wish to travel in the countryside, price for air transportation will be added on the complex services as follows:

Air transportation to and from the Gobi Desert is 180,40 US dol. Air transportation to and from Hujurt is 145, 00 US dol. All expenses should be paid in cash in US dollars to Zhuulchin. Herewith enclosed a visa application form, please, send it to us in triplicate with photos a month before your arrival. You can get a tour visa in Irkutsk, Russia at the Mongolian Consulate. Please indicate the exact date of arrival and the period of your stay in Mongolia. We look forward to hearing from you promptly.

Sincerely yours,

Zhuulchin

There were many flimsy papers from Mongolian officials, and Japanese consulates, letters from hotel managers and tour operators, as Barbara desperately tried to travel the way she was used to. Each letter she writes during this trip, was marked with a red letter ready, to add to her autobiography.

Barbara had already started writing the introduction to what would have been her ninth book, which despite extensive research, doesn't appear to have been published.

Rendezvous in Korea
by
Barbara Toy

Barbara Toy's route to Korea took her to Moscow, across Eastern Russia, Siberia, through Omsk, Krasnoyarsk, Irkutsk on Lake Baikal with its hydroelectric plants and industrial mining projects. On to Khabarovsk on the River Amur, from where she travelled in one of the old imperial carriages to the port of Nakhodka.

She sailed for Yokohama in the Soviet ship F. Dzerinsky. Japan was experiencing the first signs of infiltration and industrial unrest. Parts of the country remained unchanged but the cities are expanding at a fast rate; Tokyo, Osaka, Kyoto, Okayama, Hiroshima and finally Shimonoseki, where she sailed for South Korea. Here her rendezvous with Kwung Sun, led to a series of unusual encounters and experiences.

There followed some months of travelling through the country by plane, train, bus and by foot. The individualistic Koreans were always accessible whether peasants or Cabinet Ministers, despite the president's growing dictatorship, the growing restrictions, and curfews in the cities.

There is a growing and steady advance in Christianity, a growing talent and appreciation of art, and the many schools and universities bear witness to the people's passion for education. The Ehwa University in Seoul, is the largest women's university in the world.

There were opportunities of seeing the affect the Americans, stationed in the country, have on the people and the economy; and to study the financial boom (solid or bubble?) which the country is experiencing at the moment.

She visited the controversial truce village of Panmunjom, on the border between North and South Korea, with its ever-present tensions that play into the hands of the Presidents iron control. He may be cutting corners in the present rate of advancement, but it leaves the countries policies open to outside criticism and propaganda.

This was a unique journey, for Barbara Toy succeeded in going from a communist country to one ardently opposed to, and suspicious of, such ideologies – an experience afforded few people and, in view of recent events in the Far East, unlikely to be granted others in the near future.

Barbara writes to her friend Marie Louise who was looking after her flat in London. Unusually Barbara was about to take her first trip without a Land Rover for company. She was to use other means of transport, which made her feel like a tourist, which she hated.

On board St George 3p.m.

I told you so – starting before the mid-day prayers. What could be worse than carrying a ton weight suitcase without a handle? It was the porters insisting on carrying the case by hand and without a trolly. And now, after scrounging rope from the news stall, and waiting whilst carpenter aboard mends a cripples' crutch and a baby's pram, he now seems to have fixed mine. Let us hope it lasts – so early to realize the utter vulnerability of being without my Land Rover.

The sea is like a proverbial mill pond, but the ship very nice. Not many people in the 1st class.

I am now cluttered with three carryalls, one of which holds four squashed eggs, three black bananas and a mouldy packet of sandwiches.

Thank you pet, for all you did. It is always a hectic run up and one gets side tracked. I shall sleep tonight, no matter what they get up to.

We all walked onto the ship, just showing a passport, no money checks whatsoever.

Now you can get on with your proper work – although it might be an idea if you became a sandwich man, and walked up and down St. James's Street, advertising the flat!

I suppose I shall stay a night or two in Yokohama, to catch my breath. I see by some pamphlet or other there is a British Consulate there. Should there be a crisis, I shall call in there, also for some information. Not that anything is likely to happen.

Lots of big fat, cheery Germans around me, swilling beer – one of them young enough to be my son, has been following me around like a puffed-up pigeon.

There was something else, I was going to say and shall of course remember it when I seal the envelope.

I hope I'm not too much of a B... bore with all my affairs, if so, I am sure Sidney will help.

Many thanks my pet.

Love, B

Hotel New Grand
10, Yamashita-Cho, Naka-Ku
Yokohama. Japan.
(A)

Dear 'Comrade,'

I held up writing as I hoped I'd formulated a plan, but am at a loss, as the letting of the London flat is a big point, could you cable if it is let?

It is the height of the season here, terribly oppressive, hotels push you out after a couple of days at any cost. Taxis won't take you short distances with luggage – it's hell. Also, just a waste of time as well as money. All my childhood prejudices still there! Once I know about the flat, I will do just one trip to the North Island, to see a vanishing tribe there, then hope to go to Korea.

Don't send anything but urgent mail, as most things get lost without Japanese writing. So, I will try to keep in touch with Embassy in Tokyo. I sent some colour Kodak film, when they come, could you let me know? I hope they are okay as the camera slipped off the seat in the train and may be damaged.

It has been brilliant sunshine since leaving England, and weather warm and perfect. The train trip and ship, wonderful. Shall write it all when things sort themselves out. Of course, there may be news in Tokyo, if I can ever get there.

<u>Later</u>

8th April, Buddha's birthday.

The first trip across Liberia was quite wonderful, and wouldn't mind retracing and stopping off at some of the places. The people were so kind and helpful and of course one met many more ordinary people, who all seemed very relaxed. It certainly was an eye opener. Unfortunately, there is no Mongolian Embassy here, but one for China.

There was a very nice Dutch couple on the train, he is a businessman here, retiring to England next year. Also, a nice elderly German couple, whose friend here brought me to the hotel, or I would still be sitting on the quay.

Took some time to recoup after the loss of sleep after my last 4 a.m. night in London, poor old Susan was well set for a few hours chat that night – the young have no imagination.

Cherry blossom is at its height now, but everyone's complaining that with the pollution and the property developers, it's not what it used to be.

Love,
Barbara

Hotel New Grand
10, Yamashita-Cho, Naka-Ku
Yokohama. Japan.
(B)

Monday

Dear Marie Louise,

Have been to Tokyo today and received your letter. I hope I mentioned I was going up, then you won't have bothered to send a cable.

Such good news about the flat, a gleam of light in the darkness. I told them to get a £100 deposit however. If they had done this with the previous tenant, he wouldn't have left owing £24. Nothing can be done now of course, and let's hope this young man's finances aren't as precarious as some freelancers we know!

I hope you can read this; I slipped on board ship and strained this wrist. I certainly envy your typewriter.

Marie my pet, thank you very much for all you have done, all that work cleaning up. I had to laugh, the Hamptons certainly are lack-a-daisical leaving the inventory for you to do. I don't think I was even put in the declaration to be signed by him, but perhaps they did?

You will certainly need that holiday. I am surprised you worry about a pain in your head, don't you think it's a chill? If you worry, then for goodness sake see a specialist, but don't be daft enough to cancel your holiday because of it.

RE Mongolia. The Russians would have to start all over again with their visa, there is no sign or stamp on my passport that I had a visa, this is very enlightening. It might take many weeks to arrange and then I really don't see that the kind of 'Tourist' conducted tour in Mongolia, could really warrant this expense. I don't think I could make it into my kind of tourisiting. The only thing is, I would like to see it, just as a matter of interest.

Shall have 'food' and think on it tonight, as I am at a loss. I've done too much travelling to be reduced to the ranks of a tourist, it's so boring, and even Korea can't guarantee accommodation because it's the tourist season! They would really be bursting at the seams with the added population in that area.

One good thing, their hotel will keep my luggage for me, and although it is expensive, not as bad as some, I'm living quite happily on a continental breakfast and half a bottle of beer a day now.

Should any query come up about the TR.V. radiator in the flat not working, I did tell Miss H., although she's probably forgotten that, because I have some good ones in the house, I am not prepared to pay for this one to be repaired.

Should I decide to go to Korea, I may cable asking for one batch of mail to be sent. By the way, do you have a 'Teach yourself Korean' to put in the envelope in both languages.

Shall write if and when I know where I am going.

Love, Barbara

Fig 34

The sign that once stood above the Spring Street house.

Chapter 16
Dear Marie Louise

(C)
Wednesday

Dear Marie Louise,

I'll start this part of the letter off, but my situation changes from hour to hour. Yesterday was the first day of bad weather, much rain. I have spent these last two days trying to get somewhere with the Mongolian situation, but it really isn't possible from this end. Firstly, the Soviets want my passport as in the UK, and this would mean I would have to stay here. Also nonplussed about my leaving for Mongolia as I really doubt, they will let me in, not already having their visa. Also, fanatical about Land Rover arrival to the date and hour etc, all this with my scanty exchange in German.

As it stands, even if it were possible, I doubt whether it would be cheaper than flying direct from home, especially as I now know the Siberian parts.

Suggest we make it an Autumn jaunt, and see if we do go for two for the price of one! Then set the wheels in motion to get the ferry to Korea. They come back with <u>all</u> the trains booked up until the 16th. Am now, annoyingly, to go the devious way with three nights stop off on route.

Do you think you could write the Mongolians, saying their letter arrived after I had already gone, and that I shall contact them on my return? This leaves things open. It might be as well to send international stamps, and a copy of their letter.

RE clarifying schedule, when ones there, I should think possible if we are on 'tourists' lines, but it buggers up the work, if one wants to differ in <u>any</u> way.

They have cameras in the cafes and banks here, they look a little incongruous in the modern buildings. Also, Kimonos, slippers and packets containing toothbrushes and *paste supplied in the bedrooms. The bag you found for me is a great help, it squashes, and having only one compartment, is less complicated when looking for things.*

There are massive cruise ships in here all the time, with Canadians and Americans.

Tokyo is quite unbelievable, so huge, everyone clogs the trains, I think it is the pollution. I go round with my destination written in their language, and am passed on from one little nodding person to another. Think I will go to the doctor tomorrow about the damn wrist.

It looks as though I shall be here until Sunday and shall keep this letter open, so that if any plans materialise, I can ask you send another batch of mail.

<u>Seoul, Korea</u>
I do hope you have kept an account of all the calls etc.? Let me know about your head, do you still worry? Perhaps it is the responsibility of have a large cat family. I saw my first cat today, they have absolutely no feeling about animals here.

<u>Later</u>
I now have all my tickets, I leave Sunday. First, I go to Tokyo – an expedition on its own, let alone with luggage. Here I buy an extra ticket to add to the collection. I have already been on the express train to Okayama, taking four hours. Staying a night here. Leave next day midday, five hours to Shimonoseki (port) where I stay two nights. Ferry on Wednesday 17.00hrs arrive next day at 8.30. I have to sit up all night as everything all booked. Have been warned, not to let my luggage out of my sight. I haven't much idea as to how long I shall be over there. Shall stay South for some time, I hope, although Seoul is the only place to cash British travellers' cheques. Might get some more dollars before I leave, as one can't get any outside the in the country.

Sorry about the scrappy letter, it isn't much fun writing, firstly with this wrist and without a typewriter. The shops aren't all that interesting, except for the T.V. Radio type of thing. Otherwise, and awful lot of junk.

Love,
     B

The card is of a dear little girl student, who was my guide in Khabarovsk, both she and her mother were reading Somerset Maughan. Can you see if there is a paper back of 'Of Human Bondage'? She wanted a 'Hornsby' English Dictionary, but it looked like a pirated addition published in Warsaw.

No rush, take your time.

Hotel New Grand
10, Yamashita-Cho, Naka-Ku
Yokohama. Japan.
(D)

Dear Marie Louise,

Borrowed this typewriter as it is easier on the wrist. Doctor says it should be in plaster as I have broken a bone, but that bone has always been broken, and I can't carry suitcases with a plaster cast on.

Off tomorrow, I should think I will spend the rest of the month being put on the wrong trains and bowed in and out of expensive hotels.

I do hope your headache isn't because of all the bits and pieces you have been doing for me? When I mention things, don't do them if it is too much. And my letters must be a bore, because I have just been writing essentials, they must sound like one big moan. Don't <u>ever</u> let me go away again without a chariot (Land Rover) of any kind. The Land Rover people have lent me a vehicle – at a colossal cost. But I've really wasted enough money on this place, that has been really over done, written – up – wise.

Have just eaten a banana from Taiwan, very nice and sweet.

My tenant sound like a bit of a pansy, I hope he is because if so, he will keep the flat clean. Hope he doesn't take all my Arab books.

Don't mention Russia if you write to Seoul as they a very anti.

Sheer bit of luck, I ran into an old boyfriend, whose been showing me the town and it's been quite fun, these big places are dreary on one's own, especially with these people who are just not interested in outsiders.

Must stop now, as it is getting too late to write.

    Look after yourself

        Love,
          Barbara.

PS. Have been writing all night with a reoccurrence of my tummy trouble – everything happens to me!

Beginning of letter missing...*Later:*

It now seems, that it almost impossible to get a ship back home, all booked up. A pity as the Ben Line has a lovely little 12 passenger craft, for this reason I may come back via Siberia after all. If I can find reasonable accommodation while waiting here for a visa. I know I said write Mongolia, but if I was in any case coming home that way, I may make a final effort, which would by then, have to be on a schedule money wise.

Do you think you could enquire at the tourist board some time, what the possibilities are having already had one visa? If they are hectic with tourist, you could phone Pavlinov at the Russian Embassy, whom I saw. Tell them how impressed I was with everything, also that I want to break the itinerary at Innsbruck and join again. This is the tricky bit.

Am thinking of Airmailing mink coat home, wish I could find a buyer here. Wrist now strapped up...rest of letter missing

Postcard
Seoul Korea

Dear Mum,
  Have finally landed up here, which is a beautiful country and the people great fun and now very 'go ahead.' Many Australians around the place and business seems to be booming.
  Hope you are all well.
      Love, Barbara.

       C/o British Embassy
         Seoul
         7/5/73
         (G)

Dear Marie Louise,

  I keep starting letters and they get out of date, and now can't remember if I have written at all from Korea?

  Sidney's batch of letters and yours, <u>and</u> the one sent to Tokyo were redirected!! SO, now I really don't know which place you go for your holiday.

  This is a lovely country, the people adorable, but have had visa trouble and can't stay after the one renewal, which means sixty days. Shall write more about country when it's easier and confine this to 'business.'

  That idiot financial advisor, sent a share cheque to <u>me</u> and Tim did the same, they must have all gone mad and now, after selling at a loss, I'm sitting here with over £1000 lying idle and in an overdraft, again I can't send anything important from here. Some mum's do ave em!

  No hope with the Ben Line ship, although on waiting list, but visa deadline makes things imperative. Was looking at the frate ships and had them in mind, but they are most likely to break down mid Pacific and I hear the food is somewhat 'uncertain.' Anyway, have ask them here to enquire for me. I don't want to hang around in Japan, and have in mind to stay here, as long as I can and then go to Tokyo and try for a transfer the way I came. But my Dutch friends say, booking from now on is almost impossible in the Autumn. The detour is just not on and I shall contact the Professor in Leeds when I return. It is rather unintelligent to go in just as a tourist – at that cost.

Did you get a letter asking you to write them, saying I had already left? I do want to keep the ball rolling.'

Hope you can read this, wrist much better but it gets sudden sharp jabs. Wonderful weather here, warm and sunny, only a few dull days.

It was a small self-drive car they were going to hire me! Did I mention, the Ainu tribe to you? One of the reasons I wanted to come to Japan, was to go to Hokkaido Island, where they claim the last of the tribe[62] now live, very few of them, and they have now turned themselves into a money-making tourist attraction.

That's another bubble burst!

You may remember the day before I left, I telephone my insurance, about missing luggage and asked them to send it to you. I don't want it sent here because of the cost. Another thing, could you telephone to make sure they are not just sending copy letters to the tenants of Ben Ezra, and ask when the tenancy is up. They have already broken a pair of Wedgewood dishes and a good alabaster lamp. I want it all valued before asking for damages. They seem very clumsy, I feel we may find complete carnage there.

Another thing, could you buy me a copy of 'Teach yourself French' and, when I know plans, send it on?

Many Thanks for all you have done.
       Happy Holidays,
       Barbara.

---

[62] **The Hokkaido Ainu** native people, Sakhalin and the Kurils, mostly hunters and fishermen.

Hotel
Kwang Hwa Moon
Seoul, Korea
15/5/73
(H)

Dear Marie Louise,

Your letter came yesterday, I hope you received the one from me from around the 6/7th. Most incoming ones, especially bulky ones, opened.

I really do want my tenants out, but need them to stay for the time being and help my finances. I shall be back, I am sure by the end of July, even if by some miracle, I could find a ship, which isn't likely. There are literally queues outside the airline offices all the time! You haven't a clue what it's like.

My plans, wrongly, are to stay the two months here, which takes me to about the 16th of June and then to Tokyo, and try and return the way I came. As I mentioned, it is a pity I can't put things in motion from here. Alternatively, I will fly. Have left suitcase and fur coat in Yokohama, shall ship them as cargo.

I do hope your foot has cleared up; I would be infuriated if I had to cancel a trip. Please do not run around after me if it is too much.

Have had an agonising week as it looked like the traveller's cheques had gone astray, as they are not signed by me, they are as good ordinary money. Turned out the bank hadn't sent them, and now after the trouble it has caused, phone calls and cables, I can't have them sent here! I am trying to get them to send everything to Yokohama, as I have to go there for the suitcase and coat. Fortunately, they are not quite so urgent, as I am now not going by ship.

There is a peony bush outside my window twelve feet high! This place grows on you, and the city is full of fascinating bits. I am having quite an interesting time, and, of course, everyone here speaks a little English. Outside the city can be difficult but everyone is very kind.

Love,
B

PS *it was not drink that caused my wrist accident, a great oaf knocked me down, I could have been killed.*

Hotel
Kwang Hwa Moon
Seoul, Korea
16/5/73
(I)

Dear Marie Louise,

I do hope the news about your toe is good, so that you can be off on your travels. I am still concerned about what wreckage I shall find on my return. The House really has been messed around.

It looks pretty certain I shall have to return the way I came. I do now hope I can, the sooner the better.

Excuse the messy writing.
Love
B

Hotel
Kwang Hwa Moon
Seoul, Korea
22nd May
(J)

Dear Marie Louise,

Just a hurried note. I leave her for Pusan in the morning. There now seems to be complications with the ferry to Japan, as it is now going into dry dock until my visa runs out, and no vacant seats on a plane until July. I will have to try to get on the last ferry. Never a dull moment!

I have had my Leica camera stolen with the valuable wide-angle lens on it. I left the other one in Japan. However, curiously enough I hadn't taken many photographs.

I will send the insurance my address.
Sorry for the hurried note
I hope the foot is better.
Barbara

Pusan
25/5/73
(K)

Dear Marie Louise,

I collected all your letters just before leaving Seoul – what-a-to-do, perhaps the honeymoon is over.

I have been worried you, are doing too much for me, for goodness sake don't worry about my things. I bought a copy of 'Of Human Bondage' here, and will send it up myself. The rest I shall sort when I get home, not important.

Many thanks for bothering about the cheques. I shall have a lot to do-workwise-when I return. I may go further by train which will be stuffy and hot. The train trip to from Seoul to Tokyo was wonderful, the countryside was heavenly, with paddy fields lightening up the scenery. There were cart loads of strawberries being sold on the streets and all the silk worms had been busy.

Perhaps anyhow, it is better in regards to getting back as I have done the spade work with several government ministers.

Hope things go well for your holiday.
Love,
Barbara.

Pusan
28/5/73
(L)

Dear Marie Louise,

Today, most unexpectedly, it is raining, quite a relief, as I don't look as out of place in my navy blue.

This is just a such note, there is a faint change, again, that I can to get a ship after all. If so, I desperately need the 'Teach yourself French' book. I shall try myself, but I haven't much hope. Apologise, but all I can say is it is very important. I don't mind if I double up on it. So sorry, but it would be a heaven-sent opportunity if things come off with the ship.

I am afraid that you are doing too much for me already, I do apologise, absolutely nothing else I have mentioned matters at all.

Love,
    Barbara

Pusan
29/5/73
(M)

Dear Marie Louise,

Have defiantly settled to travel in the frate ship leaving here on the 4th or 5th June. They can only take me as far as New York, I may be able to persuade the captain to take me further on. I wish I had as much power as people seem to think I have! Decided on this, as the remaining journey wasn't hopeful from Tokyo and I couldn't face spending hundreds waiting around there, and then having to fly after all. I think the ship is the EURYSTHENES, V-4 arriving roughly in New York on the 18th or the 19th of July.

  I am terribly worried about you, but could you make an urgent effort to send the Hugo's 'Teach yourself French' sent to Yokohama.

  I am going to have one hell of a scramble to get the suitcase and coat, and having to go to Tokyo for my traveller's cheques, seems I will only get to stay in Yokohama for 24hrs. They have been sweet here, and very helpful. I fly back to Seoul, as I have to get a USA visa. Then back here on Friday to see the Captain on Saturday morning. More about that later.

  Sorry darling, but is there any way I could get the Hugo's, it would be wonderful. I'll have very little time to search in Tokyo, after this shall not worry you until I am home!

  I am suddenly relieved to finally have something settled at least half way, and it is a fine chance to see my siter-in-law, who is unwell and saves a special journey.

  In haste.
    Love,
      Barbara

<u>Back in Seoul.</u>
1/6/73
(N)

Dear Marie Louise,

  As all my mail sent from Pusan hasn't arrived <u>here,</u> shouldn't think there is much chance of yours getting though, so I'll recap. Have decided to go on the MARCHESSINI line ship, which only has berth as far a New York, then if nothing found, will either transfer ship or fly home, leaving most of luggage on board. Leave Pusan 4th June, calling at Kobe and Yokohama. Pusan agents say we stay 24hrs in Yokohama, Seoul ones say four days, and two days in Kobe. Hope this letter is right. I wrote you urgently and shall try to cable, can you send the Hugo's to Yokohama.

Sorry about this, but will not have much else to do, and it is a heaven-sent opportunity. Decided on this course, having worked out that the return journey, the way I came, was almost impossible.

Am back here in Seoul, to get USA visa and return to Pusan today. Excuse the hurried note, hope your foot is better.

Love,
Barbara

Seoul.
(O)

Dear Marie Louise,

This might just reach you before you leave on your jaunt. I do hope the old toe is better and that you're all set to go…

…Sorry about the cable but mail from here seems most erratic.

I was all ready to set sail today, packed and everything, and then the ship just didn't arrive. All the other folk to do with the shipping just roar with laughter when I say what ship I'm sailing in, talk about lack of up keep etc. only hope the plumbing and kitchen work. If we stay long enough in Yokohama, I hope to make enquiries with BOAC about charter flights from New York.

Was very sad to leave Seoul, as was having a lot of fun and getting around a lot. This place isn't all that interesting and because of the uncertainty, couldn't go very far afield. Have met a very nice and attractive young journalist here, and so have been doing the rounds. The women really are quite lovely and seem to be much more intelligent than the men. My darling Keang Sun in Seoul was really lovely.

I have written to Mrs Boghurst saying no reconstruction to be done to the dining room until I return, just in case they have had the nerve to touch the structure, although I don't really think they could have. I will be glad to get them out, have never had such an odd couple as tenants. Poor old Ben Ezra.

They have cartloads of raspberries in the streets now, and the pansies in boxes all along the pavements, still blooming. They eat dog soup here in the spring, it's called 'health soup' and clears the blood!

Wonderful fish market and all the fisher folk, men and women, quite tough and different from all the others. They have a curfew at midnight in all the towns, kind of Cinderella cities.

They are such a lovely looking race; I spend hours just wandering around looking at them. Apart from the wrist, I feel terribly well, and have got quite brown walking around. The air is very dry, and the weather near perfect and sunny all the time, with a slight nip in the air night and morning.

Look after yourself,

B

M.S EUYZOCHUS
Yokohama
12th June 1973
(P)

Dear Marie Louise,

We docked yesterday and have come right out to 'Bunker' so haven't been into the town.

Received your letter and book, for which a _million_ thanks. It will be a great boon.

THE ship is a bit ramshackle, Greek officer and Philippino crew. All a bit hit and miss. Food unimaginative but the crew willing. Three other passengers so far, and we are praying that there will be no more, as cabin accommodation would then be acute.

A recently returned couple, both musical professors from down South, and a very nice widow from Maryland, wants me to go stay with her. We are supposed to stay here for about five days, then a nineteen day stretch to Panama – no stop and five days to New York, which by my reckoning, would put us in NY about the 10th or 12th July… that is if we don't break down. Am still hoping they may be able to take me on to the U.K., might know more today, as still haven't paid for my fare!

I really think my affairs have been too much for you, and they have accumulated to cause you trouble.

I shall try and find out if one can get a cheap flight – from New York, if I have to go that way. I could pay by London cheque, but such a waste of money.

Shall write again before we leave, when I might have some more news. Hope this arrives before you depart and that you have a good holiday. Your itinerary seems rather strenuous.

Love,
Barbara

By now Barbara's mother's health was deteriorating. Aged 100yrs, Nellie was unable to write to Barbara herself, due to her blindness. Her last letter to Barbara was transcribed by her nurse. Later Barbara's sister Sadie takes up writing about her mother's slow decline. There were no more of Barbara's letters directly to her mother in Barbara's archives.

Northridge
10/7/75

Barbi Darling,

What a miserable selfish thing I am for not writing sooner. For not answering your letter sooner, and for not realising how worried my last letter about mum must have caused you to be. Really the days and weeks just fly by almost without me noticing. Since I last wrote to you of mums 'turns' she hasn't had one, and seems to be getting stronger every day though she finds it difficult to take more than a few steps at a time, and then with help. In herself, she seems much better. Also, she was so thrilled to hear from you, she loves to get your letters.

Re the trouble with your cookery measurements used in recipes, it's easy to see you haven't done much cooking. I'll write them and you can cut them off and keep.

Happy lamington baking darling, I'll keep you posted about mum.

    Lots of love,
        Sadie

1/2 cup of flour - 4oz
1 cup of butter – 8oz
1 cup of sugar – 8oz
1 cup of liquid – ½ pint

1 scant dessert spoon butter -1oz
1 tablespoon of sugar – 1oz

Measure level cup all ingredients, a spoonful is rounded, ½ a spoonful is level, ¼ spoonful is divided lengthways.

    Much love darling,

        Sadie

Northridge
17/9/77

Here I am again,

Hospital funds are as much as a home nurse, so mum now at home instead of sending her to a nursing home. The Government pays sixteen dollars a day! So, with her pension and the money you send, which I have let accumulate for emergencies, we were doing very nicely. Then she got ill and the nurses had to come twice a day, pushing the bill up to eight hundred dollars, just at the time you sent the money for the curtains, so it came out of that. Still no refund from the hospital, goodbye to that.

She may have to go into a nursing home but we are holding up pretty well, and when she gets her pension it will cover everything. I hope you can decipher the above.

You do amuse me when you talk of me having brains – my God – I have never done a thing in my life except just mooch through time. But talking of cursedness - do not walk across the Sahara – the very thought of it is exhausting – I would say someone is exploiting you!

I'll be going now Mum is waiting, I'll write again soon, promise.

Well, lots of love,

Sadie

Northridge
20th November 1977

Barbi Darling,

You are quite right; mum's birthday is the 15th December. Tal made arrangements from this end, to have the telegram sent from the Queen. Anyway, it wouldn't matter if it came a few days early, we would just keep it.

I'm afraid I am a wash out as far as being helpful in choosing something for mum, she has so very little needs really. I haven't thought what to get her myself. I will get her the scented flowers from you, but it will mean so much when she gets the telegram from you.

I do hope your trip to France was a success. When you have a moment, I would love to hear about your new book, and how far on you are with it.

Perhaps next year you will be able to get a pension. Over here everyone is entitled to it when they turn 70, no matter what their circumstances. I thought it was so in England also.

I will write to you next month and certainly will, if I can think of anything mum would like.

Lots of love,

Sadie

Northridge
17th December 1977

Barbi Darling,

Nellie has asked me to drop you a note to tell you she received all your presents, and also a cable from you. She was thrilled to receive one from the Queen, but I am afraid it had to take second place to yours.

The chocolates are lovely, and she is going to bed every night with your cushion, like a child with its favourite teddy bear.

She got some very nice flowers delivered on the day, and added to that, all the presents made her feel like it was Christmas.

She is sending you the enclosed voucher for you to buy some little thing, and asked to say Merry Christmas and much love.

Lots of love.

From your Mum

Northridge
17th December 1977

My dear Barbara,

The enclose voucher is sent with my best wishes for you to have a very happy Christmas.

Your mother's 100th birthday was celebrated in very extended style – she was delighted with your presents and telegram – talking of telegrams (about 25) there was one from the Governor General, the Prime Minister and the State Premier and the local Mayor etc. etc.

Her room looked like a very well stocked flower shop. We had about 44 guests for the night party, apart from many people who called in during the day – she was in good form and apparently enjoyed every minute.

We are all well here and hoping you have a very happy Christmas.

Much love,
Tal (Sadie's husband)

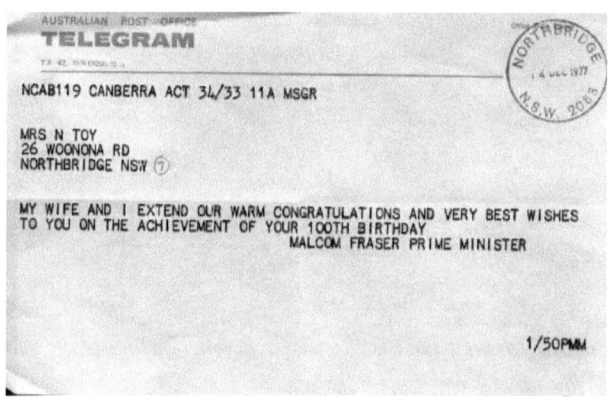

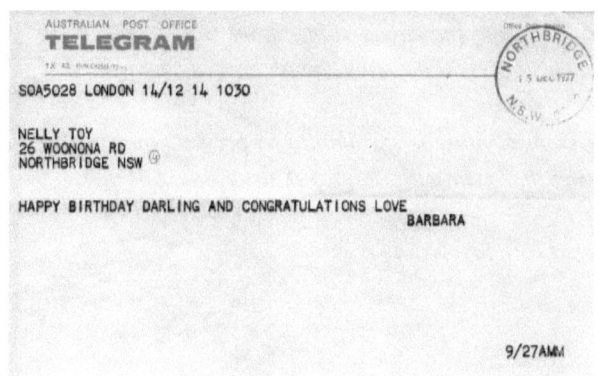

```
AUSTRALIAN POST OFFICE
TELEGRAM

SCA4966 BUCKINGHAM PALACE 38 14 1030

ETAT
MRS N TOY
26 WOONONA RD
NORTHBRIDGE NSW

THE QUEEN IS MUCH INTERESTED TO HEAR THAT YOU ARE CELEBRATING YOUR
ONE HUNDREDTH BIRTHDAY AND SENDS YOU WARM CONGRATULATIONS AND GOOD
WISHES
          PRIVATE SECRETARY

                                              9/25AMM
```

Northridge
8th January 1978

Barbi Darling,

Many, many thanks for the cheque from you, you are really generous and with mum's birthday you must have spent a fortune.

Instead of buying individual things from you, I bought the turkey and some trimmings and a bottle of cider for mum, we all toasted you again at Christmas dinner.

At the moment mum is surrounded by presents from you and others, although she agreed with me, that some curtains for her room would be nice.

I hope you can read this, my writing is so awful.

Love,
Sadie

Northridge
12th January 1978

Barbi Darling,

Really!!! Here you are taking an advance on your book because you need the money, and then proceed to give it away! I got the notice from the bank the other day, so I can tell you exactly what it came to here, and it is absolutely absurd. I will get the curtains for mum and put the rest in your account. You said you like to keep one here. Anyway, darling thanks.

Lots of love,

Sadie

Northridge
22nd February 1978

Barbi Darling,

Hope you haven't suffered too much with the awful weather you are having over there. It is difficult for us to imagine at the moment as we are all nearly dead with the heat. I have never known such heat!

Lots of love,
Sadie

Northridge
20th May 1978

Barbi Darling,

How is the wrist? I do hope it is much better. I'm afraid our clan has been having bad vibrations over the last six weeks or so. In fact, it has been quite a nightmare a times.

The pleasant news is the Dennis and Robyn got married on the 12th with not much warning as to dates, as they had to be fixed to accommodate his trips. At the present moment they are away – Hong Kong – for a week or so. At the time of the wedding Mum was pretty sick, so we arranged for someone to stay with her for a couple of hours, while Tal and I got to be at the ceremony, we all went to Robyn's girlfriends flat for a drink etc. afterwards. It worked beautifully, and Mum was looked after well. But a few days later she had a bad turn and for which, we have a nurse coming in three times a day. It is funny how things work out.

You sent that ridiculous amount of money for mum's curtains, which cost less and the remainder is in her purse.

Last Sunday night she was very ill, and the doctor called in early Monday morning, she was in hospital within the hour. Expense wise, she is covered by insurance. The doctor thought she might last a couple of days, but yesterday she had a shower and has been sitting up in the chair and seems quite well. I will keep you posted as to how it all goes.

Re Denny and a present from you, I really think cash would be better than a present… I really must go now, as I go twice a day, lunch and dinner time, to help mum eat her meal because of her eyesight.

Robyn is the sweetest thing, and reminds me quite a lot of you to look at.

Love,
Sadie

Northridge
21st June 1978

Barbi Darling,

I feel such a heel, not writing to you before, knowing how worried you are about mum. But honestly, I have found it impossible to sit down to write. Mums' pneumonia cleared up and physically she is getting along well, but the poor old thing is just terrified of the hospital. All of the nurses, to put it mildly, are bitches.

Ever since she went to the hospital, I have gone each day to give her lunch and be with her. Then go home for an hour or so to do some shopping for the house, and then back to give her tea. She can manage quite well really with some supervision, but very blind and in a place, she is unfamiliar with, she is quite panicky.

To be honest, I have not been a tower of strength to know what to do. The doctor says it is impossible for me to nurse mum properly at home, although she isn't ill, she needs 24 hr medical supervision.

I fret about mums' prospects and the nurse says she thinks I could cope with mum quite well. The only thing which would have been difficult, would have been if she were a big woman because of the lifting, but there is not a problem there.

Forgive me, I did not ask how you book was going.

Love,
    Sadie

Northridge
21st July 1978

Barbi Darling,

You will be pleased to know mum has gone into the home I told you about. She has been there a couple of weeks now and is doing really well, they are so good and kind to her.

The last six weeks has been hell, poor little thing was just terrified of the hospital, I was literally nearly out of my mind. I spent most of the days at the hospital with her. In fact, one day after an incident, I was in such a state I frightened myself. I hot footed it to the doctor and he gave me lecture on looking after myself. Then in a couple of days this vacancy turned up.

Mum is in a two-bed room for the time being, as that is all that was available, and we couldn't afford to miss the opportunity. Because of her condition, not being able to see and her hearing not as good as it used to be, she should be better in a room with more people, as there would always be someone to call for her, if she got into strife. It is also too expensive, but we have enough to see us through till another vacancy comes up in a ward which they have promised. They are very understanding about it all.

I have still been going in twice a day to help her with her dinner and tea, although I am gradually weaning her off the expectation and haven't been the last few nights. The matron told me I couldn't keep it up, I know I can't. For the last 8 weeks, I have done nothing in the house and am in a hectic mess. Tall is in a bad way and can do very little with his arthritis, as I said, I will do it gradually so she doesn't feel dumped. She knows she will never come back to her little place that she loved, it is all too sad.

Den was disappointed you hadn't the time to come and see him, we had all hoped to get some first-hand knowledge of you. But I can imagine how busy you must be and am sorry I have not got any more information about you.

If you left England, would you be coming back to Australia? The trouble is after all these years you would have very little friends here.

Funny quite a few times recently, I have thought how I would love to hear your voice, though phone calls are usually most unsatisfactory, and one thinks of all the things to say afterwards.

I always edit your letters, cut out the bits that might worry mum, and read them out as if they are written to her, she does love to hear from you.

I will write more often now, and am sure they will have brighter news. Good luck darling with your book

Love,
      Sadie

Northridge
1st August 1978

Barbi darling,

    What rotten luck missing your phone call yesterday, I arrived home just a few minutes after Tall rang off. I am sorry for my letter, must have worried you a lot. But things are much better and mum is very comfortable in the new place. They are all very sweet to her and are looking after her wonderfully well. Of course, she is sad, knowing she can't come home again, but that awful fear she had in the hospital had gone.

    I still go practically every day but realise it will be better if I break it down a bit, as yesterday as I walked into the room where she was, as she heard my footsteps she said "is that you Sadie?" All the others smiled, and said she called out my name when anyone came into the room. I can see she won't relax if she just sits and waits for me all the time. I will go up for a while later this afternoon. Luckily the place is only ten minutes away by car.

    Tal said you asked about the cost of everything, it is working out well and won't be quite as much, once she is on a bigger ward which will be better for her also. She will have more people around her.

    Tal said it took him quite a while to realise who you were....
...I hope things are going well with your book.

    Don't worry about things here, you have quite enough on your mind, I will let you know how things are from time to time.

    Lots of love dear.

        Sadie

Northridge
24th August 1978

Barbi darling,

It was wonderful to hear your voice last night, the surprise must have thrown me completely, because I didn't say any of the things I wanted to. For quite a while, I have been longing to hear your voice and then you rang. I hardly thanked you for concern about the many matters, or asked you how your back was, and your work, or even if you were ringing from London or the country – in fact I just waffled on like an idiot. When I put the receiver down, I just sat and stared at the phone for some minutes wishing I could start it all again. – and say "wait a minute, don't go". Also, there was no reason to say mum hadn't been that good that day and leave you with the worry. As predicted, when I went up yesterday, she was right as rain, and didn't remember anything about the upset. She was so thrilled to know you had rung.

Anyway darling, when Tal goes into hospital, which I hope will be anytime now, I'll give *you* a ring.

I am sorry I haven't been more useful with information. How is your back? You always play down anything wrong with you, and as you say, we are not as young as we were; I really can't believe I am nearly 75 years old. I get quite a jolt when someone calls me elderly, of course, compared to me you, are just a chicken.

Good – bye pet, and forgive me for spoiling your phone call.

Lots of love,

Sadie

Northbridge
9th October 1978

Barbie darling,

It seems so awful for you to have to sell your ring, and help with Mum, £500 is a great deal of money, are you sure you can really afford it? I must admit that your generosity is making things so much easier. They have put nursing home fees up by $7 a fortnight, going back to 1st Sept which was worrying, but we wouldn't have got by without such a large amount from you. Also, I had a look round the 'big wards' yesterday, though there is no vacancy as yet, but what I saw made my blood run cold. They are quite nice rooms with curtains around the beds, which means that except for the one near the window, they are a little like cells. But the worst feature is 98% of the inmates are senile and little dramas and unpleasantness are happening all the time. They wouldn't be any help to mum at all and not being able to see, she would be in a state of confusion and anxiety all the time.

Mum's room is very nice. Also, she is next to a large window with such a nice big tree, full of birds. So, I feel with the extra help from you, if a ward room becomes vacant, we will turn it down.

Tal goes into hospital on 7/11/78 and I do hope he will be as fortunate as your friends, and it will certainly be good to have it over.

I am glad you have heard from Molly. I really should write to her, but I rarely seem to have a spare moment. I see Mum practically every day, which breaks into my time and things have backed up in the house work area, When I come home, instead of getting on with work I am writing letters or ringing people up. I am inclined to be lazy and put my feet up.

Thanks again darling, and perhaps when this is all over there maybe some of your cash to go back to you.

Love,
Sadie

Northridge
1ˢᵗ May 1979

Barbi darling,

Mum's funeral was on Friday, it was a little later because of the Anzac Day holiday on the Wednesday. It was quiet and, in a way peaceful, although we were all sad, we said it was good she was at last resting.

Some of the family came down from the country a couple, just her family. I got some beautiful flowers from you, and put them on her coffin, as you were never far from her thoughts, I put them nearest to her.

I really can't realise she has gone and find myself suddenly thinking "I must hurry up to mum." But I know things will soon fall into place.

How are you darling? I keep thinking of you all on your own over there, with no one to share your sorrow. Now you no longer have the responsibility you took on for mum, perhaps you could take a holiday and have a good rest, perhaps do something for yourself instead of everyone else.

I will write again soon dear and do look after yourself.

All my love,

Sadie

Sadie and Barbara's mother Nell.
1876 – 1979.

Chapter 17
Journeys end

Barbara Toy in a radio interview, believed to be for the BBC, found on a cassette tape in her house. No reference to its origins exists:

'I found my second trip around the globe, that there were so many more people in the world. Especially in America and Australia. I mean my first journey across, when I arrived in Fremantle, in Western Australia, I had gone across the planes, the long desert to the East. I went from one homestead to the next. When I went this last time, I went from one motel to the next and that's progress.... People go expecting it to be the same and it won't be same, nothing is. Anyhow you are different aren't you, you have changed, and you are probably looking for other things. I just look back, for instance, on my time in Southern Arabia, it was an enchanted time and I really enjoyed it, bit of a lotus eater shall we say. I know it won't be the same, but that's okay. I think a lot has changed for the worst but that is politics really and we can't help that. And there is always, everywhere you go, a little group who are upsetting the whole scene, so to speak, but I don't feel as much can be changed by people as I used to.

I think I have become a more self-contained person; I have had to use my own initiative and stand entirely on my own two feet. Before my real travels started one was dependent on different people, now I know I can look after myself, so I think it changes you quite a lot. I am a nomad now, there is no question of that, I get irritable if I am unable to go and do things.'

Barbara was seeing the end of an era of travel as the world opened up to the movement of more and more people. The radio interview discussed the loss of the explorer to new territories and the diminishing of undiscovered lands, as the world of travel became easier for all. Although Barbara saw it as inevitable, her tone changed as she spoke.

Alone in Chipping Norton, Oxfordshire, her travels were never far from her mind, but her age and that of her Land-Rover 'Pollyanna' saw them both too risky for the insurance companies.

Barbara's last letter to her nephew Ian Seymour Wells, writing from London:

2000

Dear Ian,

I have spent another morning trying to decipher the London telephone system, but to no avail. I am hoping the written page will do a little better.

Firstly, I want to explain my haphazard approach to the 'festive season'. ...I am going around like a mole, with my eyes in far worse condition than before.

To simplify life, I've become a Muslim, at least over Christmas and so can ignore the whole farce, and as we are in the middle of Ramadan, it deals with the farcical procedure of all the rush and over eating etc - you should try it sometime.

You will be speaking to your brother and his wife, Robyn and Den I suppose, so give them my love. (It is a wonderful being ninety-two, you can be as eccentric as you like.)

Love, Barbara.

I'd stood among remnants of a life, dipping into the lost years at random, working out the sequence of each letter and the placement of each photograph, in a timeline that brought Barbara Toy to life for me. The dreaded black chest gone. The broken and rusted cameras and the film canisters of unusable edits housed within, archived and stored. Now the attic room held neat folders of Ian's work, leant against the newly painted walls, no more to discover of either Barbara or Ian. The room I had spent so much time in had changed, it had been made clean and neat with new carpet and freshly painted book shelves and walls. Ian's work was the only thing left, stacked and in order for Terri to look at, when nostalgia got the better of her. I had helped her to have the room for herself and her beloved Ian. With an exhibition and sale of Ian's previously unseen work, I'd seen the joy on Terri's face at the sell-out exhibition. Unsure if Ian would have approved, Terri assured me, she knew it should have happened when he was alive, but the feeling of unworthiness left after the cancelled exhibition in Australia, would have seen him refuse such exposure.

The day of the exhibition Terri told me her heart sang to see his work admired and alive on the walls of the gallery. I had done as promised, voluntarily taking on a task beyond expectation, swallowing my time and thoughts for months. But my heart sang too, to see this widow's wishes fulfilled and the love and pride for her artist husband swell beyond her grief.

My task was not done there. I had been given so many artifacts of Barbara's I wanted to pay homage to her too. I had after all this time, come to know her so well, not just for the amazing adventures in her books but the amazing adventures in every aspect of her life. Saved from destruction, her story lay at my feet, a privilege and a burden. My adventure was about to begin.

Terri too is now gone; lung cancer had swept through her fragile frame too quickly. I felt her absence more keenly as there was no longer any follow up chat to my final visit.

The house that had been Barbara, Terri and Ian's last resting place, now sold and housing new lives, changes to the inside soon became changes on the outside, the plaque 'snails' gone, the garage that sheltered all Barbara's archives, gone. As Barbara said:

> 'People go expecting it to be the same and it won't be same, nothing is. Anyhow you are different aren't you, you have changed…'

The past few years of research and archiving have revealed the strong and driven woman Barbara Toy, capable of things unachievable now, and not heard of then. The world has changed, climate crisis, natural disasters and conflicts are changing landscapes and borders.

Barbara courted danger and placed herself apart from the warnings she was frequently given, by those who had gone before her. Imposing herself on authorities, she disregarded the hindrances of any cultural suppression of women and strode forward across inhospitable lands. Meeting the tribal people, in an effort to preserve and record their lifestyle, while yearning for a better way of living for herself. She spent time studying different religions, moved by the rules and dynamics of the rich and poor, the generosity and happiness of those with little compared to the avarice and discomfort of those with plenty.

Discovering herself along the way, her freedoms against the odds of her time with her choice of partners, to a completeness of self-sufficiency, answering only unto herself. It was a brave journey, as the freedom she found was also a lonely place. In her later letters, we see the searching and longing for the 'magic' of companionship and devotion. Her capacity for the romance of travel and the romance of human contact went hand in hand, her searching never ending.

As middle age creeps into my own life, I am assured by the tenacity of Barbara, that searching is never over; there is no end to learning and loving in whatever capacity is true to yourself. Myself from a small family of farmers, in another small town, was taken on a world adventure with Barbara. I'd felt the heat of the dessert, looked at the eyes of the street children, cursed the restriction on women. I'd seen the strength and tenacity built into the character of this tiny lady, a spirit to admire and live by. Caution and warnings were words to inspire and move with, achievement and knowledge gathered on the way, taken on as life's lessons. Enjoyment of the human spirit, whoever you are, wherever you are, prevails if you let it. Borders are manmade, we are all the same whatever colour, nationality, religion or sex. We are all Human KIND.

In 2001 Barbara had been thrilled that a TV company wanted to make a documentary/interview with her. She saw the journalist off from her home with her diaries and films packed into her car, planning to meet up again once the editing was ready for her voiceover and interview.

Among the letters in the archive was one from 9th July 2001, that stung with sadness as I read it, I could only read half way before clinging the letter to my chest in grief. The news would have been crushing for Barbara.

A young boy had stolen the reporter's car from outside her house, setting fire to it with all of Barbara's effects still inside. Nothing was recovered of her diaries, photographs and films. The police had no evidence and despite a reward being offered, in case anything had been removed before the fire, nothing of Barbara's was ever found.

The reporter, traumatized by the event, had asked Barbara to call her, something she didn't feel able to do herself. At the bottom of the letter Ian had written:

'Rang on 6th Aug 01…. she was devastated.'

It was only a few days after receiving the reporters letter that Barbara was found collapsed outside her front door. Miss Barbara Alex Toy died on the 18th July 2001, just before her 93rd birthday in Banbury hospital, 9 days after the loss of her life's work in the car fire.

Barbara had lived a life full of adventure, being mostly self-educated, she'd acted on the London stage, wrote for stage and film and was a theatre director and repertory manager for the Rank Organisation during the war. She circumnavigated the globe, published eight books and was a fellow of

the Royal Geographic Society, winning the prestigious Land Rover Award.
(Fig 35)

Later she was invited to be Vice President of the Land Rover register and a member of the Marco Polo Society.

She was a fellow of the RSPB and collected specimens, on her journey's, for the Royal Botanic Gardens.

From Barbara's own list of places visited:

Australia, Tasmania, Algeria, Austria, Belgium, Burma, Cameroon, Cyprus, Cambodia, Congo, China, Canada, Denmark, Egypt, England, Estonia, Ethiopia, Eritrea, France, Finland, Lapland, French Cameroon, Greece, Germany. Holland, Italy, Sicily, Iran, Iraq, India, Java, Japan, Jordan, Kenya, Libya, Tripolitania, Cyrenaica, Fezzan, Lebanon, Lithuania, Luxembourg, Malaya, Singapore, Morocco, Tangier, Spanish Morocco, Nigeria, Norway, Portuguese East Africa, Poland, Pakistan, India, Panama, Portugal, Republic of Central Africa, Republic of Tchad, Rwanda, Sweden, Saudi Arabia, Sudan, South Africa, Spain, Swat, Syria, Thailand, Tanganyika, Turkey, Switzerland, Uganda, USA, Yugoslavia, Kuwait, New Zealand.

Islands: Hawaii, Tahiti, Malta, Gibraltar, Bahrein, Corsica, Sardinia and Iceland.

Freya Stark, Sir John Philby, Sir Laurens Van De Post, the crime writer Ngaio Marsh and Agatha Christie were among her literary friends and colleagues.

Barbara's Eulogy:

'...A woman, who if she were to have a conventional burial would probably be best served with the epitaph 'I did it my way.' ...

Barbara was an extraordinary person living in an ordinary world. She was extremely intuitive and seemed to have a unique ability of sensing when something was wrong with those she loved. One might say, that Barbara was in a sense a visionary, most likely a woman who was way ahead of her time, a pioneering adventurer. A woman who took as much as humanly possible from every experience she encountered in her life, took those experiences, put them into text form, and shared them with everyone. A person who led a quiet life and yet bought so much to so many. Barbara had a profound love of un-chartered territories and would venture into the most remote places in our world, only to come away and share them with the populous. She has been in the company of Kings and tribal chiefs, the rich and the poor, and to her credit found value in all walks of life. Her respect of life and with all whom she came into contact, won her love and admiration.

Never daunted, she ventured deep into places like the deserts of Africa and Arabia, usually in her beloved Land Rover 'Pollyanna', she found peace in isolated areas of this Earth even though, they sometimes threw obstacles in her path that would be considered life threatening. Her quest for life and to live it to its fullness was the fuel that kept her inner fire burning for such a long time. Even in her nineties she was planning her next adventure although there were not many remote places for Barbara to find peace in, had she been younger, she may have even put herself forward to be Britain's first woman in space. There was another side to Barbara; she was a woman who, if your paths crossed, touched your life in such a way, that for as long as you lived you, would never forget her.

Barbara was a kind considerate woman and had a warm sense of humour, particularly evident in her fit of giggles that made her eyes dance, her face lit up like stars of the night, and was infectious to all those close by. She has loved and been loved, enjoyed a life most of us only dream of, but had the foresight to put her experiences into book form so our minds could follow where she had boldly gone before us.

Although she has come to the end of her road of life, it should be for comfort that as she approached those final steps on life's road, she did so with the wonderful knowledge, that she never had to use the words 'if only. Rejoice for Barbara, for while her remains will now be at rest, her spirit is just beginning a new adventure which will take her to a place not even she, could have dreamt of. She is with her God as she understood God.

Taken from the Buddhist scriptures:

'She has completed her voyage; she has gone beyond sorrow. The fetters of life have fallen from her and she lives in full freedom. The thoughtful strive always; they have no fixed abode, but leave home like swans from their lake. Like the flight of birds in the sky it is hard to follow the path of the selfless. They have no possessions, but live on alms in a world of freedom. With their senses under control, temperate in eating, they know the meaning of freedom. Even the gods envy saints, whose senses obey them like well-trained horses and they are who are free from pride. Patient like the earth they stand like a threshold. They are pure like a lake without mud and free from the cycle of birth and death. Wisdom has stilled in their minds and thoughts; words and deeds are filled with peace. Freed from illusion, and from personal ties, they have reached the highest. They make holy wherever they dwell, in village or forest, on land or sea. With their senses at peace, and their minds full of joy, they make the forest holy.

Words from the Bhagavad-Gita:

Part of myself is the God within each creature, keeps that nature eternal, yet seems to separate... When the Lord puts on a body, or casts it from him, he enters or departs, taking the mon dans senses away with him, as the wind steals perfume from the flowers.'

Chinese saying:

> 'Yet you are indeed my friend, then in the end, there is one road, a road I have never gone, and down that road you shall not part alone. And there is one night you'll find me by your side. The night that they shall tell me you have died.'

Ian Seymour Wells and Terri Beale.

Courtesy of Guy and Tom Pickford.

Fig 35

Inscription reads: The association of Land-Rovers
Presidents Trophy 1962,
Miss Barbara Toy
Trophy now tarnished and dusty.

The Officers & Board of Trustees
have enrolled

MISS B. TOY M. J. I.

as a member of the
National Geographic Society

JANUARY 1, 1994

In recognition of your support of this nonprofit scientific and
educational organization chartered in 1888 for diffusing geographic
knowledge and promoting research and exploration.

Gilbert M. Grosvenor
President

William Graves
Editor

Photograph by Paul Tanqueray

Miss Barbara Toy
1908 - 2001

Books by Barbara Toy:

1955 **A Fool on Wheels** - Tangier to Baghdad. (Dedicated to her mother).

1956 **A Fool in the Desert** - Libya.

1957 **A Fool Strikes Oil.** - Kuwait to Saudi Arabia.

1958 **Columbus was Right!** - Turkey and Pakistan, Asia to Singapore, to Perth, Australia by boat, trans-Pacific shipment to the United States from California to New York.

1961 **In Search of Sheba** - The Sahara, from Libya to Ethiopia, The Congo to Lake Victoria and the Nile River. Khartoum in Sudan, Ethiopia and Kenya. (Dedicated to her mother).

1964 **The Way of the Chariots** - Algeria to Mediterranean and Niger and Libya.

This was the journey that received, from the Long-Distance Land - Rover Association, the trophy only once before awarded.

1968 **The Highway of the Three Kings**. - Arabia, South to North. (Dedicated to Bill, possibly 'Billy' Bailey).

1970 **Rendezvous in Cyprus** - Turkey, Cyprus.

Books by Barbara Toy:

1955 **A Fool on Wheels** - Tangier to Baghdad. (Dedicated to her mother).

1956 **A Fool in the Desert** - Libya.

1957 **A Fool Strikes Oil.** - Kuwait to Saudi Arabia.

1958 **Columbus was Right!** - Turkey and Pakistan, Asia to Singapore, to Perth, Australia by boat, trans-Pacific shipment to the United States from California to New York.

1961 **In Search of Sheba** - The Sahara, from Libya to Ethiopia, The Congo to Lake Victoria and the Nile River. Khartoum in Sudan, Ethiopia and Kenya. (Dedicated to her mother).

1964 **The Way of the Chariots** - Algeria to Mediterranean and Niger and Libya.

This was the journey that received, from the Long-Distance Land - Rover Association, the trophy only once before awarded.

1968 **The Highway of the Three Kings**. - Arabia, South to North. (Dedicated to Bill, possibly 'Billy' Bailey).

1970 **Rendezvous in Cyprus** - Turkey, Cyprus.

Bibliography:

A History of the Modern Middle East. W Cleveland & M Bunton. Pub. Westview Press. 2009

GENDER, RELIGION and CHANGE in the Middle East. Inger M Okkenhaug & Ingvild Flaskerud. Pub. Berg 2005

The Sahara. Jeremy Swift,
Pub. Time-life Books, 1975.

London's War. Sayre Van Young
Pub: Ulysses Press. 2004

Traveller's Prelude. An autobiography. Freya Stark
John Murray. 1950

The letters of Gertrude Bell Vol I & II
Earnest Benn Ltd. 1927.

A Fool on Wheels. Barbara Toy. Pub. John Murray 1955

A Fool in the Desert. Barbara Toy. Pub. John Murray 1956

A Fool Strikes Oil. Barbara Toy. Pub. John Murray 1957

Columbus was Right! Barbara Toy. Pub. John Murray 1958

In Search of Sheba Barbara Toy. Pub. John Murray 1961

The Way of the Chariots Barbara Toy. Pub. John Murray 1964

The Highway of the Three Kings. Barbara Toy. Pub. John Murray 1968

Rendezvous in Cyprus Barbara Toy. Pub. John Murray 1970

Acknowledgements

Many thanks to the readers, editors, encouragers and believers for their patience.

Tom Palmer, Jill Festa, Esther Wildman, Tom and Guy Pickford,
Sarah Hutchinson Jarman,
Louise Crotwell

Dennis and Robyn Wells.

Andrew Wildman for his technical assistance and support.

Louisa Keyworth at Maps International.
The Bodleian Library

To the Wells family of Australia
for allowing me to bring back into the literary world
the works of Miss Barbara Toy.

All required efforts have been made to obtain permissions for usage of letters, photos, drawings, maps, newspaper articles and book quotes.

About the Author

Lesley Wildman – Studied English, American and Irish lit and a graduate of the Royal College of Art, she now turns her creativity to writing, inspired by the discovery of over 300 letters Barbara wrote home to Australia, culminating in a full biography of Barbara Toy.

Lesley is currently in the throes of completing her own autobiographical novel after the death of her twin brother.

www.ingramcontent.com/pod-product-compliance
Lightning Source LLC
Chambersburg PA
CBHW020512080526
44583CB00013B/573